IRELAND'S GREAT WAR

To the Forgotten Soldiers of Ireland, 1914–18

IRELAND'S GREAT WAR

Kevin Myers

THE LILLIPUT PRESS
DUBLIN

First published 2014 by
THE LILLIPUT PRESS
62–63 Sitric Road, Arbour Hill,
Dublin 7, Ireland
www.lilliputpress.ie

A CIP record for this title is available
from The British Library.

10 9 8 7 6 5 4 3 2 1

ISBN 978 1 8435 1 635 4

Set in 12 pt on 16 pt Dante by Marsha Swan
Printed in Navarre, Spain, by GraphyCems

Contents

Illustration: Map of the Western Front by Tim O'Neill appears between pages 7 and 10

Sources and Acknowledgments

By chapter: 1, 'Opening Shots', *The Irish Times*, 11 November 1980; 2, 'Sligo and the Great War', talk, Ballymote, 10 August 2012; 3, 'Athy in the Great War', talk, Athy, 13 September 2012; 4, 'Kilkenny and the Great War', talk, Royal Irish Academy, Dublin, 1 November 2012; 5, 'Kerry in the Great War', talk, Dingle, 28 August 2014; 6, 'Armagh and the Great War', talk, Armagh, on the 100th anniversary of the outbreak of the Great War, 4 August 2014; 7, 'The Mound', unpublished; 8, 'Gallipoli', unpublished; 9, 'Business in Great Waters: Jutland', talk, The Gate Theatre, Dublin, 2 October 2014; 10, '"Billy Gray, Billy Gray, will you not come to me?" Ireland and the Somme', unpublished; 11, 'Verdun: Where No Birds Sing', *The Irish Times*, 2 March 1991, 12 November 2002; 12, 'The Leinster Regiment', unpublished; 13, 'Francis Ledwidge', talk, Slane, 10 April 2014; 14, 'Robert Gregory: Airman', talk, The Central Library, Dublin, June 2009; 15, 'Glasnevin Cemetery', talk, Glasnevin Cemetery, 11 November 2012; 16, 'From "An Irishman's Diary"', *The Irish Times*, various.

IRELAND'S GREAT WAR

Introduction

The first time I went looking for the Memorial Gardens for the Irish
dead of the Great War, almost no-one in Kilmainham seemed to know
where they were. The year was 1979, eighty years on from the Treaty of
Versailles and after the meeting of the First Dáil, and the first shootings
of the 'Anglo-Irish War' (in which both sides were of course Irish). In 1919
Europe had gone one way, and independent Ireland had gone another,
the journey of the latter taking it to a condition of utter amnesia about
the very war that was central to its foundation-myths. For without the
Great War, there could have been no Easter Rising, and no gallant allies
to support it. Yet it had nonetheless been completely forgotten, and so
totally that not merely had people forgotten, but they'd forgotten that
they'd forgotten. So complete was the eradication of any knowledge
of Irish involvement in the war, that yards away from the great park to
honour Ireland's war dead, no-one admitted to knowing of its existence.

Or maybe they just didn't think of it as a park, because by that time it
had been turned into an urban tip-head, with Dublin Corporation lorries
disgorging the city's rubbish onto vast mounds of spoil. A score or more
tinkers' caravans were parked on the edges of the park, and alongside
them were the rusting hulks of scrapped cars. Piebald ponies grazed in

the foot-high weeds, children scavenged through the waste, and Lutyens' great granite columns were covered with graffiti. In the muck, almost invisible, lay the two elegant granite obelisks meant to represent lapidary candles, now felled, and almost invisible.

The plinth beneath the memorial obelisk declared then, and declares still, that 49,400 Irishmen died in the Great War. This foundation-falsehood has survived the decades, and is even now being recited as a fact by government ministers. It is simply could not be true, for with casualty-rates running at 11 per cent, this would imply that 500,000 Irish had served – out of an island of under four million. However, the figure is an interesting example of how an attractive myth – 49,400 gives the appearance of 'fact', because it is so close to 50,000, yet scrupulously isn't – survives deconstruction.

As I cycled away from the tiphead that the park had now become, I made a vow to do what I could to get it turned into a decent park again. The first thing I had to do was to get the facts right – so I spent months going through the Memorial Records that had been compiled in the early 1920s – at a staggering cost (then) of £5000 – to assess who was actually Irish amongst that 49,400. The records had been put together under a committee led by Eva Bernard, of a prominent unionist family, and it seemed that – to put it mildly – she wanted to maximize Ireland's involvement in the war, and thereby maximize Ireland's devotion to the union. So, the memorial records counted as Irish anyone who had served in an Irish regiment, regardless of where they were from. Admittedly, the question of who is Irish is not easily resolved. Many Irish people – such as Willie Redmond MP, who was born in Liverpool – cannot be called non-Irish simply because of their place of birth. Infuriatingly, one primary source for the Memorial Records – and for all subsequent analysis of this time – 'Officers Died in the Great War' – unlike the companion volumes, 'Soldiers Died in the Great War' – does not give the place of birth of the men it lists.

The figure I came up with, first published in a feature article in *The Irish Times* in November 1980 (see 'Opening Shots,' p.19) was roughly 35,000. Such is the power of the press, and of my colossal influence therein, that this figure of 35,000 has had absolutely no impact whatever. Quite simply, people still prefer the mythic – and perhaps Vedic: who knows? – number of 49,400. But having since discovered the disgraceful War Office pension-saving policies of discharging injured soldiers from the army, and then not counting their deaths from war-related injuries as meriting a place in SDGW or ODGW, I feel 35,000 is too low. Furthermore, it is now clear that the military bureaucracy – like the War Graves Commission, a generally meticulous organization determined to honour the dead – was sometimes overwhelmed by the scale of the catastrophes confronting it. And this is understandable, for it had to record the same basic details for every single dead man: name, rank, number, regiment, battalion, cause of death, date of death, location of death, place of birth, place of residence, place of enlistment, decorations and former regiment. That is at least 240,000 separate facts for the 20,000 dead of the first day of the Somme alone, and without a pause for counting, because on the second day, there were 1438 dead, and on the third, 2338, and on the 135th day, 13 November, there were 2504 dead; and from 1 July to 13 November, covering the duration of the Somme, there were 122,466 British dead alone, yielding at least 1,469,592 details to be recorded in S/ODGW. How does any organization, using just clerks with fountain pens and paper, manage such a feat, while all able-bodied men are being sent off to war? So, allowing for such human failings, I would now confidently say Ireland's war-dead number 40,000.

Glimpsing such appalling statistics is, however, like a doctor peeling back a bandage, noticing a wound but then smelling gas-gangrene, for there's far worse than you can see. It has been the besetting sin of belligerent Anglophone countries, in which community Ireland has now claimed full membership, to see matters only through their own experiences. On 22 August 1914, the very day that the 2nd battalion, the Royal Irish Regiment suffered their first casualties near Mons, 27,000 blue-coated, red-trousered French soldiers were killed, in the first day of the 'Battle of the Frontiers'. The cult of the uninhibited offensive á l'outrance was now treading out its daily harvest of garnered youth through the wine-press of war. By 29 August French losses totalled 260,000, with 75,000 dead. The British army never had a week like that or even a month in the entire war.

Consider the night-assault by the Ottoman army, starting on Christmas Eve 1914, at Sarikamish high in the Caucasus. At minus 35 degrees Celsius, the troops had been ordered to discard their greatcoats and backpacks for greater speed. Some 25,000 men disappeared in the advance, and those not butchered by the waiting Russians froze to death in the rout that followed. The Russians found 30,000 bodies in the snow, and another 25,000 wounded apparently dragged themselves away and perished on the mountainside.

That is, over 50,000 men froze to death over a just a couple of nights. Come the spring thaw, the wolves of the Caucasus grew exceeding fat.

Sacrifices like this could only have been possible if human attitudes, and especially those of men, were unrecognizably different from what we know today. This was true of all nations. Ludwig Frank, a Socialist Deputy in the Reichstag, who had feverishly (and successfully) lobbied for his party to abandon its pacifist policies and support of the war, wrote on 23 August: 'I am happy; it is not difficult to let blood flow for the Fatherland, and to surround it with romanticism and heroism.'

Frank was a Jew, and was the only Reichstag Deputy to die in the war, whereas three Irish MPs – two nationalist and one unionist – were to die. (Lt Tom Kettle of the Dublin Fusiliers who is often cited as an MP was no longer a member of the House of Parliament when he was killed at the Somme.) Even that most clinical of Austrians, and Frank's fellow-Jew, Sigmund Freud, admitted to the almost insuperable power of what he called the 'libido' that he felt for his homeland. Yet what perhaps distinguishes Ireland most from all of the subject territories in what, after all, was an imperial war, or rather, wars, was its exemption from conscription. Poles were especially lucky, for, depending on where they lived, members of an extended family could be forced to fight for the Romanov Tsar and the Hohenzollern Kaiser and the Habsburg Emperor. On mobilization, Czech conscripts marched away bearing (the rather-Czech) banners, declaring, 'We are marching against the Russians and we do not know why.' They were not the only unhappy soldiers that summer. Dublin gunners on exercise in Athlone in early August 1914, demonstrated, in uniform, against the Bachelors Walk shootings in Dublin, but they of course were not conscripts. Moreover, public anger at the shootings seems to have been largely dissipated with the public enquiry that followed within a fortnight, and which resulted in the now forgotten dismissal of the Deputy Head of the DMP who had illegally mobilized the army, and the reinstatement of policemen who had mutinied rather than obey what they considered illegal orders. The only political demonstrations of Irish soldiers from that point onwards were by groups of uniformed Dublin Fusiliers in the pubs and streets of Naas in September 1914, celebrating the passage of the Home Rule Bill into law. These nationalists would then of course serve and die for crown for which many felt little or no loyalty, and would duly be forgotten by all.

Readers of the pages that follow might be forgiven for criticizing any apparent lack of analysis of the motives of the Irish soldiers who served. This is not a careless omission so much as an admission of utter incapacity. I am quite unable to explain my own motives for almost any aspect of my life, including this book: it would therefore be slightly presumptuous of me to impute motives to long-dead Irishmen of whose culture and personal circumstances I know nothing. Indeed, it cannot be repeated enough how different people were, even in European 'democracies' (though no real democracy would exist in Europe until after the war). Most working-class people lived in tenements without privacy or personal privies, washed seldom, ate no fruit, were cold from September to April, shared a toilet with a hundred strangers and used scraps of newspaper if they were 'well-to-do', and their imaginations if they weren't, wore filthy, shit-encrusted underwear (if they wore any at all) and for much of winter lived in the dark, which they shared with vermin, bodily and rodential.

In those tenements, as in the great houses of Rathmines and Rathgar, and the Georgian palaces of the gentry, lived another matter for general omission from this selection of thoughts on the Great War. It is the women: the mothers, the wives, the sisters, the sweethearts, whose tale is still untold, and indeed might never properly now be told, such was the silence about grief – through reticence, pride, social status, illiteracy or nationalism – that governed so much Irish life. I have referred to some of the women: to Agnes Montresor, who lost both her father and her new husband within a couple of days early in the war; to Mrs Bruce, lover of Henry Desmond O'Hara; to Kathleen Shine who lost all three of her sons, and Agnes Collins, who lost four of hers. In no way, however, could that satisfy my own expectations of how properly to convey any sense of a woman's grief, bereavement, loss and emptiness, never mind those of a women's group. Quite simply, it is beyond my power to talk about the emotions these women must have felt.

I am reminded of a woman in Rathgar whose brother Reggie had been wounded in the war. Her name was Violett – two t's – and poor Reggie (my reason for visiting) was well beyond any useful interview. After I had spent an hour trying to talk with him, she and I had a cup of tea, and I made to go. But we stayed talking at her front door, on the high granite stoop of her house on Frankfurt Avenue.

She told me how she had lost her fiancé Nigel in the battle that had maimed Reggie.

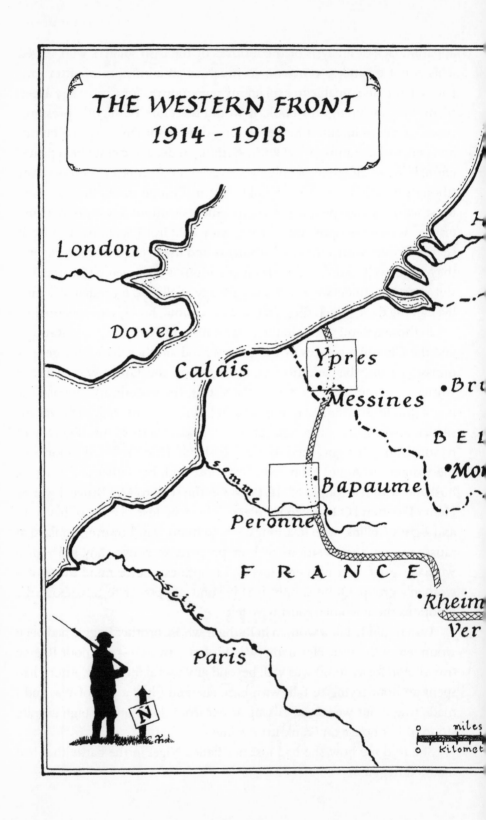

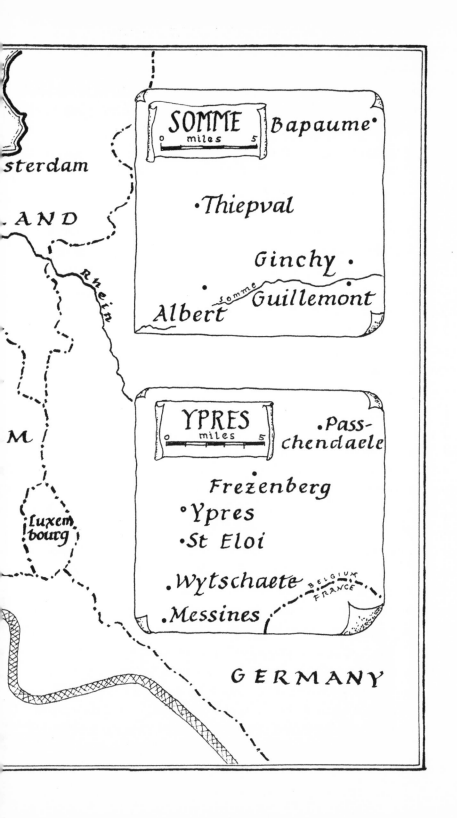

'I don't wish to be rude,' she said, 'but my bowels were never right after the telegram arrived. Never. A terrible impediment. I couldn't really trust myself to go out. So you see, I know so little. These days, of course, Nigel and I would have … you know … but we were God-fearing folk, very proper. So we never. Anyway, I never had a boyfriend after that – just as well, really, because Reggie was never right again after he got home. And he couldn't hold down a job. So I looked after him. God's will, I suppose. We have a little money put by. Just a little.'

Her social life consisted solely of attending Rathgar Presbyterian Church on Sunday mornings, sometimes with Reggie, sometimes not, the only time she had the confidence to stray far from a lavatory. Most of her family and friends had emigrated; now the pair of them lived in decaying gentility in a house that smelt of urine and mothballs.

'I must be going,' I said. 'It's been a real pleasure.'

I leaned down and kissed her cheek, and she reeled in astonishment. She was silent for a moment or so.

'No man has kissed me, even like that, since my Nigel kissed me goodbye at Kingstown,' she whispered.

He died in 1917; it was now 1980.

So, no I cannot do justice to the feelings of women in the war. I have neither the emotional clarity, the imaginative powers nor the language to undertake such a task. I confess my guilt, and move on. However, I feel a little more confident when dealing with the many trite and commonplace judgments on how stupidly the war was conducted. For this was a new kind of war, that was begun with cavalry and four years later was finished with computer-ranged artillery, tanks directed by radio-equipped spotter aircraft, while ground-attack aircraft ranged deep behind enemy lines, dive-bombing targets of opportunity. The *Blitzkrieg* was born in 1918, after four years fighting that had begun with dragoons' sabres along the Sambre, and in those forty-eight months, every single general, battalion commander, platoon subaltern, section leader, from top to bottom, was a novice, and the only lessons that could be learnt were through the grievous expenditure of human life. The alternative, against an adamant foe – and all the participants were certainly that – was unilateral surrender, and such capitulation is not in the nature of great or imperial powers. One can deplore this fact, just as one can the vileness of human nature, but not usefully.

It was a depressing reminder of the Irish appetite to find themselves the most oppressed people ever that one of the first manifestations of an awareness that the Irish had served in the war was when our political classes started campaigning for the British to 'pardon' the executed Irish. Now I confess I have a certain proprietorial interest in this subject: aided by the researches of those two admirable men, Julian Putkowski and Julian Sykes, in 1989 I published the first ever list of Irish soldiers who had been executed (see 'Shot at Dawn.' p.220). I could never have predicted that a political class that had come into existence on a campaign of murdering often unarmed and helpless policemen, and which had assured the safety of the fledgling institutions of new state by 'executing' – ie murdering – seventy-seven captives, might now get exercised about the deaths of a few British soldiers who happened to be Irish.

The first execution of a British soldier (an Englishman, actually) occurred within two weeks of the first outbreak of fighting. Contrary to much mythology, the British army had in general fought extremely badly in its first encounters with the Germans; the mix of a battalion consisting of between 40 per cent regulars and 60 per cent reservists simply didn't work. The reservists were often unfit, slow and reluctant to do anything, except hobble homeward on blistered feet. Armies are not nursing homes. They will employ any device to make their men fight, including murder: 10 per cent of all executed soldiers were not even represented at their trials, three of which are dealt with in this volume.

The issue of the executed Irish is not as simple as nationalists / republicans today apparently believe. In the new wartime divisions, two men of the 16th (Irish) Division were executed; both of them in Northern battalions, and certainly one of them, Wishart, was a Protestant. Four men of the 36th (Ulster) Division were executed. That means all six of these war-time recruits were northerners, and certainly five of them were Protestants. Looking at the executions from a regimental point of view, five of the executed came from the Royal Inniskilling Fusiliers, five from the Royal Irish Rifles and two from the Royal Irish Fusiliers – that is, twelve from Northern regiments. Eight men from the southern regiments were executed during the war, three Dublin Fusiliers, three Leinsters and two Munsters. The execution of poor James Daly in 1920 in India, for leading a munity in which an innocent man was killed, quite simply does not belong in the same category as wartime executions for desertion, which is a far lesser crime. However, the really large question over the executionsis raised by the 29th Division, in which there were never more than three Irish battalions, more often two, out of initially twelve battalions, more latterly nine: six of the eight executions were of men from Irish battalions, a grossly disproportionate number. However, the initial charges were brought by the men's own officers, who were themselves usually Irish, which complicates matters somewhat. Were Irish officers more unforgiving than officers from Britain? In the absence of more work on the subject, I simply cannot say.

Initially when looking at this unbearably painful subject, I suspected the anti-Irish hand of Lieutenant General Aylmer Hunter-Weston, who had commanded the 29th Division in Gallipoli, before passing command to Lieutenant General H. de Lisle, a well-known savage, but still answerable to Hunter-Weston, commanding officer of VIII Corps. I am grateful to Julian Putkowski for the following story, about one particular Irish-English soldier from Yorkshire.

On 19 August 1917 nineteen-year old Gunner William Casey, from Sheffield, married Margaret Connor at St Mary's Catholic Church, Newcastle upon Tyne. She was eight months' pregnant, and Gunner Casey had deserted his unit at the Front to ensure that the baby would be born in wedlock. On returning to his Royal Field Artillery unit, he was tried by Field General Court Martial for what was a capital offence. Margaret Casey, who was illiterate, persuaded her mother to write a letter to Casey's commanding officer, pleading for clemency. The letter was read out to the court and after news of the proceedings reached General Sir Aylmer Hunter Weston, he wrote to Margaret Connor.

Allow me as the commander of the Army Corps in which your husband is serving to send you a cheque with which to buy a wedding present ... your husband's Court-Martial happened to come to my notice, & though of course his commanding officer had no option but to try him for the very heinous offence of being absent without leave & the Court Martial on the evidence had no other course but to condemn him and sentence him to severe punishment, yet, I am glad to say, it has been possible to commute the sentence and suspend its execution. So your Husband will not be punished. I rejoice that when he was forced with the necessity of committing a fault, your Husband had no hesitation in choosing that fault which would bring punishment to him and not to you. You fully realise, I hope, that in coming home thus to marry you he ran a very great risk of being found guilty of desertion & being shot; so he faced death for your sake.

Though I do not know him personally, I feel sure he must be a fine fellow & a good soldier, & I congratulate you very heartily on having gained his love. He went through much and took great risks in doing the right thing & coming home to marry you. I respect him for doing this & coming back again to do his duty straightway thereafter, & I am certain that you will always remember his fine qualities & this great proof of his love for you, and that you will make him a real good wife… I feel confident that you must be a really nice woman, and I think he is a lucky man to have you for a wife.

Send your husband my greetings and best wishes for his success as a soldier.

No stereotype survives a letter such as that, complete with a cheque; nor their aftermath, for General Hunter-Weston took his own life in 1940. Moreover, I repeat, armies are not nursing homes. In August 1914 the French government accorded its military authorities the unquestioned right to use the death penalty whenever necessary. On 1 September, after some French units had broken under fire, the French Ministry for War instructed officers to carry out death penalties within twenty-four hours of any offence, with no trial needed. That autumn, faced with the very real prospect of his army collapsing and the last corner of his country capitulating, King Albert of the Belgians issued an Order of the Day that declared that any soldier who fled the battlefield would be shot by special marksman posted to the rear, whose duty was solely that; officers claiming to be sick would be court-martialled, and general staff officers shirking their duties would instantly posted to the front line.

Since executions have become something of an obsession both in Ireland and in Britain, it is worth remembering that during the war, one and forty thousand men deserted from a British army totalling seven million. Twenty thousand British soldiers were convicted of offences carrying the death penalty. Three thousand were sentenced to death. Three hundred and twelve were shot. By contrast, 493 RIC men were shot by the IRA, 1919–22, and 77 IRA prisoners shot by Free State firing squads, 1922–23. People who justify such killings are perhaps on slightly questionable ground when they complain about executions by the British.

Perceptions of the war, and not just in Ireland, have in recent decades been almost hopelessly contaminated by an entertainment industry that prefers spurious fiction to sober fact. First World War generals – who actually managed to inflict military defeats on the Germans and sent them packing across the Rhine, to be followed by an allied army of occupation – are still widely seen as being legitimate target for lampooning in a way that contemporary politicians, and later generations of British generals that had achieved no such victories, are not. The wanton lies of agitprop theatre such as *Oh What a Lovely War!* and of the *Blackadder* television caricature, have a ready market, which is in itself a cultural curiosity: for though it cannot be healthy to worship war, it cannot be much healthier to revere such falsehoods. Yet these perceptions are as widespread as those other caricatures, 'the lions led by donkeys', and 'chateaux generals'. No German generals ever accused the British army of being led by donkeys: how could they, who had lost the war? As for chateaux generals, well that's exactly where generals should be – behind the lines, just like Henry Ford then, or Bill Gates today. Nonetheless, *over one hundred* British generals were killed in the Great War.

The war poets are another matter, because they have been hopelessly traduced by subsequent politico-critics who have often imposed a pacifist or left-wing agenda on their words. For the most part, these men were warrior-bards; they were sensitive humans who were aware of the barbarism of war, yet nonetheless served as bravely as possible in a cause that they thought right. The most cherished of them all, Wilfred Owen, won a Military Cross for seizing a German machinegun, turning it on its former owners, and killing them. His biographers have usually turned this into 'capturing them'. Our own Francis Ledwidge (see elsewhere in this volume) is a fine example of the warrior-bard, for he expressed so many of the conflicting emotions of the thinking man engaged in a righteous war. Naturally, Irish cultural republicanism, while implicitly denying the very existence of the main body of his wartime poetry, nonetheless conscripted his 'Lament for Thomas MacDonagh', as if that was his poetic and moral essence. It wasn't. He was proud to be a soldier in the allied cause.

> *It is too late now to retrieve*
> *A fallen dream, too late to grieve,*
> *A name unmade, but not too late*
> *To thank the gods for what is great;*
> *A keen-edged sword, a soldier's heart*

Is greater than a poet's art
And greater tha a poet's fame
A little grave that has no name,
Whence honour turns away in shame.

The war, after all, was actually being fought in Belgium and France, which had not generously lent some neutral jousting-ground for the two sides to test their imperial martial prowess, but instead were the unwilling hosts to a war of both conquest and liberation. Now, one can certainly argue that the liberation of those lands was not worth the dreadful price that was paid. That very valid point does not – and cannot – answer, the questions that follow: what would have become of Europe if Germany had been allowed to hold onto the conquered territories of Belgium, with all its ports looking out onto the North Sea, and much of the industrial heartland of France? Perhaps, even more serious, what would Germany have been like if the barbarous war of conquest launched by the Kaiser and his military caste had triumphed? Are such people sated by victory, or made hungrier? And how else does one explain the ferocity of the worst battle on the Western Front, Verdun, where France was fighting for the survival of itself as country, and Germany was fighting against a defeat which, it knew –considering its many crimes in the conquered territories – would result in a ruinous settlement?

After Irish independence, the political heirs of the insurgency were mixed in their attitude to the ex-servicemen. Kevin O'Higgins, one of whose brothers Michael Aloysius was killed in France with the 2nd Leinsters, and another, Jack, served as surgeon-commander on Admiral Beatty's flagship HMS *Lion*, was both conciliatory but adamant: 'No-one denies the sacrifice and no-one denies the patriotic motives which induced the vast majority of those men to join the British army to take part in the Great War, and yet it is not on *their* sacrifice that this state is based, and I have no desire to see it suggested that it is.'

Every single one of those assertions could be contested. Many republicans did – and furthermore would increasingly – deny that the very term 'sacrifice' could apply to those who had served in a foreign army which they had themselves (if only intermittently) fought. Many within republicanism most emphatically did deny the patriotic motives of those who had served the crown, as did, at the time, Sean Lemass – an attitude for which, some forty years later, he was to regret and also offer, rather generously, public contrition. As for the third assertion, I would maintain that it was the very evidence that so many nationalists had served the crown in the Great War that made the creation of an independent state, on boundaries agreed by John Redmond in 1915, tolerable for the British. I am, I accept, on challengeable grounds here. Either way, given the bipolarity of the British imperial psyche, it was surely better for the Irish to address, and be addressed *by*, the malleable democratic pole than the purblind imperial one, which, almost without blinking, in the summer of 1920 had lost the lives of over eight thousand of its own soldiers in the subjugation of the new-found imperial booty that was Mesopotamia. Moreover, the Treaty was largely being negotiated on the British side by a leadership that had supported the Home Rule Bill, and was also aware of the losses nationalist Ireland had suffered in the Great War. The faith in *that* Ireland must have generated a goodwill in the heart of the democratic pole that outweighed any military threat that was posed to the ruthless imperial pole by the likes of Tom Barry and Dan Breen. It was this latter pole to which Lloyd George was (and not very obliquely) referring when he effectively finished the Treaty talks with his promise (flourishing an admonitory envelope), 'If I send this letter, it is war, and war within three days.'

However, post-independence Ireland was not composed solely of Kevin O'Higgins, as he himself was to discover. Several county councils, including Wexford, Cork and Tipperary, voted not to employ ex-servicemen, and also, in a particularly noble gesture, even to withhold all educational-scholarships from their children. Thousands of unionists, unwilling to stay in a state created by the violence that had claimed so many of their own number, departed, causing a housing slump in their former strongholds of Rathgar, Rathmines and Pembroke. Since up to 40 percent of all *Irish-born* infantrymen – it varied with the regiment: higher in the west than in the east – were themselves emigrants who had been recruited in Britain, to where, presumably, they would have returned after the war, and since diminished job-opportunities at home would have caused higher emigration amongst returned ex-servicemen, the number of veterans remaining to participate in Irish life, and most of all, *to tell their story*, must have been disproportionately far smaller than the Irish experience of war actually merited.

So, though 1920s Ireland was deeply aware of the losses in the war, and – as Keith Jeffrey pointed out in his wry study on the subject, *Ireland the Great War* (Cambridge, 2000), 20,000 veterans paraded in front of 50,000 people in Dublin on Armistice Day in 1924, and the British Legion announced that it had sold half a million poppies in Dublin. As for this last figure, I rather think it compares with the highly creative statistic of '49,400 war-dead'. Yet over time, it simply became firstly unfashionable, and then impossible, for ex-servicemen to speak out. The redoubtable Jack Moyney VC told me that he had long since learnt to keep his mouth shut unless utterly sure of his company. When I first tried to get veterans of the war to discuss their experiences, some told me that they were in fear of their lives from the IRA. Absurd though that might now seem, that was the culture that had emerged. Moreover, neither schools nor universities – not even Protestant-ones, or Trinity, which between them must have lost a thousand officers killed – broke ranks with the emerging nationalist orthodoxy of silence. In a land that was most comfortable with an all-embracing consensus, forgetting the missing 40,000, and the equally accomplished vanishing-trick with the 200,000 that survived, proved to be relatively easy. Official Ireland had no problem studiously not knowing about the uncomfortable part of its history: and southern Protestants meekly went along with the new fiction, reserving their memories for the semi-secret rites of Remembrance Sunday, and the poppy discreetly sported under the overcoat. When I started writing about the Irish and the Great War, and *repeatedly*, in *The Irish Times*, the then editor Douglas Gageby sent his deputy, Ken Gray, to ask me to desist.

I readily agreed to do just that – the moment when the Irish state acknowledged the dead of the war.

'Good man,' whispered Ken, patting me on the shoulder, and returning to put some gloss on my reply, Douglas Gageby – who, to be fair, never spiked a single column on the issue, even though he heartily disliked what I was doing. Perhaps he thought that my efforts were in vain and quixotic – and for good reason, for it is hard now to convey the utter ignorance that was the norm. When I spoke to a women's group in Killester in Dublin in 1990 about the Irish in the Great War, not a single person in the room was aware that Killester had orginally been founded in the 1920s as a home for ex-servicemen; likewise in Athy, a garrison town that had about one hundred men killed in the war, but by 1993, when I went to discuss its role in the war, the local sheet was blank, the slate wiped clean: I could have been talking to Peruvians about their granddads' time in Flanders.

The transformation since then has been extraordinary. Right across Ireland, community-groups have been striving to re-discover the hitherto-forgotten names of the local war-dead of a century ago. That phenomenal beast, the Irish collective memory, has been stirred from its artificial slumbers, and alert and keen once again, is examining its inner recesses, as tales whispered long ago are compared with the written record.

It is almost impossible to exaggerate the raw power of this amazing memory. At around the time of my trip to Killester I came across the grave of forty-seven-year old Private Thomas Carthy, Royal Irish Regiment, killed in April 1915, in Poelcappelle Cemetery in Belgium. The cemetery register said he was the husband of Mary Carthy, of 34 River Street Clonmel. I wrote to the occupants of that house, asking if they knew what had happened to the Carthy family. In due course I got a letter from a woman in Nenagh who was the great-grand-niece of Thomas Carthy. She told me the family history. The Carthys were poor, small-town Protestants, and her great grandmother had been Carthy's youngest sister. That girl was already married when Carthy died, but with a new name, address and religion, having become a Catholic on marrying and later moving to Nenagh.

Such is the might of the Irish collective memory, which through the long dark centuries of dispossession cherished the tales of the Fianna and Knights of the Red Branch, and helped, not always construcively, the Ireland of the twentieth century. Now, one hundred years on from the war that everyone once forgot, it is reminding us that amnesia in Ireland can sometimes be no more than a deep morning mist on an entire landscape of personal knowledge, which yet might yield before the warming sunlight of honesty and disclosure.

1. *Opening Shots*
11 November 1980

The first shots to be in Europe by a British soldier in the First World War came from the carbine of Corporal E. Thomas of the Royal Irish Dragoon Guards. He thus opened accounts for a conflict that would devastate the manhood of the British empire and, to an unrecognized degree, of Ireland. Four years and three months later Corporal W. Ellison of the Royal Irish Lancers, who had been at Mons with Thomas, was killed as his picket of Royal Irish Lancers seized a canal bridge not far from where Thomas had fired his shots. He was the last outright British fatality of the war. A fellow lancer, Thomas Farrell, from Navan, was fatally wounded, and died the next day. The two lamentable events, the start and the finish, are commemorated by plaques in Mons. Ironically, unlike some 35,000 Irishmen, Thomas survived the war that he, if only symbolically, began.

It is one the curiosities of history that most people believe that the stories of German atrocities in Belgium were a fiction got up by British propaganda. This is simply not true. German soldiers did actually shoot priests as an example to the rest of the population of the conquered lands. In Tamines they shot and bayonetted to death 384 men, women and children – the youngest three weeks of age. At Seillies 50 civilians were shot, at Aershot 150, at Audenne 110, and at Dinant 664. All of these killings were in cold blood. But the deed that shocked the world was the sacking and burning of the medieval city of Louvain and the random killings of hundreds of its citizens long after it had surrendered to the German army.

This was what turned Tom Kettle in favour of the war effort, and the loveable Willie Redmond MP, who was far too old to join up but managed to get a commission in the Royal Irish regiment in order to be able to tell young men: 'Don't go, but *come* with me.'

Unionists throughout the country, north and south, gave generously, but so did nationalists. In all 108 Dohertys, 182 O'Neills, 200 Ryans, who could belong to either identity, were killed. So too were 40 Patrick Byrnes, who were probably all of nationalist stock.

The professional and footballing community of Dublin formed the famous 'D' Company of 7th battalion Royal Dublin Fusiliers. They were the cream of the Dublin middle classes, and included some GAA players as well as the better-known rugby players. One of the original 'D' Company, Lieutenant C. Paul, of Howth Road, Dublin, was to bring back the dying Willie Redmond during the battle of Messines. Paul was then a member of the Royal Irish Rifles attached to the 36th Ulster Division. Within a short time he too would be dead.

John Redmond was passionately pro-war, and the Redmondite National Volunteers flocked to the Colours. So too did the poor of Dublin's city centre, Summerhill and Gardiner Street in particular. For such people, a soldier's income of 9 shillings a week, plus separation allowance for his family, was a small fortune. In a world in which one child in six died before the age of one, the hardship of military life apparently seemed a small disincentive.

And sometimes soldiers' motives were not always clear. One recruit for the Leinster Regiment kept bawling, 'To hell with them bloody French anyway.' A large number of under-age boys managed to join, and wangle their way to the front. James Rathband, from Gardiner Street, Dublin, was such a volunteer, and was killed on the Somme at the age of sixteen in 1916.

The strange thing about those days was that much of the animosities of the recent past had died down. National Volunteer and UVF bands would parade together through the towns of Donegal or Down. Crime just about ceased everywhere. Magistrate after magistrate took the bench in empty courts: likewise circuit court judges regularly donned the gloves of White Assizes. 'It was formerly an army of occupation,' quipped Tom Kettle of the RIC. 'Now, owing to the all but complete disappearance of crime, it is an army of no occupation.'

By November 1914 120 fishermen's houses had provided the Royal Navy with 156 men, and 165 National Volunteers from Manorhamilton were already at the Front. Youghal had 800 men at the Front, Castlebar 100, and from the Athy area it was reported that 1600 men had joined the British army.

Of course recruitment was proportionately highest in Ulster. Between August 1914 and October 1916, of the 130,241 recruits in Ireland, almost 67,000 came from Ulster. They were by no means all unionists. Thousands of nationalists joined the Connaught Rangers, the Leinsters and the Royal Irish Regiment, and the 36th Ulster Division was never wholly unionist or Protestant. Moreover, recruitment remained more successful in Britain, and some Irish service battalions were amply filled with Englishmen – Yorkshire men in the Munsters and West Countrymen in the Leinsters. Even the 36th Ulster Division needed topping up with English and Scottish recruits. However, Irish recruitment was by no means confined to Ireland. Roughly 40 per cent of Irish infantry recruits were of Irish-born living in Britain.

Most of these men are listed in 'Ireland's Memorial Records', which contain the name of 49,400 men killed in the Great War. However, these records are not very accurate. Some 11,000 of the men listed in the eight volumes are stated to have been born outside Ireland. Generally, then, these men may be said to be not Irish, though the rule cannot be hard and fast. Willie Redmond, for example, was born in Liverpool, and presumably there must be a fair and incalculable number of Irishmen like him.

The non-Irish lists are swelled by the fact that Irish cavalry regiments were Irish in name only. The unfortunate Ellison, for example, came from York, and the extraordinarily fortunate Thomas came from a London family. Also included in the Memorial records are the dead of the nominally Irish regional regiments in England, such as the Tyneside, London and Liverpool Irish. Most of these men had no real connection with Ireland.

Another category of names in the Memorial Records is even harder to decode. Some 7240 men are given no birthplace. One such is Tom Kettle, whose Irishness is unquestionable, another is John Kipling, Rudyard's son, of whom the opposite could be said.

About 31,000 Irishmen born in Ireland are reported to have been killed in the war. It is difficult to be more precise than that, because not merely did Eva Bernard, the compiler, allow great latitude in her definition of 'Irish', she allowed great latitude in her definition of the First World War. This included civilians killed in the 1916 Rising, perhaps a legitimate inclusion, since its instigators had proclaimed the Germans as 'their gallant allies'. But many soldiers have been listed twice. And there are anomalous cases that defy explanation. William Jennings Bryan, accorded no birthplace, rank or unit, and who died in Colorado Springs in 1916, is in the Memorial, as is Demosthenes Guilgault, of the Royal Canadian Mounted Rifles, who died of heart failure in Canada in 1919. So is Henry Beddowes, ex-Dublin Fusilier, and Richard Smythe, who drowned in 1919 while bathing, respectively, in Dublin Bay and off Jaffa.

There are some listings that are doubtful on other counts, such as 'Daniel Collins, rank Private or Corporal, Connaught Rangers, died of wounds, April 29th, 1915 or April 29th, 1916, born New York or Ireland', or 'Thomas Curran, died at home, December 17th 1915, or killed in action France, March 21st 1916.' That these are open to later clarification does not reduce the uncertainty they bring to the Bernard *modus operadni*.

One more complication. Some who are listed who would probably not thank you for calling them Irish, Kitchener of Khartoum from his watery grave being one, though admittedly he always felt his Kerry birthplace gave him an understanding of Irishness, though not an empathy with it.

There can be no doubt, however, that about 35,000 Irishmen died in the Great War. Ireland's Memorial Records, their margins decorated by Harry Clarke's sombre, sinuous designs, therefore make terrible reading, as brother follows brother, with consecutive numbers, to the grave.

When war broke out, 51,000 Irishmen were serving soldiers or reservists. They had no choice but to fight. The 250,000-odd men, though this figure is still unclear, who joined them were volunteering to fight. Of the 35,000 or so Irishmen who died for little Belgium, for Ulster, for Home Rule, for the King or his shilling, one in sixteen died on the first day on the Somme, 1 July 1916. About the same number died in the Gallipoli campaign.

The story of the 36th Ulster Division at the Somme needs no retelling. It is part of the Orange folklore, occurring as it did on the anniversary of the battle of the Boyne. However, the stories about the men of the division donning Orange sashes before they went into action is almost certainly a post-battle myth with no foundation in fact.

Other myths are not remotely baseless. So, it is doubtful whether, apart from specific and obvious occasions, such as the outdoor relief work during the Famine, or during the closing weeks of the battle of Stalingrad, that so many people have been so miserable for so long as were the soldiers of all the armies on the Western Front.

'The men stood motionless in water up to their waists for two days and nights without food and on relief marched out if they were capable of movement.' – 'It was not advisable to grope in the slime. The substratum was chiefly rotting corpses.' – 'Bent double with cold, streaming with water from the waist down, and caked with mud from the waist up, strong men would sob like children.'

Thus run three descriptions by Irish officers on a routine winter duty. Sanitation often consisted of using empty bully-beef tins, with the contents being thrown into no man's land only to ooze back with the mud that slid constantly into the trenches.

The 2nd battalion, the Royal Irish Regiment, was effectively twice wiped out in the war, as was the 2nd battalion, the Royal Munster Fusiliers. On one day in October 1914 50 per cent of all British army deaths on the Western Front were of Irishmen, and there were probably some forty-five days in which the Irish dead and fatally wounded numbered over a hundred. The 1st Leinsters lost 2000 men during the war: its full strength was seldom more than 800. At 'V' Beach near Sed El Barrh, in the Dardanelles, near-catastrophe awaited the Dublin and Munster Fusiliers. A naval flier, Commander Sampson, reported that the bay was red with blood. It was Irish blood.

It was reported later in the campaign that men of the 10th Irish Division captured a woman sniper in Gallipoli and she was shot. It is impossible to separate barrack-room myth from military bravado or the truth. 'There was a Hun on the end of my bayonet,' reported one Irish officer in Belgium, 'but I fired and he dropped off.' An NCO reported: 'We got at close quarters with them. Some fled, the others put up their hands. We spared none.'

Interestingly enough, censors did not see fit to remove such material from the newspapers of the time. War seldom elevates the human soul.

Saxon regiments on the Western Front were often rebuffed in their attempts to befriend men of the Leinsters. After one failed truce effort a German peered over his parapet: 'A bullet between the eyes soon settled his hash, and no truce,' reported the regimental historian with grisly satis-faction. Andrew Dunne, father of five serving soldiers, received a commu-nication from Buckingham Palace on the deaths of three of them; it ended: 'Their Majesties congratulate Mr Dunne on having been able to send so many sons to the war.'

'All honour to those who found recruits, trained them, and sent them out, qualified for saving the skins of fools,' observed one Irish officer when it was all over.

Recruitment actually increased in the immediate aftermath of the 1916 Rising, in large part put down by Irish garrison troops, who were also among the first casualties, perhaps explaining their keenness to seek revenge. It was a Royal Irish sniper who shot and wounded James Connolly, and men of the regiment seized the tricolour from the GPO.

The whole ghastly mess became even more complicated in the wake of the executions. So concerned was the British about the loyalty of Irish regiments that in 1917 they were all withdrawn from Ireland. That year Ireland lost the poet Francis Ledwidge, who had joined the Inniskilling Fusiliers to prove, among other things, that he was not pro-German. But as with most motives, his were mixed: his sweetheart had got pregnant by another man, and later died in childbirth, along with the baby. Ledwidge was killed on the first day on Third Ypres, an epic of futile horror that even today defies proper description, in which one by one all Irish regi-ments fought. Then in March 1918 the Germans broke through the allied lines and almost destroyed the 16th Irish Division. One battalion was left with just three men.

The end of the war did not bring peace to all Irish soldiers. Some Irish units were sent off to fight the Bolsheviks, others to occupy Istanbul or Cologne – so much for Little Belgium – and those Irishmen who returned home found themselves amid the rising tide of another war. By 1919 248,000 ex-soldiers were back in Ireland. A few joined the IRA, others the RIC, the Black and Tans and Auxiliaries; yet others joined the A, B and C Specials in the North. Scores of ex-servicemen were murdered by the IRA for the crime of having served the crown. In time many joined the Free State Army, and in doing so, effectively decided who was to win the Civil War. However, most veterans elected not to fight in any more wars.

They are almost gone now, largely forgotten in their own country, the hundreds of thousands of Irishmen who left these shores to fight other people's battles. But the dilemma that nationalists like Ledwidge felt has found its laureate in Seamus Heaney and these closing stanzas of his 'In Memoriam Francis Ledwidge', moved in childhood by the cold bronze of a Portrush war memorial:

> *In you, our dead enigma, all the strains*
> *Cross-cross in equilibrium*
> *And as the wind bores thrugh this vigilant bronze*
> *I hear again the sure confusing drum.*
>
> *You followed from Boyne water to the Balkans*
> *But miss the twilit note your flute should sound.*
> *You were not keyed or pitched like those true-blue ones*
> *Though all of you consort now underground.*

2. *Sligo and the Great War*

In early 1914, a little working class girl called Mary Pilkington ran into the path of car in Thomas Street, Sligo, breaking several ribs and badly injuring her hand. The driver Henry L'Estrange, and his passenger, Captain W.H. Parke, sub-sheriff of the County of Sligo, brought the injured girl to her modest home in Distillery Lane.

Three years before that incident, the local regiment, the 2nd battalion, Connaught Rangers, were brigaded with the 2nd Royal Sussex Regiment in Dublin; and this presumably was how young Geoffrey Russell Fenton, of Ardaghowen, son of the Crown and Peace Officer for the County of Sligo, first met Agnes Millicent Montresor, daughter of the Sussex's commanding officer, Lt Colonel Ernest Montresor. The Montresors lived in some splendour in an apartment in in Hampton Court Palace. For Irish gentry, this was a good marriage indeed.

Courtship in those days must always have been a rather parlous business, but the wooing of the daughter of the commanding officer of a regiment with whom one's own battalion is brigaded must have constituted shark-infested waters. One way or another, Geoffrey Fenton was able to pursue his prize, and to win her. The couple were married in a quiet ceremony in London in September 1912. Eighteen months later the scion of another grand house was to encounter a young woman of a drastically different background.

On the declaration of war, both the Sussex and the Connaughts, with Millicent's father and husband in their respective places, rushed to the front. By August 1914, as elsewhere in Ireland, the Volunteer movement in Sligo was split overwhelmingly in favour of the National Volunteers: 4000 as compared to the 280 of what was loosely called the Sinn Féin faction. The National Volunteers were heavily dependent on the enthusiasm and the military skills of army reservists, and it was these very talents that were to rob the INV of its most important men as they were called up for wartime service. Initially, support in Sligo for the allied cause was very strong. Local priests and politicians denounced the German atrocities in Belgium, and such they were, for they were not the invention of British propagandists, though these certainly elaborated upon what was a solid body of truth.

Thus we read that on 10 September 1914, 'A most enthusiastic meeting for the purposes of recruiting for Lord Kitchener's army was held in Collooney. Organized by Captain Bryan Cooper DL, it was attended by all creeds and classes. Captain Cooper said that Sligo was asked to raise one battalion, and 350 of the 1000 required had joined. (Cheers) He had volunteered for the Connaught Rangers. And if local men wanted to join him, he'd be only too glad to help.'

Michael Gallagher county councillor, seconded by Mr Alexander Slim, proposed the motion: 'That we are fighting a just war for the vindication of the rights of small nations, and the sacredness of Treaties, and we shall carry it on until the arms of the allies are victorious and the future peace of Europe assured.'

Reverend J. Doyle CC, supporting the resolution, considerably broadened the scope of the war beyond the Schlieffen Plan, asserting that if the Germans won, they'd even stop the old age pensions and land reform, not in Belgium but Ireland. If ever the British empire had fought a war stamped with the hallmark of justice it was the war in which the Irish and English soldiers were engaged on the Continent, he proclaimed, and they all hoped that the Germans would get such a licking that they would never again be in a position to endanger the peace of Europe. Canon McCormick then supported the motion, which was passed unanimously

Bryan Cooper separately announced that all rents below £10 a year would be waived for the families of volunteers, and above that, £10 would be deducted. Appeals to claim to the concession were to be made to Mr L'Estrange, who would drive recruits to Boyle in his now perhaps infamous car.

Meanwhile the BEF was facing the almost irresistible juggernaut of the German right hook through Belgium. Only a naïve adherence to treaty obligations, and the impetuosity of the continentally inexperienced could have allowed the British Expeditionary Force to be exposed to being outflanked and even annihilated by such overwhelmingly greater forces. The first horsed skirmishes near Mons on 22 August that were almost redolent of ten centuries of cavalry war gave way to ferocious infantry clashes the next day, as von Kluck's First Army fixed the BEF, while it was being simultaneously outflanked. Retreat was inevitable.

Millicent's father and husband were mobilized in August 1914. On 14 September, Millicent's father was killed in action and, six days later, so too was her husband. Neither body was ever found. The two of them are commemorated at La Ferte Sous Joucerre Memorial.

And also killed on 20 September, the same day as Geoffrey Russell were Sligomen John Meehan and John Dunleavy of the 2nd Connaught Rangers, John O'Connor, of the Highland Light Infantry, Dominick Battles of the Manchester Regiment, John Walsh Royal Irish Fusiliers, and, upon that forgotten element the sea, William Guthrie, of HMS *Hogue*.

The first Ballymote man to die was Thomas Brennan, Irish Guards, on 22 September. In October Lieutenant F.R. Robinson, aged nineteen from Woodville, County Sligo, was killed in action with the South Staffordshires. He was the nephew of Sir Edward Carson, and the younger son of St George Robinson.

They say that the first casualty of war is truth. No doubt. But running it a close second is common sense. That same October Judge Wakeley at Ballymote Quarter sessions, in a case in which Major McClintock RE sought compensation for damage to his meadow in June, said that if the Germans were victorious, 'our land would be made a German colony. It would be a bad thing for the blackguards who committed these deeds, for under German occupation, they would be shot.'

That bit was probably true; 6500 Belgian and French civilians were murdered by invading forces, not in battle, but as captives, to set an example. Over the coming years thousands of civilians from the occupied countries were sent as slave labour to work in Germany, but there's absolutely no indication that the Germans had aggressive territorial designs on the Irish, or their land.

People do not lightly forgive arrant nonsense from their rulers, and I suspect it was during this time, with the exaggerated threats to Ireland, that both British rule in Ireland, and its supporters, began to lose legitimacy in the eyes of the common people. But for the moment Sligo appeared to remain pro-war, of course, and the largely unionist War Distress Fund was able to raise enough money to buy an ambulance for the army.

The Irish Times reported in November 1914: 'At the beginning of the war, 500 reservists belonging to different regiments left the town. Since then there has been a steady flow of recruits, from all classes and creeds. On four days last week, some 70 recruits were accepted and left for the depot at Boyle, Sligo was believed to hold the recruiting record for a nationalist town.' This was journalistic and unionist enthusiasm, perhaps hoping the majority population would recover their senses and become imperialists.

Mayor Jinks was a nationalist who supported recruitment throughout the war, as did Bishop Coyle of Elphin and Canon Quinn of Ballymote. By now the National Volunteers in Sligo had almost ceased to exist: based reservists, they were at the front. Here duty created a self-defeating policy: the more pro-British or pro-Home Rule recruits were drawn from the town, the less influential would they be outside church gates and in pubs.

On 17 February 1915 Captain F. Wood-Martin, youngest son of Colonel Wood-Martin, of Clevenagh, Sligo, was killed with the Suffolk Regiment. Three weeks later his brother James was killed in action with the Northamptonshires. Also serving in this regiment was Captain Guy St George Robinson MC, Woodville, Sligo, whose brother Francis had been killed the previous October.

By March 1915 recruiting in Sligo, as elsewhere, was faltering. Lord Justice Moriarty, a Catholic, told the Spring Assizes that 350 recruits had joined the colours in the county, as had 200 reservists. Sligo town had provided 279 of the 350 recruits, which meant that only 71 recruits had enlisted from rural areas.

Of the 200 reservists, he said, 152 were from Sligo town, which had a population of 10,000. This was poor. Nonetheless, he referred with pride to the Irish Guards and Connaught Rangers, and mentioned local men who had fallen: the Wood-Martins, Lieutenant Geoffrey Fenton, Lieutenant Edward Robinson, and Captain Perceval, who'd been badly injured. He spoke of Private Bracken a Sligoman in Irish Guards, who he said had been commissioned in the field

Actually, Bracken wasn't a private, but a drill sergeant. The Irish Guards that January had discovered their real enemy was mother nature. Just in the process of getting to the front-line trenches, seven men got stuck in the mud and it took six hours to get them all free. As Kipling said, the job of front line troops was like navigating canals. One reason why the men were getting stuck was the weight of their packs: each soldier had to carry all he needed for two days, because once in the front line re-supply was impossible. It was therefore absolutely necessary to keep the German heads down. Drill Sergeant Bracken came from an extended family of gamekeepers who worked several estates in Sligo. Using perhaps the first telescopic rifle seen by the Irish Guards, he set about establishing local dominance. By his own count, he killed three Germans and wounded four. The wounding would not have been through inaccuracy or mercy, but ruthless common sense. In the appalling state of the communication trenches, the evacuation of a wounded man required a carry of at least six soldiers; four for the stretcher, with a reserve shift of two. The economics of this are clear: a single bullet immobilizes at least seven enemy, possibly for the duration of the Micks' stay in the trenches. Bracken's seven bullets meant that there were at least thirty-one fewer Germans to fear. Bracken was awarded the Military Cross and commissioned in the field in the King's Liverpool Regiment. Against the odds, as both a senior NCO and a subaltern, he survived the war.

Judge Moriarty continued his splenetic tour of the assizes of Ireland. In King's County he observed that 688 men had joined the colours, 367 reservists and 321 new recruits. With a male population of 29,800, Moriarty thought the county's record might be better. *The Irish Times* agreed with him: 'Irish farmers ought to remember that they stand to lose everything, their freedom, their land, their political rights, if their country is beaten in this war.'

Frankly, I just don't think that the majority of people, never mind Sinn Féiners, accepted this argument. Sligoman Michael Doherty certainly didn't. He was charged with interfering with recruitment. He had apparently rescued his son from the recruiting officer at the railway station in Boyle, calling, 'You won't go into the army.' He was then charging with obstructing recruitment.

Meanwhile the judges continued their rather eccentric contribution to the cause. That spring Judge Wakeley told Grand Jury of Sligo Quarter Sessions that he was adjourning the business of the day so that they would all attend a recruiting rally. They were, he said, fighting not only for the safety of their property but for the safety of their lives.

On 27 April 1915 the band of the Irish Guards toured Sligo. Enthusiastic crowds, it was reported, welcomed them everywhere. Major O'Hara told a rally that thirty recruits had gone from Sligo since their last meeting, which showed their efforts were not in vain. J.J. McLoughlin, National Director of Recruiting, then declared that if the men of Sligo loved their land, their churches, their wives and children, they could not refuse the call that was being made to them. Sligo councillor McSharry next said that the countrymen should join the army, and, as he apparently thought they were doing, not take the jobs of the townsmen who had earlier joined. Sligo town had done well but the country had done little.

Meanwhile, the catastrophe of Gallipoli was unfolding and reaching into the westernmost parts of the United Kingdom for its harvest. Bryan Cooper's recruits had been formed into a battalion that had been sent there. But amongst the first Sligomen to fall were three men recruited in Scotland : John Murphy, with the King's Own Scottish Borderers, James Conlon with the Royal Scots, and Patrick Feeney with the 1st Dublin Fusiliers.

This last battalion had made what was to become initially a legendary and later a completely forgotten landing from the *River Clyde* steamer in Suvla Bay, on 24 April 1915. The Dubs and the Munster Fusiliers suffered such huge casualties that the two battalions were amalgamated into a unit called the Dubsters. And Henry Desmond O'Hara from Sligo was the Dubs sole uninjured officer after the landing. He took part in the assault on the Turkish for at Sed El Barrh, for which he was awarded an imme-diate DSO. This was only one of two DSOs given to the Dublin Fusiliers in Gallipoli, despite a regimental death toll of one thousand men. It was widely believed within the regiment that the divisional commander, later Corps commander, Hunter-Weston, disliked Irish troops, in particular the Dublin Fusiliers, and so blocked the award of any further DSOs.

As the only officer still standing O'Hara not merely was commander of the remaining Dubs, he was also unit censor, which meant there was no else to censor his own letters to his fiancée. In these, he was remarkably frank about the military failings of army command, as well as the low morale of the troops under his command. After the futile attack on Gully Spur, he said his men were bordering on lunacy.

The other end of the social spectrum was represented by Bobby Burnside, perhaps the most famous soccer-player in Sligo. He enlisted with the Connaught Rangers, was sent to Gallipoli in Cooper's battalion, was wounded there and died of his injuries in Britain. His funeral in Sligo was one of the largest the town had ever seen. Other deaths followed. Private Thomas Timoney, nineteen, son of a Crown and Peace Officer of Union Street Sligo, had joined the Pals battalion of the Dublin Fusiliers, and died of dysentery. Also with the 7th Dubs, Lance Corporal J.W. Little, Castlegarren, Sligo, died of wounds. And of course the fighting continued in France, where John Patrick Stokes, Irish Guards, twenty-six, only son of Maria Stokes, a widow, was killed in action.

Bizarrely, work continued on the Midland and Great Western Railway's new £30,000 hotel for tourists at Rosses Point, and every bit as bizarrely, work on it was halted by strike by ITGWU. Nonetheless, the campaign to promote Sligo as a tourism resort continued, with a press trip around the county for Dublin journalists. Alderman Jinks, Mayor of Sligo, welcomed them off the train, and they were driven round the county by none other than Mr L'Estrange, whom we first met as he ran over a little girl. And they were greeted at Sligo Golf Club President Mr Wood-Martin, who had lost his sons to the war.

We get a sense of the utter strangeness of the time, and an insight into why the Parliamentary Party was heading into trouble, during a recruiting meeting in Sligo addressed by Tom Kettle, formerly an IPP MP, and now a lieutenant in the Dublin Fusiliers. He began by referring to 'the pointless vulgarity' of Colonel Moore of the National Volunteers, essentially, his superior officer twice-over. Well, they all knew that Colonel's Moore's family had a talent for vulgarity, said Kettle, and he left that field uncontested (laughter). As an Irish nationalist, he was well content with the work he had been able to achieve against the foul megalomaniacs in Berlin. (Applause). This war for European freedom which had made so many soldiers of civilians, had found Colonel Moore a retired soldier, and left him more retired then ever (hear hear). He was seeking for recruits to reinforce and support his old comrades in the Connaught Rangers.

But that of course was the old regiment of the man he was mocking: surely a fairly counter-productive way of drumming up recruits.

As recruiting collapsed in Ireland, the Lord Lieutenant became Director General of recruiting in Ireland, with a Captain Kelly as the chief organizer. Fears of conscription, though, were already abroad. The Liverpool Correspondent of the *Weekly Despatch* reported large numbers of young men arriving from Ireland, especially from Boyle and Ballymote, and heading for America to avoid conscription. Soon afterwards, for this very reason, Cunard banned all Irish emigration to the US. No doubt for related reasons, the recruiting campaign became even more hysterical. In November a Mr T.P. Gill told a meeting at Nenagh that the war was a fight for the farmer's sons and their land, and for the farms that have been purchased for them. If the war were lost, Ireland would be planted, priests arrested, the banks seized and so on (*sic*).

He spoke of how a friend back from the front had told him of a captured German officer who was found with a map of the part of Sligo the Irish officer was from, including his farm, but on it were two wells he didn't recognize. When he got home he checked, and sure enough the wells had been dug on his farm and had found their way onto the officer's map.

The absurdity of a German officer carrying a map of Sligo into the murderous bogs of the Western Front is too self-evidently preposterous to require refutation; yet clearly, for the pro-war lobby, it all seemed self-evidently true; so perhaps such cognitive dissonance is not merely a symptom of war, but also its enabler.

The pro-war lobby was having little impact on the remaining young males of Sligo. In November Patrick Dywer arrested for having an anti-recruitment document signed by thirty-three shop assistants in Tobercurry. It said that they were willing to enlist for military service under a free and independent national government, but were prepared to resist conscription with our lives. 'We earnestly urge all able-bodied men of Sligo County to arm themselves with effective weapons without delay and give the so-called leaders who want to send them to bloody fields in foreign lands a very wide berth.'

Something strange is afoot when even *shop assistants* talk about sacri-ficing their lives. Dywer was so fundamentally law-abiding he even took the arresting officer from his bedroom to his place of work and showed him the document, and asked for it back. D.I. Walsh testified that he was a quiet unassuming individual, and would not even describe his conduct as 'hypothetical treason'. He understood the expression 'while Ireland is under foreign rule' as to mean until Ireland got Home Rule.

Imprisoning Dywer for a month, the magistrate said that if the same thing had happened in Germany, the corpse of the accused would be lying before a firing party of troops. The growing disparity between much of the ruled and their rulers was further revealed after schoolteacher Alec McCabe appeared in court on a charge of possessing gelignite at Sligo railway station. He testified that he had it for fishing and the jury acquitted him. Meanwhile, a more traditional form of dissent had returned, with judges hearing compensation claims after outbreaks of cattle-driving and hay-burning. The past and the future were meeting and synthesizing.

Sligo seems to have been lucky during the dreadful gas attack on the 16th Irish Division at Hulluch at the end of April 1916. Of the 494 enlisted Irish soldiers and twenty-six officers who were killed between 24 and 30 April, just two were from County Sligo. And the county was not really involved in the 1916 Rising, which occurred that week: in time some sixteen men from the county were interned, and later in the year were given a warm welcome on their return. The mood was changing.

On the first day of the Somme, 1 July 1916, six Sligo men were killed, three with the Dublin Fusiliers, two with the Tyneside Irish, and one, Charles Eyre, with the 36th Ulster Division. He was resident in Coleraine, so he enlisted when most Protestant men of his age, namely his peer-group, were joining up, and though Sligo had a large unionist population, there was very little sign that it aligned itself politically or any other way with the unionists of the nine Ulster counties

That summer Captain J. Ritty, 7th Royal Inniskilling Fusiliers, the son of Lieutenant J. Ritty RM, and Jenny Ritty, Harbour View, Sligo, was awarded the MC for gallantry during the gas attacks at Hulluch. He was recuperating from injuries when the award came through. He had already twice been mentioned in despatches. He returned to the front in time for the attacks by the 16th Irish Division on the Somme.

Seventeen soldiers from County Sligo were killed in these attacks, including the recently decorated Ritty. In the meeting of the council, Mayor Jinks proposed and Councillor Smyllie seconded a motion of regret over his death, but, curiously enough, over no others. Ballymote suffered heavily during the year. It lost seven men killed in the 16th's attacks in September, fourteen during the Somme overall, and twenty-one in the year 1916.

That October John Redmond unveiled a statue to Patrick McHugh MP in Sligo town. At the railway station in Longford, he was welcomed with an address from the council. At Collooney Reverend W. Dooley assured him he had the support of the people. At Sligo he was greeted by the mayor 'and a few' members of the Corporation. Bonfires were lit, but some younger people were hissing and booing.

In September 1917 Mr S. Kelly, Master of the Dromore Workhouse, applied at a meeting of the guardians for leave of absence in order to enlist, and was granted half-pay while he served, with the promise that his job would be kept open. The following month £10 was collected at Mrs O'Hara's garden fete to raise money for the comfort of the troops, and she gave another £3. Snow fell soon afterwards, and two local men, Michael Chambers and Pat Connor, were charged with carrying guns without permits under the Defence of the Realm regulations, Despite the seriousness of the charge, they were allowed out on their own recognizances for judgment within twelve months. Judge Wakeley for one clearly felt he was on the losing side, when he declared in November that people were so accustomed to illegalities that they took no notice of the law.

And so it was to prove. In March 1918 Alexander McCabe arrested at the railway station as he was boarding a train and taken to Sligo Jail, prompting the assembly of large crowds in the street, with shots being fired in the air, and the resulting disturbances were reported to be greater than those at the high of the Land League agitation. When McCabe appeared in court there was uproar. Soldiers were called for, and they arrived with fixed bayonets while the RIC used truncheons on protesters.

For soldiers at the front who heard about these events, these must have been perplexing days, for the great offensive by the 'gallant allies of the 1916 Proclamation' was soon to fall most heavily on the men of the 16th Irish Division. Over ninety men of the Connaught Rangers died in the battle, fifteen of them from County Sligo, and while another seven men from Sligo town were killed serving with five different regiments. One of the dead was Trooper Arthur Gorman of the South Irish Horse, son of John and Elizabeth Gorman, the postmaster at Ballymote. Four other sons were at the front. However, the Gormans were Church of Ireland, as presumably, were most of the Ladies Sandbags Committee.

In the final hundred days of the war, twenty-four men from Sligo town were killed. Many men who had enlisted in the Connaught Rangers had been transferred to the 2nd battalion the Leinster Regiment, a regular battalion which, though now full of wartime recruits, still prided itself on its pre-war, professional standards. The Ranger-transferees suffered disproportionately high casualties, thirty-three dead out of some hundred, perhaps because their fighting skills were cruder, or because many were Northern nationalists, and their legendary impetuosity in battle brought predictably tragic results.

But it was a Sligoman and former Ranger, Martin Moffat, whose measured courage won a Victoria Cross in the assault by the Leinsters on the Belgian town of Ledegem (see 'The Leinster Regiment,' p.149).

By this time the conscription crisis had completed the transformation of Irish politics. Into this tragi-comedy sails the heroic figure of J.J. McLaughlin of the Recruiting Council, announcing that conscription would be introduced in Ireland unless the Viceroy's figure of 50,000 voluntary recruits by the end of September was achieved: a figure, he declared, that was so generous in its moderation that he would not dare to propose an extension.

By 25 September 1918 the number of new recruits stood at 7290. Whereas Sligo's quota was a preposterous 1600, or three times the recruitment for the first three months of the war, the county managed just 138 new recruits, namely 8.6 per cent of the target. On one day when Sligo recorded no recruits, Dublin had thirty, Limerick five, Waterford three, and Belfast 111, but even this last figure was way below requirements. The Ulster capital had a total a 2595 recruits, 6000 below its quota of 8500. Dublin, with a quota of 8500 was 6000 below that. And the army wasn't getting what few recruits there were: of the seventy-three Dublin recruits on one day, sixty-six were for the Royal Air Force.

The public face of Sligo was now altered beyond recognition. In mid-September Sinn Féin supporters broke up a meeting in the town hall. Most of the county grandees were present, but proceedings soon became a farce with catcalls and people shouting 'Up Germany!' An attempt to finish with 'God Save the King' was drowned out by the cries of the Sinn Féiners. Shortly afterwards the self-styled Countess Markievicz and

Count Plunkett (my how these 'republicans' loved royal titles) were made freemen of Sligo.

However, the conscription crisis did not stop all conscription in Sligo or the country generally. Young men with American citizenship obeyed the instructions of the US consul in Dublin to report for military service.

And even with war's end, there was little enough charity in the air. In December a reception to welcome home Martin Moffatt, VC, was boycotted by the new Sinn Féin mayor, and most councillors.

To sum up. Some 167 soldiers (not officers) born in Sligo town were killed in the war, just forty with the Connaught Rangers. The fate of exiled Sligomen explains why that latter figure is so low, For example, of the twenty-one Sligo town-born men who died and who had enlisted in Glasgow, only two joined the Rangers. And of the thirty-eight County Sligo-born recruits who were killed having been recruited in Scotland, twenty-three were serving in Scottish regiments; in other words, these are Irish recruits who appear in official statistics as actually being Scottish. This is true overall: 44 per cent of Sligomen killed with the British army in the war were recruited abroad. They enlisted in fifty-six different places, and served in thirty-five different regiments, so that there really is no common 'Sligo' experience of the war: 140 soldiers from Sligo town died in the European theatre, fifteen at Gallipoli, and nine in the Middle East. The figures from the Commonwealth War Graves Commission tell us that 313 Sligo men died in the war, 279, or 89 per cent, with the British forces, the rest with the Commonwealth. Sligo town's deaths came as follows: 1914 – 15, 1915 – 32, 1916 – 41 1917 – 34 1918 – 20.

The years 1916 and 1918 were equally bloody, so Sligo losses for 1918 reflect the smaller proportion of Sligomen still serving. One Sligoman, Francis McNally, a Catholic, was actually killed serving with the 14th battalion of the Royal Irish Rifles, formed from the Young Citizen Volunteers of the UVF. At least thirteen Sligomen died with the Royal Navy.

Some fifty-seven men from Ballymote were killed, in twenty-four regiments or branches of the services, seventeen Connaught Rangers and nine Irish Guards. The annual figures are: 1914 – 6, 1915 – 10, 1916 – 21, 1917 – 5 and 1918 – 15 (ten in the final hundred days). Seven were from Gurteen, two from Grattan Street, four from Teeling Street. Only three of the Ballymote dead are listed as married, and none of these was living locally. Of the nine Tobercurry-born fatalities, three were in the Rangers, and four in British regiments: five had enlisted in Britain. In other words, many Sligo recruits were already lost to the county by the time of their enlistment. Those who survived returned to homes in Britain, and so were not present in the county to form a narrative of their own.

The historian for the county over this time, Michael Farry, quotes Russel Fenton as saying the working class had done 'magnificently'. Mr Nelson, a jeweller, said the 'corner boy element' had all gone to join up. It was a commercial transaction, said Fenton, and so it probably was, and would remain so, within the new dispensation. Farry shows that ten Free State soldiers in 1922 were from Holburn Street, which was where the footballer Bobby Burnside was from, and these were probably former British soldiers.

The Ritty family, who had lost their son in 1916, moved out of Ireland after independence, to the Solent in Hampshire. Disconsolately, they named their house after the battle in which he had died: The Somme. And of course the war didn't end in 1918 in Ireland, but took on another and more personal note. On 3 November 1920 RIC sergeant Patrick Fallon, who was a popular and much respected man in Ballymote, was shot dead on Market day as he walked out of his digs. He was one of just nineteen people killed in Sligo during the troubles of 1919–21; eighteen by the IRA, and one IRA man by crown forces.

Bryan Cooper, who had helped raise a battalion of Connaught Rangers, returned to Ireland to find his wife had conceived and given birth to a child while he was away. Later elected unionist TD for South Dublin, and throughout the period in question an alcoholic, he died in 1930, and was given a military funeral by the Free State army, with a union jack and tricolour on his coffin. Captain Perceval, who had been invalided out of the army in 1915 with a ruptured diaphragm, actually survived to 1976. Judge Wakeley, who had fulminated often enough about poor recruitment in the county, in 1922 held his court under an Irish tricolour. The rebel Alec McCabe became a successful politician and businessman. In 1946 Martin Moffatt VC took his own life, the day after being sacked by Sligo Harbour Commissioners.

But I began this tale with the story of Mary Pilkington being run over by Henry L'Estrange. He represented the passing order, and she, quite coincidentally, represented the one that was about to triumph. For her older brother William was the most dynamic IRA leader in the conflicts of

1919–23, and in time was to represent the twin forces of Catholic triumpha-lism and ideological Fenianism, for once the fighting was done he became a Redemptorist priest. And it was those forces, more than any other, that so successfully obliterated almost all memory of the four hundred or so Sligo men who died in the Great War, and in their stead commemorated and even celebrated a conflict in which just nineteen people in the county were killed, and all but one by the IRA.

To the victor, not just the spoils, but also the conch.

3. Athy in the Great War

Though Athy was a garrison town, most Athy soldiers did not enlist here but in Naas or Carlow. Of the eighty-seven Athy men killed as plain soldiers, just thirteen enlisted locally. This was not so unusual. Labour was mobile in those days, with men travelling widely in search of work – and when that was hard to come by, the military option beckoned.

Three regiments recruited in this part of Kildare: The Royal Dublin Fusiliers, the Leinsters and the Irish Guards. It was this last regiment from which the first Athy dead of the war came, Private William Corcoran, on 1 September 1914, at the battle of Villers Cotteret, in the final stages of the retreat from Mons. It was the first time that the Irish Guards had ever been in action, and in addition to losing their commanding officer, Colonel Morris, from Killannin, County Galway, thirteen plain guardsmen were killed. The next Athy man to die was also a Mick: Patrick Heydon, of Churchtown House, on 4 September, still in the Villers-Cotteret area. Edward Stafford, a member of the Dublin Fusiliers, and a near neighbour of the Haydons, was the next Athy man to lose his life, on 24 September. Under a month later, on 20 October, the town's Michael Lawlor fell in an epic slaughter, of the Leinsters at Premesques, in which the Irish suffered some 120 dead.

The war already had had an immediate impact on the economic and cultural life of Athy, with the South Kildare Agricultural show having to be cancelled that August 1914, primarily because the military who were at its core were on their way to the front. As was the case universally in Ireland at the time, soldiers leaving for war were sent off from the station by large and enthusiastic crowds of well-wishers waving union jacks. The economic upturn in the town, reflecting a general increase in prosperity in Ireland generally, meant that when the urban district council sought tenders to build thirty-seven houses for working-class tenants, there were no tenders, not least because recruiting was reported to be heavy. The Athy Board of Guardians voted that all men going to the front should have their positions retained for them until the war was over.

However, not everyone was satisfied with the men of the town. In mid August a pro-war women's rally was organized by Lady Weldon, whose husband, Lord Weldon, was at the front with the Dublin Fusiliers. Lady Weldon said she could raise a battalion of women for the front, and complained about the numbers of able-bodied men still visible on the streets of Athy. These were different times indeed, as we can see when her son, Sir Anthony Weldon, said he would look after any recruits who joined the Leinsters. To which someone cried, and not sarcastically: 'God bless you sir.'

Mr P.J. Murphy proposed vote of thanks and a motion supporting the war was passed by acclamation. The mood remained bellicose. On 16 October Athy Board of Guardians passed a vote in support of the Irish National Volunteers' stance on the war. A Mr Dunn said that the Irish National Volunteers must defend both Ireland the empire. And in December a concert for the welfare of Athy soldiers in a packed town hall ended with a rousing rendition of 'God Save the King'.

March 1915 saw perhaps the high point of pro-war feeling in Athy. Several thousand soldiers of the Munster and Dublin Fusiliers marched through the town. Mr E. Doyle, JP, chairman of the Urban District Council, gave an official welcome to the troops, and announced that 1000 men from the Athy area had already joined the army. Echoing a sentiment that was widespread across the country at that time, he declared that final peace between Ireland and England had been achieved.

The following month, Doyle declared that every able-bodied man in Athy was at the front. This was probably true of both the small-town poor, and of the Catholic middle classes of the town. Dr John Kilbride, son of the most eminent doctor James Kilbride, had joined the Royal Army Medical Corps. His uncle, Denis Kilbride, was an Irish parliamentary party MP, and another uncle was an RM. John Vincent Holland, son of the local vet, had enlisted too, commissioned in the Leinsters. Two of the sons of the Protestant businessman, and well-known unionist, John Hannon, also joined. A concert in the town that same April 1915 was provided entirely by local soldiers home from the front, from many different regiments, on this occasion most not even Irish regiments, and largely cavalry.

In May 1915 Athy gained a certain notoriety after the urban district council came out against the general restriction on drinks sales, perhaps because farmers had money to spend. Certainly for them, things were going very well; the first cut of hay that summer fetched up to £5.10 a ton, twice that of the harvest of the previous year.

That same month the Mallen family learnt that their boy was missing in action, but later found he was alive, a POW. The Hannons of Ardreigh House learnt that their boy Norman Leslie was also missing. In due course they discovered he was dead. He was just twenty. He had been at Trinity College when war was declared, and a member of the officers training corps. He had promptly enlisted and was posted in the King's Liverpool regiment, in which his brother John Coulter was already serving. They both took part in the assault at Festubert, one of many costly but largely forgotten offensives in the year of 1915.

That summer, the Irish National Volunteers held a morale-boosting meeting. The INV in Athy, as elsewhere, were discovering the counter-productive consequences of their polcies: the more successful they were at recruiting, and the more men went to the front, the less influential they were in the town. Canon Mackey told the meeting that the war was one of right against might, of justice against inequity, of purity against lust and barbarism. (This was not unusual. Across Ireland at the time, much the same message was being repeated by Catholic clergymen.) Denis McBride MP told the rally that conscription would never come to Ireland so long as the Irish Parliamentary Party were in Westminster, A vote of sympathy was passed for INV soldiers killed at the front, and another vote of sympathy for the allies was passed unanimously.

That summer it was learnt that a local man, Surgeon Peter Burrowes of the Royal Navy had been awarded the DSO for his work at the landings at Sed El Barrh at Gallipoli the previous April. Educated at Castleknock, he was the son of Gilbert Kelly, clerk of the Crown, Meanwhile, Athy UDC retained their reputation for truculence when they refused to pay for gas from the Athlone Gas Company, declaring that it was too expensive. And so the town went dark, and effectively stayed dark for the rest of the war. At one stage twelve oil lamps were erected 'pending a supply of electricity', which at that time in the war was not dissimilar to awaiting the Millennium.

That September support for the war was still evident. Large numbers of people attended a horse-jumping contest to raise money for local prisoners of war, aided by cavalry regiments, and raised £165, a large sum indeed, which went to local men at the front and to Athy POWs. (Sgt Pender last wrote from Germany to thank Lady Weldon for her work for prisoners, so clearly some proceeds found their intended destination.)

It was now being reported that that some 1500 men from Athy, out of a town of 4000, were at the front. It's likely that some statistical massaging was going on here; and whereas the poor and middle classes had responded, a recruiting meeting was told that farmers' sons and shop assistants were still not joining up, yet at the end of the meeting another large number of recruits enlisted. One of the new recruits was Mr M.J. McLaughlin, vice-chaiman of Athy Board of Guardians, who joined the Pals battalion, of the 6th RDF. When he appeared at a meeting of the Guardians in uniform, he was widely applauded. Generally, local government officials were doing their bit. For example, the assistant to M. Doyle, JP, Joseph Spiddal of the South Irish Horse, was soon afterwards reported missing in action. In November another recruiting meeting was staged and yet more joined up.

They were needed. That autumn Private Albert Mullen, aged eighteen, 2nd Irish Guards, who had been reported reported missing in September, was now reported dead. 'Safe in the arms of Jesus,' said the death notice. The son of a former policeman and now small farmer, he was an exception to the rule about farmers' sons not enlisting, but being from a Church of Ireland family, the general rules would not have applied. However, they would have applied to the son of another farmer and police pensioner, Christopher Fitzpatrick, twenty-one, whose family were Catholic, 2nd Irish Guards, and who died in the grim and ceaseless slaughter at Loos.

As local casualties grew, so too did a certain restlessness in the town.

At a meeting of the UDC Mr Dunne complained that of eighty Irish MPs, only four had joined up. A Mr Byrne said they were sensible to stay at home. The clerk of the session pointed out that sixty of them were over age, which in the longer term was of course to help bring about the downfall of the IPP, as it lost touch with the rising nationalism amongst the younger generation.

The weather proved a harbinger of things to come. On New Year's day 1916 both a monsoon and a hurricane struck that part of Leinster, the worst in memory. The Barrow overflowed and hundreds of farms were flooded. However, agriculture generally prospered. Pigmeat was now selling at more than £3 a hundredweight (50 kilos), an unheard-of price. So many were away at the war that five public houses in Athy closed. With 1600 men at the front, the town was receiving £250 a week in separation money.

But life went on. Several people were fined for cycling without lights in this now lightless town. The boys of the Christian Brothers school performed *Julius Caesar*. In neighbouring Carlow, White Assizes were briefly held for the donning of the gloves. All was well in Ireland. But in fact, catastrophe loomed. A manmade answer to the evil weather on New Year's Day was unleashed on the Western Front as the 16th Irish Division was exposed to the horrors of gas warfare. From Athy, Sergeant Ryan and privates, Mulhall, Stapleton and Whelan, were reported to be among the 632 Irishmen missing. All three were found, alive but wounded.

Athy was lucky. Few towns escaped the slaughter of Huluch as it had done. And the great gas attack had coincided with the Easter Rising in Dublin. But this too largely passed Athy by. In June 600 republican deportees were transported to British prisons: not one man from Athy was adjudged to be dangerous enough to merit exile. Yet the drip drip drip of casualties, J. Hegarty, IG, wounded, P. Dowey, IG, wounded, Cpl Kavanagh wounded, was eroding faith in the war, and not just for the British. Surgeon Peter Kelly had been decorated for bravery in Gallipoli. Now his brother Gilbert who had also served in Gallipoli was killed with the New Zealanders. Another Gallipoli veteran, Sgt James Price, son of James and Eliza Price Ballylinan, of the 1st Royal Dublin Fusiliers, was killed in action shortly before the battle of the Somme began. In Athy Show in the summer of 1916, the prize for the best three-year-old gelding went to the local vet John Holland. The prize for the best four-year-old went to the Hannons – they who had lost a son in action. Three weeks later the son of the vet, John Vincent Holland, led a team of twenty-five bombers in an attack on German positions between Guillemont and Ginchy, as the 16th Irish Division took their position in the Somme battles. Only four men were still standing at the end of the assault, but all German positions had been taken, with some fifty prisoners. John Vincent Holland was later awarded the Victoria Cross, and in November Athy UDC unanimously passed a vote of appreciation for his heroism.

But there was already a measurable distance between local feeling and central government. That summer the Local Government Board in Dublin asked Athy Board of Guardians, which had initially been so pro-war, to reconsider its recent appointment of Dr McLennan as Monasterevin Dispensary, saying he should be in the army. But the Board of Guardians declined, and reiterated its determination to appoint him, with the apparent figleaf that he was not fit to join the army

The same summer Athy UDC, wayward as ever, voted to supply all children with a hot meal every day, and to clothe and shoe all children in the town. This was the Mother and Child scheme some thirty years earlier, and it only makes sense when viewed in the light of the rise of republican sentiment after the Rising: it was apparently a frantic attempt by the forces of Redmondism to regain favour among an increasingly restless electorate

Recruitment was clearly not soaking up quite as many men as the war-party maintained, That summer 110 men from Carlow and Kildare were summonsed by the RIC for cockfighting and all were fined.

Increasingly, therefore, we get the picture of two Irelands, even viewed from the relatively narrow lens of Athy. In one Ireland, 2nd Lt John Hannon youngest surviving son of Mr John Hannon of Ardreigh House, as noted, had been reported killed in action. In the other, De Valera and Arthur Griffith attended a large rally in Athy, with men in uniforms with tricolours and hurleys. And even some of the UDC had changed Irelands, for UDC member Mr Peter Doyle presided. De Valera's speech was punctuated by cheers – for it was in part an anti-conscription meeting. 'England will not conscript us,' he declared. 'We will sell our lives dearly, We would fight conscription, if only using 10 ft pikes.'

Here now, was language, with its imagery of 1798, which would strike a chord amongst the young men of the county. He continued unapologetically: 'I believe in physical force, in Ireland.'

Denouncing the Home Rule Bill, 'that unfortunate worthless bill' he sneered, presumably in that careful, measured way of his, 'Redmond believes that fighting for France was fighting for Ireland.' The sarcasm was well rewarded with laughter.

If they were staunch and knew their rights, and were ready to sacrifice all, freedom lay before them. He appealed to people to join the only army, the physical force army, the moral force army, they had the people on their side. More loud cheers erupted from the crowds.

Arthur Griffith presciently added that under the new franchise the IPP would not get half a dozen MPs elected.

Later there was a special meeting of the Athy UDC to make a presentation to De Valera, with Mr Joyle JP presiding. The defection of official Athy from one Ireland to the other was complete, even if some of the pretences for doing so were unconvincing. Mr Mahon, for example, declared that De Valera was not in favour of violent revolution: he had been misquoted. Messrs Malone Mahon and Baily agreed, declaring that Athy's new hero was not for physical force (even though he had in their hearing said that he was). His opinions had been falsified by the press, but – De Valerean casuistry clearly proving infectious – if he was in favour of force, it was justified.

The forces of Redmondism – represented by Mr M Doyle JP and Dr O'Neill – opposed the motion supporting De Valera, and amid scenes of confusion and uproar Mr M. Doyle stood down from the chair, the town clerk took over, and it was he who decided that the presentation should be made. Later, the Athy Board of Guardians also voted to make a presentation to Dev. The dominoes were collapsing.

When uniformed men bearing tricolours and hurleys attended a Sinn Féin rally in Stradbally, Father Doyle, the parish priest of Athy, presided. He read out an address from his fellow local priest, Father Burbage, who described Redmondism as a pernicious unionist faction that had misled the Irish people. Redmondites believed in Up England, Up the Union Jack, which is another way of saying Croppies Lie Down.

The meeting ended with a resolution calling for the breaking up of grazing lands, especially of the Reverend Mr Butler's. In other words, the new Ireland pretty much resembled the old one, complete with anti-Protestant sting in the tail.

So the politico-cultural revolution, able to call on so many historical strands, was well under way. In June 1918 Athy number 2 Rural District Council elected Thomas McHugh of Sinn Féin as chairman, and Mr Malone as vice-chairman. That summer a local schoolteacher, J.J. O'Byrne, was arrested, for participating in illegal rallies, and seen off by large crowds on his way to trial in Dublin, with Sinn Féin flags on the station that just four years before had been bedecked with union jacks. And whereas the 1914 agricultural show had been cancelled because the army had departed for the front, in 1918 the show could resume, now with a large contribution from the army.

For now Ireland was well and truly garrisoned.

But of course the war had been going on all this time. The Third Battle of Ypres had occurred; four Athy men had died in Flanders that August. Two more Athy men died in the great German offensive in March 1918. That summer came the great allied counter offensives. In all these melancholy affairs, I would guess that Athy casualties were barely registered by a town whose sympathies had gone in an entirely different direction.

One of the last Athy men to die was twenty-five-year-old Private Thomas O'Brien. Perhaps aware of the change in national mood, his family put on his war-grave headstone just two words: 'A Volunteer.' Officially the last man to die was Hugh Fenlon, of the Royal Dublin Fusiliers, then of the Labour Corps, who died on his injuries in a Hampshire hospital on 29 October 1918, and whose body was returned to Ireland for burial. But we can be sure that others died of the long-term complications of war.

Death was sometimes not satisfied with a single visit. One of the first Athy men to die was Edward Stafford of the Dublin Fusiliers, killed in September 1914. Two years later his parents, Thomas and Julia, learnt of the death of another son, Thomas, twenty-four, killed in the battles in which John Vincent Holland would win the Victoria Cross. Another early death that September 1914 was of Patrick Heydon, Irish Guards. Three years later his brother Aloysius was also killed with the Micks. Their mother, Margaret Heydon of Churchtown House, was now left with just one son.

Two Kelly brothers from Athy also were killed. The sons of John and Mary Kelly of Chapel Lane, John was the first go, being killed in action on the ruinous fields of Festubert in May 1915. He was aged just twenty. His brother Denis was killed just over a month before the war ended. He was aged eighteen. Another Kelly from the town, Owen Kelly, must have been in the same recruitment queue as John – one was no. 3626, the other no. 3636 – and they died just a couple of weeks apart

The two Hannon brothers who had been killed in 1915 and 1917 were joined in death by their cousin, Reginald, in December 1917, serving with the Shropshire Light Infantry. He was resident in London though his Commonwealth War Graves notice emphatically declares him to be of Athy.

Finally, we come to the Curtis brothers: all three had enlisted in Glasgow, where they presumably were living. Patrick Curtis, Irish Guards, was killed in action in December 1914. He is the only Irish Guardsman buried in Sanctuary Wood outside Ypres. The cemetery register names his parents as John and Margaret Curtis of Kilcrow Athy. Two other brothers were to die. John Curtis, Royal Horse Artillery, killed in action in January 1917, and Laurence, killed in action in December 1917: but the cemetery registers make no mention of any family connections. Was it because these two men had been killed after 1916? Or was it because the family was just too devastated to supply details, as sometimes happened? I don't know.

The last Athy man to be directly killed in action was William Corrigan, formerly of the South Irish Horse, and latterly the Dublin Fusiliers, who died on 14 October 1918, in one of the last actions of the war – the liberation of Ledegem by 1st Royal Dublin Fusiliers and the 2nd Leinsters, in the course of which two Irish VCs were won. William is buried in Ledegem cemetery seventeen miles east of Ypres. In the same cemetery and killed in that same action is Coman O'Malley, nineteen, who enlisted in England and I suspect had run away to do so. He was one of six brothers from the Redmondite O'Malley family of Glenamaddy to have served. Their father was a local GP there. Had history been different, that family would have probably turned out to be major players in Home Rule Ireland. But events, as we know, went in another direction.

The worst year for Athy deaths was 1915 – thirty-two enlisted men died that year. It's quite clear from their ages and numbers that a good deal of these men were new recruits from the year before. In the first year of the war, eight Athy men died, nineteen in 1916, and sixteen in 1917. Eleven died in 1918. Perhaps the most remarkable death is that of Christopher Power, husband of Esther, a soldier with the 8th Dublin Fusiliers, who was killed in action at Hulluch at the astonishing age of fifty-nine.

I don't know the figures for Athy officers, simply because officers' origins are not listed in the official statistics, and for the most part they weren't mentioned in national newspaper dispatches. But we know from references to the Kilbrides and the Hollands and the McLaughlins, that the nationalist middle class of Athy town did join up. But I suspect that rural Athy did not; either through Sinn Féin-type loyalties, or through an agricultural resistance to military service that was widespread in both Ireland and Britain. Allowing for the usual ratio of officers to men, it's reasonable to accept that around 100 Athy men were killed in the war. If you allow Castledermot casualties, the figure rises to well over 120

I don't know what happened to most of the people in this story. The Hannons stand as representatives of an almost doomed caste of unionists in southern Ireland. A memorial raised in the Church of Ireland church in 1919 actually says that four Hannons were killed – but I haven't been able to find the fourth. However, perhaps that number was prescience of a kind. Devastated by the loss of his sons, and with his milling business in ruins in part because of the collapse of his own mental health, their father, John Hannon, took his own life. The only surviving Hannon son became a clergyman, and married in Ballymoney in Country Antrim in the 1920s. One son of that union became a bishop, and his son Neil Hannon became the lead singer of the band The Divine Comedy. But as for the Hannons in the Republic, once so prosperous, and with five children, the line seems to have died out.

Athy at the time of the Great War had a population of about 4000 people. Whereas 1.7 per cent of the population of Britain died in the war, the figure for Athy, at 2.5 per cent, is proportionately 47 per cent higher. Yet when I first spoke on this subject to people here in this town nearly twenty years ago, almost no-one had the faintest idea about what Athy had suffered. Amnesia was total. That has changed totally now – and I think that is almost entirely due to the efforts of local solicitor, Frank Taaffe, and his family.

If we owe any duty to these men of the Great War, and I emphatically believe that we do, it is simply that as a society we must never, ever hide the truth again.

4. *Kilkenny Families and the Great War*

In the beautiful St Symphorien Cemetery in the southern Belgian city of Mons lie the remains of the first and the last of the British army's victims of the Great War. Lance Corporal Thomas Troy of the Royal Irish Regiment belongs to the former category. He was 'killed in action' on 24 August 1914. What that parenthetic term actually means, I cannot say. Was he eviscerated by a flail of shrapnel, to die in agony in a Mons street? Was he caught by An Uhlan's scything sabre? Was he sniped from far away, never knowing who or what had brought about his end, or quite how? We cannot know. He lies there now, in the gentle groves that grow around the first and the last.

'Kilkenny Families and the Great War' does however allow us to see something about this man's life; he was thirty-four when it departed from his body, which, we know, was 5'5" in height with a 34" chest, weighing 9 stone 7lbs, when he had enlisted in 1898 fourteen years previously, aged twenty. At the age of twenty-six or twenty-seven he married a widow, a Welshwoman named Sarah Anne Williams, ten years older than himself, in a Registry Office in Pontrypridd, Glamorgan; so by the standards of the day he was clearly not much of a Catholic.

Perhaps the important thing to bear in mind about this soldier, was that, like so many others to fall in these early days, he was a reservist. He was thus called from the colours to serve in a war that must have come as a very bad shock indeed. He had initially been discharged from the army in Cork in 1904, and placed in the Reserve, which was legally obligatory. But now living in south Wales, in 1910, he re-enlisted as a volunteer, little imagining, I surmise, that he would ever be called to fight. The extra money would come in handy, and the yearly military exercises each August might offer the possibility of renewing old friendships. It probably never entered his head that war was a possibility.

The 2nd battalion, the Royal Irish Regiment, was mobilized on 29 July, and reservists recalled to the depot at Clonmel. Those like Thomas Troy, who had crossed over from Britian, were promptly despatched back again, to Devonport, thence to Southampton, and on to France. On 23 August the battalion was ordered to the new front line near Mons, where in close countryside bounded by banks and hedgerows they suffered their first fatal casualties of the war. There is no point in pretending that one can describe the first clash of arms between the onward drive of the German army and the first skirmishing vanguard of the British Expeditionary Force. Suffice to say, that at one stage a bayonet charge was ordered under 2nd Lieutenant Shine, which allegedly drove the enemy back with loss. Whether this is true is barely relevant, for Lieutenant Shine was lost, and so too, in the skirmishing and the utter confusion of battle, were some 150 other men, killed, wounded and missing. One was Thomas Troy.

This, remember, was in the last week of August. His wife was not told that he was Missing in Action until 27 November. Finally, on 6 June 1915, she was told that he was believed to have been killed, and though the date given for his death was usually 24 August, the day before, the day of the Shine bayonet-charge, is more likely when he died. Sarah Troy started to receive the 12/– a week widow's pension in December 1915.

Thomas, at least, is remembered officially, listed in both Soldiers Died in the Great War, and the Commonwealth War Graves Commission. His older brother Martin, a former soldier, re-enlisted in 1914, and was sent to Gallipoli with the 5th battalion of the Royal Irish Regiment. During service in the Dardanelles, Salonika and Egypt, he contracted malaria, which finally killed him in February 1919. He is on no official list of the war-dead, save that of 'Kilkenny families in the Great War': two brothers whose deaths bookend that enormous tragedy.

Probably killed at the same time as Thomas Troy was, as we've seen, John Shine, from Dungarvan, County Waterford. His brother Hugh Patrick Shine, Royal Irish Fusiliers, was to die in the first gas attacks of the war, in the spring of 1915. A third brother, James, serving with the Royal Dublin fusiliers, died amid the ocean of mud that was the Frezenberg Ridge in August 1916. The three boys were followed shortly thereafter by their mother Kathleen Mary Shine, who died of whatever it is that mothers die of when all their sons have been killed.

One Kilkennyman for sure did well out of the war. In 1914 Freddie Plunkett was a thirty-seven-year old Regimental Sergeant Major when he arrived in France. By war's end, four years later, he was an acting Brigadier General, the holder of the Distinguished Service Order and Two Bars, the Military Cross, the Distinguished Conduct Medal, mentioned in despatches too often to count, and had been twice recommended for a Victoria Cross. And if you want to get an insight into how the British army that had beaten the Kaiser's army then collapsed, the fate of Freddie Plunkett will give you a hint. At the end of the war he was put on the half-pay list as a mere major, while the army reverted to imperial mode, with all the lessons of 1914–18 unlearnt, and the glories of Dunkirk just two decades away.

The last soldier from Kilkenny City actually to be killed outright in the war was Royal Dublin Fusiliers Company Sergeant Major Patrick Delaney DCM MM. He took part in the famous landings at V Beach in Gallipoli on 24 April 1915, and in subsequent fighting was so severely injured that an arm had to be amputated. He could therefore easily have opted for discharge through incapacitation, but he chose to remain with his battalion. Loyalty to one's fellow soldiers, and the comradeship of the trenches, are difficult things to define or express – but what else explains a man making such a decision – and moreover, winning a DCM while the owner of just one good arm, as he did for bravery during Third Ypres in 1917?

A year later the 1st battalion Royal Dublin Fusiliers took part in a frontal assault near the Poperinge area, with the one-armed CSM Patrick Delaney amongst those in the lead. And finally, along with a young officer commissioned from the ranks, Lieutenant Nolan MC, DCM, he was fatally wounded. Twenty-five men died with them: even at this late stage of the war, twenty of them were Irish. Those who were killed outright, such as

Lieutenant Nolan, were buried at Birr Cross Roads Cemetery, so named by men of the Leinster Regiment, while those who expired of their wounds, like the gallant CSM Delaney, son of Michael Delaney, Collier's Lane, Kilkenny, were laid to rest at Haringue Cemetery, Poperinge.

Not all Kilkenny men, or indeed, all Patrick Delaneys, proved to be such adept soldiers, though perhaps my favourite was a tinsmith, more commonly known as a tinker then, and a Traveller now. When he enlisted in the summer of 1915, this particular Patrick Delaney was just 5'3" tall, with a 34–" chest, and weighing 118 lbs, under 54 kilogrammes. Perhaps not the ideal build for a soldier, in a Flanders plain where the mudpools could consume the weak or unwary in a trice and only begrudgingly yield them up in a century or so later, if even then, but clearly sufficient for what he was really heroic at, which was being a deserter. This he managed to be for two years, as well a drunk, a thief, and after serving 168 days hard, labour, was discharged with ignominy, having forfeited his Boer War medals. Yet despite this, such was the manpower shortage, that he was allowed to re-renlist in 1916, and served for some two years in the Labour Corps, whose ardours he survived. To tell you the truth, I rather admire the pluck and ingenuity of Patrick Delaney, who finally claimed his two Great War medals in 1935.

Some 145 men who were born in Kilkenny City died in the war, having enlisted in 52 places, and in 40 different regiments; and far from this being an especially Irish characteristic analysis of a similar cathedral city, namely Litchfield, revealed comparable patterns within England. However, in all, fifty-five, or 38 per cent, of the Kilkenny dead were recruited outside Ireland: twenty-four in the north of England, FOURTEEN in Wales, seven in Greater London, and three from Scotland. They ended up in the following regiments: twenty-four in the Royal Dublin Fusiliers, nineteen in the Connaught rangers, twelve in the Irish Guards, and FIVE in the local regiment, the Royal Irish. This figure of approximately 40 per cent of local volunteers actually being recruited in Britain applies both to most Irish regions and most Irish regiments. The failure to perceive this is one of the reasons why Irish recruitment is persistently under-estimated. Of course, volunteers in Britain, where enthusiasm for voluntary recruitment lasted well into 1915, would have experienced different social pressures to enlist than those that existed in Ireland.

The reasons for regular soldiers to have joined up are probably simply stated: economic, family tradition, and regimental pride, which for the case of the Royal Irish Regiment, the oldest Irish military establishment in the Army List, would have been considerable. Both gentry, such as the Catholic Redmonds, and commercial families, such as Smithwicks, the brewers, seem to have taken for granted that the Royal Irish Regiment was the proper billet for a younger son.

And then there are the almost invisible, unseen in life and forgotten in death, who have been brought back to view, if only briefly, in this memorial volume. Let us remember now Edmund D'Arcy, a private in the 1st battalion of the Royal Irish, who was born in Kilkenny and who enlisted in Merthyr Tydfil in Glamorganshire. He had no known date of birth or home when he enlisted. He disembarked in France in January 1915 and was killed just two weeks later. He has no known grave. He was posthumously awarded (as were all soldiers for that time) the 1915 Star and the British War and Victory Medal, but these were returned, unclaimed.

We know something about Edmund's last days on this earth. The 1st Royal Irish were doing front line duty at Trench 19, near St Eloi, Belgium, in the astonishingly vile winter of 1914–15, for which the army was totally ill-equipped. 'Stand-to' usually occurred an hour before dawn, and the parapets manned against a surprise attack. 'Stand-down' was ordered once day had broken, and the rest of the day would be spent skulking in the mud-filled trenches, which at this point in the war were not the exotically constructed earthworks they were later to become, but a series of interconnected lateral pools of bitterly cold water. Men standing in them were up to their knees in water, and unless they moved, gradually sank. Brushwood, straw and planks were placed on the trench-floor to give men support. But these usually sank also. So men slept on the firestep, on which also stood the sentries. Little was done in daylight; little could be done. The unwary would pay the price, as did Lieutenant Stackpoole and Sergeant Mahoney, both of whom were shot through the head in Trench 19, probably by the same sniper. At night, men slept, if they slept at all, leaning against the back of the trench in a standing position, their legs deep in freezing mud. Two men drowned in the communications trench leading to Trench 19. A front-line tour of duty lasted forty-eight hours; how long is that in such conditions?

Edmond D'Arcy disembarked in France on 25 January. He was in the front line two weeks later when the 1st Royal Irish were ordered to relieve the Royal Irish Fusiliers. But then orders came through for them to attack: Trench 19 alongside The Mound had been lost, they must retake it with the forces available; two companies, which should have been around 250 men, but in fact numbered just eighty-five strong. Major White had reconnoitred the ground. Parallel with Trench 19 was a deep and muddy and impassable ditch, but with a plank bridge across it, leading to a hedge. He proposed getting the attacking force across the bridge in the dead of night, assembling it in the cover of the hedge and then storming Trench 19.

At 8.45 p.m. the attacking troops set off, and successfully crossed the bridge, but the Germans must have been alerted, for flares and star-shells were fired, and the assembled soldiers beside the hedge subjected to heavy fire. In moments fifteen men were killed, including Major White, and twenty-one wounded, one fatally: nearly half the attacking force. Support fire from their own machine-guns was impossible, because they were jammed with mud. Among the dead was Edmund D'Arcy, age, home and family unknown, as is also his grave, a sepulchral anonymity that he shares with the eleven other enlisted men caught in the hedge before Trench 19. Let us remember their names perhaps for the first time in history since that mini-massacre: John Bates and James O'Neill of Dublin, Martin Jackson and Thomas Long of Waterford, Patrick Meara and William Quinn of Limerick, John Healy of Thomastown, Kilkenny, Patrick Leacy of Enniscorthy, Michael Daly of Ballina, and James Brabston and Patrick Meara of County Tipperary. Their bodies vanished in the ditch and slime and they are commemorated at the Menin Gate in Ypres.

The body of Major William White, of Dublin, was recovered, and is buried in Dickebusch Cemetery. Lieutenant Philip Anderson, of Buttevant, County Cork, latterly living in Harcourt Terrace, Dublin, died of his wounds, and is buried at Baileul Cemetery.

Trench 19 was finally taken the next day by survivors of the Royal Irish, supported by other regiments. Next month Trench 19 was retaken by the Germans. This led to a counter attack by the Royal Irish and 1st Leinsters. The Royal Irish lost another thirty-five men killed, including Lt Brendan Fottrell, whose uncle was a prominent Jesuit in Dublin. The 1st Leinsters lost forty-five men killed in this same attack, including Captain Robert Bowen-Colthurst, whose brother a year later was to be responsible for a series of murders in Dublin during the Rising, and whose aunt, the famous Mrs Lindsay, was herself murdered by the IRA in Cork in April 1921.

All shall pass, but the Mound remained, also luring the 2nd battalion of the Royal Irish towards Trench 19 and the terrible warfare for it. In May 1915, during what the battalion war-diary called a 'comparatively quiet' period, casualties varied from four to eighteen a day. One of these was Patrick Phelan of Kilkenny, like much of the army now on the Western Front a reservist in his forties who had been rudely recalled from civilian life. He and his son Kieran arrived together in France on 21 October 1914. On 14 May 1915, in view of his boy, he rose slightly to light his pipe in a front-line trench, and was instantly shot through the head and killed, to be buried near where he fell by his son.

At 2 a.m. on 24 May the battalion was stood-to on Belleward Ridge. A sinisterly gentle breeze blew from the east, bearing clouds of chlorine vapour. Although men had been issued with gas-masks and sprayers, these were not effective against such intense concentrations of gas. No useful record exists of the calamity that befell the 2nd battalion. Most of its officers were killed and injured, including their OC, Lieutenant Colonel Redmond Moriarty, and Captain Gerard O'Callaghan, whose father, Major General Desmond O'Callaghan had been the first Irish Catholic to have been appointed Colonel Commandant at Sandhurst. The broken remnants of the battalion were rallied by RSM Plunkett, mentioned earlier. One of the dead was Kieran Phelan, who succumbed to his injuries a couple of days later. Royal Irish losses in this gas attack numbered 400. This though was almost modest compared to the fate of the 2nd battalion, Royal Dublin Fusiliers, which in a place they fondly called Shelltrap Farm had suffered over 100 per cent casualties in the course of a month of gas attacks: 33 officers and 1078 men of the battalion having been killed, wounded or missing.

Such numbers and such a scale of suffering are almost meaningless, save in this regard: they were completely forgotten within a generation, and enfolded within this blanket of miasma was not only the grief of poor Mary Phelan, of Walkin Street, Kilkenny, who had lost her husband and son within a few days. Also affected was the rather grander Connellan family of Thomastown. Peter Martin Connellan, serving with the 1st Hampshires, was in the front-ine trenches when a shell fragment pierced his neck and lodged in his spinal column, killing him within minutes.

His cousin, Roger Slacke, serving with the East Kents (The Buffs), was killed in the May offensive that wrought such havoc on the British army generally, and more particularly from our point of view, the Irish regiments. A third cousin, Henry Desmond O'Hara, whose fate is dealt with more comprehensively in the chapter on Sligo, died of wounds in June 1915. And a fourth cousin, Percy Gethin, a celebrated artist, brings the absurdity of war into an especially acute focus. For he was a forty-two-year old lieutenant, who had initially been in the almost oxymoronically-named Artists' Rifles before transferring to the 8th Devonshires. One of his fellow officers was the poet Noel Hodgson (twenty-three), who penned these words that summer of 1916:

> *I, that on my familiar hill*
> *Saw with uncomprehending eyes*
> *A hundred of thy sunsets spill*
> *Their fresh and sanguine sacrifice,*
> *Ere the sun swings his noonday sword*
> *Must say goodbye to all of this!*
> *By all delights that I shall miss,*
> *Help me to die Oh Lord*

Percy Gethin was killed two days before the Somme offensive began, to be followed on the opening day of the battle by Hodgson himself.

Let me close these observations on Kilkenny and the Great War with a look at the career of soldier Johnnie Cahill, and the impact he had on other lives. The son of minor Catholic gentry, originally from Freshford, Johnny was a son of the regiment, his father having been CO of the 4th Royal Irish. From the outset he was a highly promising career-soldier. A captain at twenty-four, he was made instructor at the school of musketry at Dollymount Strand in Dublin in May 1915, and in November of that year he led a recruiting drive in Castlecomer, County Kilkenny. We can trace what happened to these men by their near-consecutive numbers. One of them, William Booth, from a very humble Church of Ireland family, was put into the hard-hit 2nd Royal Irish, which had effectively been wiped out at least twice. The battalion was in the 4th Division that entered the battle of the Somme in early July 1916. In the opening engagements, the nights of 5-6 July, among those to be killed were Captain Robert Bell, from Tipperary, and Lieutenant Gerald White, son of the Bishop of Limerick. Forced back from the German wire, the Irish made three more attacks, led by Captain H. J. O'Reilly, but to no avail.

Eight days later the battalion was back at the front, near Mametz Wood. Their advance seems to sweep all before them, and the battalion was in a state of high exhilaration. The men stood around the empty German trenches, savouring the moment of victory, when a machine-gun opened from the windmill, cutting the Irish to pieces. Among those caught and killed in the renewal of fighting were 2nd Lieutenant Finlay from Clondalkin and Captain Tighe. Lieutenant Arthur Denham Deane from Belfast led a bayonet charge into the windmill, and was killed in the hand-to-hand fighting that resulted. His body was later found, stripped naked and mutilated. A Kilkenny man, Anthony Brennan, reported in his account of the battle around this time that another unit murdered captured German prisoners, but it's reasonable to speculate that, considering the emphasis made by the regimental history on the fate suffered by young Deane, the killers might well have been from the battalion. Either way, one of the dead of the day was Private 7830 William Booth, the first of Johnnie Cahill's Castlecomer recruits to die.

In early September the 2nd Royal Irish made their third trip to the Somme battle. Now ear-marked for the the Ginchy-Guillemont sector, they advanced to the sucrerie where Lieutenant Tom Kettle of the Royal Dublin Fusiliers was to be killed a few days later. Despite the deployment of six Lewis guns by the attacking companies, the assault failed, in large part because of a faulty map, and among the dead was 2nd Lieutenant Bevan Nolan from Cahir, County Tipperary, and Private 7833 George Stone, aged twenty, the son of Julia Stone of Market Street, Castlecomer.

Six days later the 6th battalion of the Royal Irish attacked a strongly held German position outside Ginchy. They were repulsed by five machine-guns firing over the parapet of their target trench. One of the dead of this attack was 2nd Lieutenant Eric Hackett, of Ballycumber, all of whose three brothers and one sister were to die before war's end. And also to lose his life was Private 7827 Denis Connell, son of Margaret Connell of Love Lane, according to the 1911 Census, their family all being members of 'The Church of Rome'. The fourth of the Castlecomer men to die was Private 7861 James Stone, also Church of Ireland, killed in the great German offensive on 21 March 1918, in which the 16th Irish Division was almost destroyed.

The man who had helped bring these youngsters to an early doom, Johnnie Cahill, unusually for a southern Irish Catholic, had in 1916 been transferred from the Royal Irish Regiment to the 13th Royal Irish Rifles, which was based on the County Down Ulster Volunteer Force. Despite their differing religious backgrounds, the officers actually had much in common with the Kilkennyman, being largely interested in bloodstock and hunting, and they appear to have got along well together. Ahead for the 16th Irish and 36th Ulster Divisions, alongside one another on the Frezenberg Ridge, lay the tragedy of the battle of Langemark, in August 1917. The two divisions were to suffer 8000 casualties in this epic of brutal stupidity, and their failure to achieve their objectives was, according to their Corps commander, General Gough, because they were Irish and didn't like shellfire. There has been much mythology about the cretinous arrogance of British generals in the war, and most of it baseless; but if one sought grounds for the allegation, they surely lay in these contemptible words.

One of those who paid the price was Johnny Cahill, killed 'gallantly leading his men', as if those words could have much meaning in the vast morass of Flanders mud. Moreover, for the Cahills, and for his wife's family, the Nolans of Tullow, County Carlow, the war was by this time a very personal affair. His two brothers were already serving. In the same year of 1917 his widow May was to lose her own two brothers to the war, while her sister Jane served as an ambulance driver in France and Belgium.

May was later to remarry a Polish count, and she moved to his country. After the German invasion in September 1939 she joined the Resistance, and was killed by the Nazis in 1942.

Thus the tragedy of the Cahills, the Nolans, the Hacketts and the poor unsung lads of Castlecomer.

5. *Kerry in the Great War*

As with any county, it's hard to be certain who precisely is a Kerryman. Take Kitchener, of Khartoum, for example, born in Kerry, but who was unlikely ever to have been seen in Croke Park. Or another, more modest example: the first of the 718 so-called Kerrymen to be killed in the war was thirty-nine-year old Daniel Dalton, with the Royal Irish Regiment. He died early – on 24 August 1914, and is buried at St Symphorien Cemetery in Mons. King's County, or Offaly, can certainly claim him, because that was where his family had moved to when he joined up, and so might Tipperary, where he enlisted, but he was born in Castleisland, as were at least eight other men to die in the war. (A word of warning: all figures on statistics must remain conditional. Recent research has generally raised Irish war-deaths by at least 10 per cent everywhere.) However, no other county has any lien of Michael Sullivan, born and resident in Killorglin, enlisted Tralee, killed – notionally anyway, and I think in the fog of war all these dates should be accepted with some caution – on 26 August 1914. He has no known grave.

Michael was the first of 340 men who enlisted in Tralee to die in the war. The day after his death, seventeen Tralee-enlisted men died: a phenomenal death-toll for a single town so early in the war, even if not all of the men were actually from Tralee or even Kerry. What largely explains this loss of life was the stand by 2nd Munsters at Etreux, beside the Sambre L'Oise Canal, protecting the headlong retreat of the British Expeditionary Force from Mons. Their commanding officer, Paul Charrier, might or might be said to be a Kerryman: thirteen out of the 130 Munsters' dead on that terrible day were Tralee-enlisted private soldiers. One of their officers was also a Tralee man, but of a slightly different class. Francis Blennerhassett Chute of Chute Hall, Tralee, was the twenty-nine-year old battalion machine-gun officer. He fell covering the retreat of a group of Munsters towards the end of a twelve-hour battle against six battalions of infantry. This epic feat of resistance enabled the British 1st Division to able to escape the encircling movement of the Germans.

I'm reluctant to emphasize the astonishing feats of forgetfulness that consumed any knowledge of this time, especially in a community that cherishes its feats of memory. How did Ireland forget the period of 19 to 20 October 1914, when 50 per cent of all British soldiers killed on the Western Front were Irish, in large explained by the slaughter of the Royal Irish Regiment at Le Pilly? Just one of this latter group, Jeremiah Dowd, from Boherbee, was a Kerryman, but clearly not an enthusiastic one as he'd gone to the trouble of travelling to Wexford to enlist in a decidedly non-Kerry regiment.

Meanwhile, the military career of another volunteer was approaching an end in Kerry. Karl Lody was a German spy, and though highly amateurish, he'd nonetheless managed to inflict serious damage on the British. Able to send a telegram to Sweden from Scotland, soon after the outbreak of war, he had warned of the imminent departure from the Firth of Forth of some Royal Naval vessels, A German U-boat was duly sent just in time to find, torpedo and sink HMS *Pathfinder*, the first vessel ever so-despatched by submarine. Amongst the 120 dead were four Irishmen. In a saga that could have come from the pen of John Buchan, Lody then fled to Killarney, carefully followed by Jeremiah Lynch, one of the many sharp Irishmen employed by Scotland Yard. Lynch finally arrested him at Killarney's Great Southern Hotel, and searching his room, found incriminating documents there.

Lody was sent to London, where he was tried, found guilty of 'military conspiracy' and shot by firing squad in the Tower. He was, by the standards of the time, simply a patriot doing his patriotic duty, which merely concluded in County Kerry. However, the definition of patriotism in the county was certainly not what London, or Dublin Castle, had hoped, as evidenced by the all-Ireland final in Dublin in December 1914. The Great Southern and Western Railway brought 8000 Kerrymen to the capital, and the presence of so many happy, robust young men in Dublin's streets, with absolutely no intention whatever of fighting for King and Country (whatever that might be), aroused some amazed indignation among unionist observers.

In this regard, Kerry was merely on the extreme edge of a nationalist spectrum, which could be seen across the country. Quite simply, farmers' sons could not be persuaded to take an interest in the war, and this is true in every county: only more so in Kerry, whose distinctiveness today is probably no greater than it was then. It was probably this county to which the Earl of Meath was referring when he declared, somewhat darkly, in the House of Lords that Irish fisherman off the west coast were laying German mines. Many things are casualties of war, but common-sense is surely amongst the most conspicuous.

The reluctance – by British or Ulster standards – to enlist was by no means universal. The small-town poor in large numbers joined for largely economic reasons, and this is clear from Tralee's figures. Middle-class Catholics joined in large numbers over much of the country, but less so, it seems, in Kerry; however, amongst the new Kerry officer class were the three Dodd brothers of Ballymacprior House, Killorglin. Their father had been the local GP whose Hippocratic duties clearly did not absolve him of his pelvic ones, being the father of eighteen children in all: and those duties having been attended to, he was, perhaps unsurprisingly, dead by the time of the 1911 Census.

In late April 1915 the Band of the Irish Guards arrived in Tralee in a recruiting-drive. Already, enlistments in Ireland were falling well below the levels required to keep the existing Irish battalions, regular and new, at fighting strength, and Tralee, being a garrison town of the Munster Fusiliers, was an improbable place for the Irish Guards to find new soldiers. Nonetheless, the band was welcomed by a reception committee led by J.M. Slattery of the Urban District Council, and a temporary recruitment office was opened in Denny Street.

We cannot now know what strange mood erupted in the town, or quite why, only that it did. Some thirty men are reported to have enlisted, at least three of them being members of what *The Irish Times* inaccurately called in its account of the meeting 'the Sinn Féin Irish Volunteers'. But this was a group that was entirely opposed to recruitment into the British army. One of them was Richard Curtayne, whose sister Alice, nearly fifty years later, was to write the first, and crucial, biography of Francis Ledwidge. She dedicated the work to Richard, specifying 'Irish Volunteer and Irish Guards'. When I first read this, I assumed that she had mis-written, and meant 'Irish National Volunteers', who of course supported recruitment; but then on an archive word-search, I found *The Irish Times* report on the rally, and the revelation about the nature of recruits. In due course, I discovered, through the 1911 Census, place of enlistment and regimental numbers, and the records of the Commonwealth War Graves Commission, something about the fate of these young men. This also tells us something of the history of the 2nd battalion, the Irish Guards, rather as the warning isotope in a barium meal identifies the locus of mortal infection.

The first of the Kerry recruits to die was Private 7656 Daniel O'Shea of Killorglin, and an exception within the group. Less than a year after recruitment, on 2 April 1916, a stray shell in Ypres landed in his party of 1st battalion of the Micks as they returned from home leave, killing him instantly and fatally injuring his warrant officer Sergeant Major Kirk MC. According to the CWGC, he was the son of James and Margaret of Killorglin: that they supplied this information suggests that he was not an Irish Volunteer. For whatever reason, he alone of the rally-recruits was in the 1st battalion.

The next to fall was Private 7655 Michael Lynch from Tralee, killed on 13 September 1916, as the 2nd battalion moved into the Ginchy area of the Somme, recently and bloodily visited by the 16th Irish Division. Even for men recently in the Ypres Salient, the much fought-over Somme battlefield was an unmitigated horror: as Kipling described it, 'the whole landscape happened to be one pitted, clodded brown and white wilderness of aching uniformity, on which to pick one detail was like identifying one plover's nest in a hundred acre bog'.

The battalion arrived at a new and poorly dug trench-system on the evening of 12 September; the following dawn, after a night's careful preparation, the German's opened up with machine-guns, snipers and artillery at the exposed Irish. Forty men were injured and Lieutenant Vaughan and 'several' men alongside him were killed by a single shell. Vaughan and his sergeant, twenty-year old Thomas Torsney from Riverstown, County Sligo, are buried in Bernafay Wood Cemetery. Private 7655 Michael Lynch might have been in that group. More probably not. Life for the battalion being made unendurable by machine-gun fire, number 2 Company was sent to deal with the enemy by hand, 'rather as one digs out a wasps' nest after dark'.

Under Lieutenant Tomkins, the advancing troops filed across the Ginchy-Morval Road, and came under enfilading machine-gun fire that killed the young subaltern, just less than a fortnight after joining the battalion. When the two-platoon attack on the machine-gun nests finally began, it was discovered that the artillery bombardment that should have cut the wire protecting the German machine-gunners had achieved no such outcome. Hemmed in by fire, seeking out gaps in the wire, while the Germans were firing at close range over ground they knew well, number 2 Company was in minutes simply butchered, with 75 per cent casualties. That first day on the Somme, thirty-eight Irish Guardsmen were killed, even before the battalion's main battle had begun. Of the dead, twenty-seven have no known graves and are commemorated on the Thiepval Monument, the eleven others are buried in three different cemeteries. Michael Lynch has no grave, and his family supplied no details to the CWGC. Of itself, this doesn't mean he had been an Irish Volunteer: of the thirty-eight Irish Guardsmen dead that day, the families of twenty-four – including Lieutenant Vaughan's – supplied no personal details, a remarkably high proportion, for which I have no explanation. One of the dead was fellow-Kerryman John McKenna of Ballinvoher, who according to the 1911 Census was twenty when he died.

The next of the Tralee Volunteers was Private 7649 Richard Curtayne, from Castle Street, Tralee, who of course prompted this search, and his fellow Tralee volunteer, Private 7653 James Sheehy. They were both with the 2nd battalion, but on this field, it really made little difference, for with the Guards' Division attacking together, 1st and 2nd battalions were alongside one another. A mis-timing of part of the accompanying artillery bombardment meant that at one point the Micks were advancing in an almost eerie silence towards the unheeding German trenches, whose occupants apparently believed something unpleasant from the British could be afoot only if they had been nearly blasted into extinction by

British artillery. Life returned to its normal decencies moments later, when the British guns finally opened up, prompting a German reply, and the advancing Micks saw an entire platoon of Coldstreamers just in front of them 'crumped out of existence in a flash and roar'.

Officers had maps of their objectives, marked with brown and yellow lines, with the assurance that once they were taken, the cavalry would surely follow, consolidate and then advance to Bapaume or even Berlin; but since no feature remained on the landscape to remind them where their objectives might be, or their lines should run, or where the cavalry could gracefully trot to final victory, they may as well have been on the surface of the moon while it was being swept by a sleet of machine-gun fire. Some 150 Irish Guardsmen died on that day, and not even the pen of Rudyard Kipling in his official history of the Micks is able to do justice to the frightful shambles of Ginchy, not least because the monstrous arithmetic of war must have meant that another 300 men were injured. And how does any army retrieve such numbers under fire, when each stretcher over broken ground requires a carry of at least four men?

Either way, Richard Curtayne was killed on 15 September and Corporal James Sheehy, having survived that day of vast slaughter, was apparently felled the next day by a whizz-bang shortly before being withdrawn from the line. Two other Kerryman were killed in this slaughter. One was Sergeant Major Maurice Riordan DCM of Kealduff. Though he could not possibly have been captured in such a hecatomb, the Guards pretended that he might have been, and posted him as 'missing', during which period of fictional uncertainty he was given a bar to his DCM, an award that could not lawfully be made posthumously. The Micks have a habit of fiddling the rules in order to honour their dead. A fourth Kerryman to die was yet another but rather older John McKenna, who had previously served in the Royal Navy for fifteen years. The families of neither Curtayne nor Sheehy gave details to the CWGC. Of Sheehy's family, I know nothing. I cannot presume the reluctance of Sheehy's family to supply personal details proves an IV membership, since the families of over half of Irish Guards who died at Ginchy were similarly non-compliant. This is a far higher percentage than one could normally expect.

With reasonable certainty, we can say that Richard Curtayne was an Irish Volunteer. The evidence of his sister Alice and *The Irish Times* report suggests as much. (That said, she could be economical with the truth:

her biography about Francis Ledwidge studiously misled her readers away from the fact that the poet's girlfriend Ellie had become pregnant by another man, whom Ellie then married, then dying in childbirth.) The Curtaynes' father was a highly skilled businessman, a successful coach-builder in Tralee, who lavished his money on Alice's education. She became a linguist and one of the first female intellectuals in an indepen-dent Ireland, if very much in the Catholic republican tradition.

A month after Richard's death, in late October 1916, Private 7654 J Dineen, of Tralee, was wounded in action. I haven't been able to trace him on the 1911 Census. The next to fall was Private 7660 Cornelius Murphy of Castleisland, on 31 July 1917, while the 2nd Irish Guards were clearing and holding a British flank prior to what was meant to be the decisive action of the war, the Third Battle of Ypres. By this time, artil-lery bombardments before an attack had become highly sophisticated and intense, depending on a meticulous fire-plan and well-trained infantry keeping close to a barrage that advanced according to a set timetable. Long bombardment wasted metal and gave an unnecessary indication of intent to adversary, for whom forewarned really did mean forearmed. A four-step barrage of sharp but paralyzing intensity would go in simultane-ously: an onslaught of shells from 18-pounder field-guns onto the enemy's forward trenches, with back barrages of 6-inch howitzers and 60-pounders into communications trenches, and a deeper barrage of the same metal into the connecting transport system and artillery batteries, accompa-nied throughout by the threshing of machine-gun batteries that filled the enemy air with lead and kept heads down. For this attack, Major Greer added an extra layer of preparation, causing models of the landscape to be made, for the officers to study carefully; and each officer had his own card, prescribing his particular duties.

And the outcome was indeed a 'victory', but by only the grotesque standards of the day; the intended real estate was taken, and held. The Micks alone lost sixty dead, including their commanding officer Major Eric Greer MC and their heroic chaplain, Father Simon Knapp DSO MC. Alongside these illustrious paladins passed Cornelius Murphy of Castleisland, cause of death now unknown. With a scrupulous modesty, his widowed mother Hanna informed the CWGC merely that he was the twenty-one-year-old son of Timothy, though his father had already gone before. This citation does not mean he was *not* an Irish Volunteer: analysis of CWGC records suggests that a widowed parent, regardless of politics, was rather more likely to supply personal details.

Now, as was the custom, Richard Curtayne's battalion number had been recycled, and quite extraordinarily, though it could have been allocated to a recruit from anywhere in Ireland, (or by this time, Britain) it actually went to a near-neighbour of his: Terence O'Regan of Rock Street Killarney, the son of the manager of Tralee Market. As members of the Catholic commercial gentry of the town the two families would certainly have known one another well, and living so close, would probably have attended the same church. And on the vast mudplain of Flanders, as the Third Battle of Ypres inched towards its dreadful, inconclusive conclusion, Private 7649 O'Regan was gravely wounded. He died in Etaples military hospital on 26 October 1917.

Third Ypres was over; before the armies hunkered down for the winter, there was housekeeping to be done. The great tank battle at Cambrai in November was ending in what looked like another victorious defeat which might just turn into that most sobering of outcomes, a debacle. The final stages of Cambrai had left the hundred acres of Bourlon Wood in German hands, and with it the high ground that overlooked allied positions. Futility is an oft-used term about this war. It is actually the godchild of utility, the urgent need for a short-term practical outcome, regardless of wider considerations. To have fought a battle merely to place your trenches close to and below well-protected German sniping-positions, from which was no protection save departure, and for an entire winter, would have been almost the ultimate military folly. So: Bourlon Wood must be taken.

The 51st Division assaulted its matchwood ramparts in late November and was beaten back. Next the 40th Division was sent in, with much the same outcome: after five days of serious winter-fighting of the very worst kind, with thousands of casualties, the Germans were left in command of all that they were able to survey, to a very far horizon. The British could, quite simply, not camp down until the springtime where they currently lay.

The Guards Division was called in, employing a new form of synchronized warfare: tanks plus creeping barrage, with the need, most of all, for *haste*, because the German strength was visibly growing and soon would be unassailable. That November, the Micks advanced to the front through a wearying, sleet-lashed night, each man with two grenades, a shovel and his rifle. The Germans knew they were coming and fired a welcoming barrage that cost the Micks forty casualties. Their CO, Alexander, later a field marshal of not great distinction, but at this level almost supreme, his leadership inspirational, brave and detailed, then briefed his officers, who in turn briefed their NCOs.

The men dressed in attack order; detonators were now inserted in their bombs. They rose at first grey light from what remained of their trenches and advanced behind their own barrage through the sleet, over much fought-over, chewed-up ground. The tanks either did not materialise or vanished on the battlefield. The Germans, naturally, were ready and waiting, their machine-guns firing blind on pre-set interlocking arcs. Some of the first trenches, manned by defenders who were cold and wet and exhausted and who preferred to shelter under oilskins from the dreadful wet snow than to fight, were easily taken. But in the broken woodland, it was difficult to be sure what was what and where was where; and some prisoners sent back to the British lines simply returned to the fray. Once that was suspected, prisoner-taking presumably stopped. All forest rides being alike even on a summer's day in peacetime, on that midwinter sleet-ridden, metal-lashed dawn, the company commanders and their subalterns could be forgiven for not knowing where they were, or more to the point, where the enemy was.

However, by noon, Bourlon Wood, seemed to have been won by the Micks and their flanking battalions, with different parties of British soldiers meeting on its outer perimeter, though within, fierce and highly personal fighting continued amidst coppice and brake. The new occupants next tried to dig trenches, but vainly amid the cold, unyielding roots of those old trees. There was good reason to dig: not a man doubted what was coming next – a German counter-attack, for that was the German way, and a damned unpleasant way it was too.

Unexpectedly, and almost unbelievably – except it wasn't really unbelievable, because after all, they were Germans – the enemy opened up with a battery of machine guns on the Micks *from their rear.* Meanwhile, German heavy guns were lobbing their ordnance with splendid impartiality into the many warring factions inside the wood. As expected, the German counter-attack began, but with an unexpected ferocity; and in one of those strange imponderable moments that can occur in battle, the entire British hold on the wood appeared to crumble, as battalions lost both contact with one another and belief in their cause. A confused retreat began as the German counter-attack gathered momentum, ending in a rout, as men streamed from the wood, in broken dribs and drabs. Four hundred and fifty men of this depleted battalion had gone into Bourlon. Just 117 came out. It was the first great defeat for the Irish Guards during the war.

Of the seventy-five enlisted deaths, there were three Kerrymen: nineteen year old Private 10545 James Magee, the son of Helen, a widow who had moved to Louth and was CWGC-compliant; Private 7764 Edward Sharkey, a former shop-assistant and son of an RIC pensioner, whose family was not CWGC-compliant; and the very last of our Tralee recruits from two and half years previously, Private 7661 William Kirwan of Kildare, but clearly in Tralee on the fatal day in 1915.

We can tell from the numbers 7649 to 7661 that probably around twelve men, possibly a few more, but not the thirty as reported in *The Irish Times*, enlisted that day in Tralee. Seven were killed and one whom we know of was wounded. Four of the men's families declined to supply family details to the war graves commission. That's 57 per cent compared to the 25 per cent norm for Kerry – however, there does seem to have been a tradition of funerary reserve in the Micks; even Major Greer's and Father Knapp's family's offered no information about their loved ones.

These men have never had any public memorial: no residue remains of the folly of their tragic decision that April day in 1915. No death notices followed then or thereafter, and they disappeared from all purview as completely as if they had never existed. Alone of them all remains Richard Curtayne, a mere mention of whose name in a frontispiece began this search. And if there is one unimpeachable lesson from this saga, it is that human motives are usually mixed and probably quite beyond clinical analysis.

Parallel with the tragedy of those Tralee recruits to the Irish Guards was the unfolding catastrophe of Gallipoli, in which sixty-seven Tralee-enlisted men died, and all with the Munsters. Nine of these men died in the famous landings from the *River Clyde*. There has been much misleading and exaggerated material written about the death-toll in the landings, to which over time I have, alas, added my share. Certainly, events at V Beach were fairly calamitous, but the oft-quoted claims by one man present that of the first two hundred men who left the *River Clyde*, 169 were immediately killed has no substantiation in fact, and nor logically could it. As it became clear to officers in the vessel that nothing was being achieved by sending more men ashore, and to their probable deaths, soldiers were ordered to stay inside the hold. Of the fifty-five enlisted men from the Munsters who were killed in the landings, only two were from Kerry. In the course of the campaign, eleven Tralee men and five from Killarney died. Gallipoli was an allied disaster, but compared to the Western Front, its impact on Kerry was relatively slight.

The county was not so fortunate in France, in the battle of Rue de Bois, on 9 May 1915. After its calamitous losses at Etreux, the battalion had been reconstituted from reservists and the first of the new recruits. Each of the four companies had its own flag (of dark green with a golden harp, with 'Munsters' and the company number inscribed below). An intensely Catholic and Irish ethos had been inculcated in the battalion, encouraged by both the officers and the NCOs. On the eve of the battle, at a wayside shrine, Father Gleeson made his famous blessing with the men formed in a follow square. They attacked at dawn, in one of the most calami-tous infantry advances the British army had yet experienced. Of the four hundred casualties, the Munsters' dead totaled eleven officers and 144 men. Of the enlisted soldiers killed, twenty were Kerrymen. It was one of the worst days the county was to know in the war.

I have no intention of discussing the Sinn Féin/Irish Volunteer activi-ties in the county; much fine work has been done on that area. No doubt the loss of some key-members to the Irish Guards in the spring of 1915 was something of a setback. Yet for all of Austin Stack's legendary if slightly chaotic charisma and organizational skills, the county was hardly in a revolutionary state in 1916. When Pearse visited Tralee shortly before the Rising, he had inspected some 250 Volunteers. The RIC estimated that of the 165,000 people in the county, around a thousand were 'Sinn Féin'. An RIC officer told the official inquiry into the Rising that there were perhaps 350 'Sinn Féin' volunteers in Tralee at the time. So it wasn't republican zeal that explained whatever shortcomings Kerry exhibited in its recruitment perfor-mance so much as that well known trait of the county, *caution*. Perhaps another word might be 'cuteness'.

Indeed, I'm inclined to think this is one reason for the largely steady nature of Kerry casualties. There were a few disastrous days after Rue de Bois, and nothing to compare with 1 July 1916, a day that spelt disaster for

Ulster – indeed, so far as I can see, no soldier from the county died on that day. But in that same battle of the Somme, now two months on, Kerry's turn would come, as the 16th Irish Division attacked at Guillemont and Ginchy, between 3 and 9 September. Of the 191 ordinary Munsters killed in that week, seventeen were from Kerry. Another eight or so Kerrymen were to die in the assault by the Irish Guards over those very same fields the following few days. Though grievous, the loss of approximately one man a day in the month of September 1916 is far from calamitous.

By 1917 most Kerrymen at the front were serving in the 16th Irish Division, but a fortuitous rotation of battalions kept the Munsters out of the worst of the fighting during the abomination of Third Ypres in August 1916. However, one Kerryman was not so lucky. Alfred Aldworth, the son of a Church of Ireland farmer from Tahilla, outside Kenmare, had enlisted in Tralee, but studiously, and most unusually, providing no place of birth or residence. Perhaps he was, if only psychologically, preparing to identify with the unit of his choosing: the 36th Ulster Division. He found himself in the 14th Royal Irish Rifles (Young Volunteers), the only battalion recruited in Belfast for the 36th Division that was not UVF in origin. It's not clear whether he served in and survived the battle of the Somme. On 16 August 1917 the 16th and 36th Divisions, after manning the front-line trenches for two weeks in quite appalling conditions, assaulted German positions at Frezenberg Ridge. The outcome was a quite terrible defeat in detail: 1100 men of the two divisions were killed, and the outcome for the 14th Royal Irish Rifles provides an insight into what had befallen so many 'Irish' battalions. For though Alfred Aldworth was certainly among the dead, he was not the only outsider to Ulster: 48 of the 116 dead were trans-fers from English regiments, mostly Londoners and Bedfords, plus five of the new unfortunate conscripts. In other words, this battalion was now only 50 per cent Ulster. Aged twenty-two, Alfred Aldworth, Kerry's only volunteer to have died in the 36th Ulster Division, has no known grave.

I suspect that some Kerry's councillors would have exulted in an 'I told you so' fashion over young Aldworth's ardent unionist sympathies. However, many previously avowed (if today now forgotten) unionists in Tralee, whose position after 1916 became rather tenuous, had already made a strategic and prudent shift of loyalty. (After all, they too were Kerrymen). In early 1917, in an attempt to secure a foothold in a state that they were certain would become independent at war's end, they voted in favour of Home Rule. The following May, Redmondite councillors submitted a motion before County Kerry Council welcoming this change of heart. It was vehemently opposed by Sinn Féin, who – notwithstanding the Tonean republican piety about Catholic, Protestant and Dissenter, et cetera, not to speak of the previous year's proclamation that cherished the children of the nation equally – declared that time was not right for any republican reconciliation with the town's unionists, and the motion was voted down.

While a new war for Kerry was brewing on a domestic front, an older one had found a new dimension. On 31 October 1917, Walter de Courcy Dodd, of Ballymacprior House, aged twenty-one and a lieutenant in the Royal Flying Corps, was shot down and killed. A year later, to the very day, his brother Francis, a lieutenant in the Machine Gun Corps, who had narrowly survived a gas attack in March 1918, though with irreparably damaged lungs that could not withstand any infection, died in the flu epidemic.

The gas attack that was to fatally weaken Francis Dodd was of course part of the great German offensive, the *Kaiserschlact,* in which the 16th Irish Division was pulverized, and effectively destroyed. At least ten Kerrymen died in the battle, most of them with the Munsters, but one, John O'Connor, fell serving with the South Wales Borderers, a regiment he appears to have gone and joined in Monmouth while still resident in Kerry. With the Tralee's Irish Guards heavily in mind, I'll hazard no explanations for that decision.

Kerry's last dead during the war, officially-speaking, included Jack Sullivan, of Killorglin, serving with the Australian Light Horse, who died at Damascus on 1 November 1918. And two more men from Killorglin were to die, both on 7 November. One was the last of the serving Dodd brothers: Lieutenant John O'Connell Dodd. He was killed in action east of the Forest of Mormal just eight days after the death of his brother Francis. The other Killorglin man to die that day was a nineteen-year-old Royal Irish Lancer, Cornelius O'Leary, at home, cause unknown. However, his family then took an unusual course of action. Though they supplied the Commission with personal details, they refused to allow a Commonwealth War Graves Commission headstone on his Kerry grave, and since the Commission is legally obliged to honour all war dead, he is remembered at Brookwood Memorial. And as anyone who has ever done any research will testify, archives are sent to try us, and perhaps also to remind us of a

world that seems impossible now: hence, the only Cornelius O'Leary at
Listry mentioned in the 1911 Census was a forty-two-year-old farmer living
with his wife Mary and *his seventy-year-old nephew* Patrick Price!

What is rather striking about Kerry's war is that its casualties tend to
be spread evenly. Rue de Bois aside, and the odd day in Gallipoli, there
are no great cataclysms of blood, such as Cork, Dublin, Sligo and so many
Ulster towns experienced. So, overall, Sneem lost four dead, Tralee 130,
Killorglin fourteen, Listowel forty-three, Killarney fifty-three, Dingle eight,
Cahirciveen five, but spread across the plain of the war, and mostly without
the statistical peaks that spell social trauma, with the accompanying possibility of memorable myth.

These figures are all based on the official record compiled in 1920–
22, 'Soldiers Died in the Great War', and though assembled with honest
intent, they are inadequate, as the example of one Kerryman will show.
Richard Morgan was a professional soldier from Kerry serving the South
Wales Borderers, transferring in his early fifties to the Labour Corps. The
monstrous travails endured by the Corps are dealt with elsewhere in this
volume (see 'Glasnevin Cemetery'); suffice it to say here that many men,
serving in atrocious conditions digging trenches and making roads in
all weathers, seven days a week and without break, contracted chronic,
exposure-related illnesses which rendered them unfit for military service.
Thus discharged, they often then died of the condition that had ended
their military careers, but because they were no longer in the colours,
their families were denied any war-pensions, and of course, their deaths
are not counted in SDGW. And so, nor was Richard Morgan's after he
died in 1919, though his family proudly declared his Kerry-origins and his
faithful thirty years' service to a country that then turned its back on him.

One measure of alienation from the war is the bereaved family's refusal
to supply information to the Commonwealth War Graves Commission
– though other factors, such as illiteracy and grief may also be reasons.
Using the experience of the 36th Ulster Division as a high benchmark of
submissions, virtually 100 per cent, and of Belfast nationalists as a low
(around 40 per cent) the families of Kerry's dead were – perhaps surprisingly, considering later developments in the county – keen to remember
their loved ones. Of the 718 dead, only 179 families – or 25 per cent –
declined to supply details. In other words, there was 75 per cent CWGC
compliance. However, as with young O'Leary, death at home, which

meant a gravestone in Kerry and possibly a cemetery register for to see, resulted in greater reticence: in those circumstances, 44 per cent refused to give details.

One of the most taxing yet most easily resolved issues is the apparent disparity between recruitment in Ireland and the Irish dead, with the former too low to explain the size of the latter. Let Tralee supply part of the explanation. Of the 130 Tralee-born who died in the war, thirty – or 23 per cent – were recruited in Britain, thereby becoming 'British' recruits, just eight of them enlisting south of a line from the Wash to the Bristol Channel, with three of these being in London. The rest were recruited in Wales, Liverpool, and industrial towns such as Leeds, Accrington, Stockport and Bolton, and three from Scotland. Perhaps surprisingly, of the fifty-three Killarney born dead, as many as twenty-five (50 per cent) were recruited abroad and unlike Tralee, largely from south of the Bristol Channel-Wash line, including seven in London. Listowel has yet another pattern. Of its forty-three dead, only three were recruited in Britain – two in Liverpool (which features surprisingly little as a place of recruitment for Irish-born soldiers) and two in Rochdale. Killorglin complies with that pattern: of fourteen dead, just two joined the army abroad.

So when one assesses the extraordinary failure of long-term memory in Ireland regarding the soldiers of the war, it's worth remembering that many Irish-born survivors would not have returned to Ireland after the war, but instead returned to the British towns where they had enlisted. And in as much as a war-narrative was created within those communities, their contributions – such as there were – would have been absorbed locally.

All statistics for the while must remain tentative, as research by such as the great Tom Burnell continues. However, for the time being, we can say that twenty-two Royal Navy sailors from Kerry died in war – a small number compared to the losses that Cork, Waterford, Dublin and Antrim suffered. Young De Courcy Dodd was not quite alone, for in all, four Kerrymen died with the Royal Flying Corps. Nor were the Curtayne group of volunteers into the Micks alone either: fifty-two Kerrymen died with the Irish Guards, but only twenty enlisted in Tralee. And two Kerry chaplains – one Catholic, one Presbyterian – died in the war.

Kerrymen won at least two Military Crosses, eleven Military Medals, and three Distinguished Conduct Medals. Among the decorated Kerrymen or the Kerry-enlisted who died, there were Maurice Riordan DCM and bar, Michael Clifford DCM, Patrick Scully DCM, Joseph Mansfield DCM, Patrick Doody MM, James O'Sullivan MM, John Prendiville MM, Patrick Barrett MM, and John Curtin MM. But none of Kerry's eleven dead O'Briens – eight army, one each with the Canadians, the Australians, and the Royal Navy – or the twenty-four Kerry O'Callaghans who died – including two with the Australians, and one with the New Zealanders – were lucky enough to have their valour recognized in life.

But to conclude with the Dodd family, which in 1914 consisted of 18 children, three of whom joined, and all of whom perished. Their mother claimed them to the war Graves Commission, in her own name, Ellen Mary, and in that of her late husband, William Henry. Peace in 1918 thus found fifteen living Dodds – yet there is today but one Dodd in Ireland, aged seventy-two: the line is thereby extinct. For the ways of war are always strange, and its full human bill certain to be beyond all recking.

6. Armagh and the Great War

Just as important as the narratives that we tell are the ones that we don't. We all know, and rightly, about 1 July 1916, and the fate of the heroic men of the Ulster Division. This is such a vast catastrophe that it really only becomes measurable when reduced to its component parts. Twenty-six men from the city of Armagh died on 1st July. It is a useful corrective to the image of the descendants of Planters going to their graves to see the names of some of these Ulstermen who died that day: James McAdorney, Joseph Shannon, Sam McGahey and James McNally. These are all 'native' Irish names.

Moreover, some thirty-six Portadown men serving with the Royal Irish Fusiliers died with the Ulster Division that day – men with planter names such as like Absalom Abraham, William Allen, William Bowles and John Brownlee. Every one of their thirty-six families later gave personal details to the Commonwealth War Graves Commission for inclusion in the Commission's official register. Another Royal Irish Fusilier from Portadown, Francis McCann, a Catholic, also died on 1st July. He was serving with the 1st battalion in another division, and his family were to provide no details to the Commission.

They were not alone. The previous April the two mainly nationalist battalions of the Royal Irish Fusiliers had been caught in the hideous gas attacks on the 16th Irish Division at Hulluch. Of the one hundred and twelve Royal Irish Fusiliers killed, the families of seventy-six – almost all from the northern side of the border, and mostly from the Armagh area – did not supply personal details to the Commonwealth War Graves commission. Thus a conjoined silence largely abolished any group-memory amongst nationalists of Irish Fusiliers such as John McConville, Patrick Haughey, Edward Turley, and James Milligan, all Catholics, all killed, and all from County Armagh. Considering what lay ahead – admittedly almost as useless a viewpoint as that enjoyed by hindsight – the behaviour of their Crossmaglen families proves to be just a trifle paradoxical. At least thirteen men from the immediate region are known to have died in the war, and the families of nine supplied information to the CWGC. One of these, Felix Gartland, at sixty-three, was possibly the oldest private soldier, Irish or otherwise, to have died in the war. Formerly of the Royal Irish Rifles, he was attached to the Labour Corps when he went down on the *Leinster* on 19 October 1918. Remarkably, his father appears to have been alive at the time. Of the Crossmaglen contingent, the families of just four, all members of the local regiment, the Royal Irish Fusiliers, did not supply information to the CWGC, whereas just two families that lost soldiers in that regiment corresponded with the CGWC. Conversely, families of men who had served in other regiments – the Irish Guards, the Scots Guards, the Royal Welsh Fusiliers, the Inniskillings – were all forthcoming to the commission, as was the next-of-kin of a merchant seaman. It's more than possible that hostility to the very memory of the sacrifices suffered during the war had not been reached in its full intensity in South Armagh when the CWGC was collating details: like many of the recently created border areas, South Armagh pinned its faith on the Border Commission, and a destiny within independent Ireland. As this never happened, in due course South Armagh effectively and violently seceded from both parts of Ireland, a virtual independence that lasted long after the ceasefires and the Good Friday Belfast Agreement.

The county of Armagh was not some regional exception. Of the twenty-seven Connaught Rangers killed in the gas attacks at Hulluch in April–May 1916, nine were nationalists from West Belfast, who had apparently chosen to join that particular regiment as a declaration of an all-Ireland identity. Six of the families of the West Belfast Rangers dead declined to supply personal details to the CWGC in the aftermath of war and the partition of the island. Another southern regiment vying for Belfast nationalists were the Leinsters, whose basic recruitment area abuts and sometimes overlaps that of the Royal Irish. To judge from SDGW, Belfast recruits were allocated serial numbers from approximately 1480 to 1790. Just two men in this sequence – both from Birr – were not from Belfast. Overall, this suggests that some 300 men from West Belfast served with the Leinsters.

The 7th Inniskillings, recruiting largely but not solely among national-ists, were attached to the 16th Division. Of the eighty-five killed at Hulluch, thirty-five were from north of the present border, and of these, the fami-lies of just eleven supplied details to the CWC. This battalion tended to recruit from the west of the province, where the Royal Irish Regiment, based in the south-east (Kilkenny-Waterford), had also been recruiting from amongst the nationalist community. Some of the northern national-ists with the Royal Irish were then transferred to the Inniskillings – one of the very northern regiments they had sought to avoid joining in the first place. Four of these former men of the Royal Irish and now reluc-tant Inniskillings were killed with the 7th battalion; two of their families offered no details to the CWGC.

The 8th battalion of the Inniskillings *tended* to recruit from among nationalists in the east of the province. Of the seventy-four men it lost in April-May 1916, thirty-five were from the six counties that became Northern Ireland. Under half the families gave information to the CWGC; of these, nine were from Belfast, three from Derry, and another three can be said to be unrepresentative: two were based post-war in Scotland, and one was the family of an RIC-man from Tyrone. CWGC-compliance was consistently in the 70 per cent bracket for families south of the border, as compared with nearly 100 per cent for the families of men of the 36th. And of course, as with the 7th, the 8th Inniskillings recruited from an area where nationalists were also being actively encouraged by the Irish National Volunteers and the effective leader of Ulster nationalists, Joe Devlin MP, to enlist in southern regiments, the Leinsters and the Connaught Rangers.

As we have already seen, to join an army is to surrender authority over one's life. So, many Belfast nationalists who had enlisted in the Leinsters in an apparent effort to avoid joining a northern regiment were then trans-ferred the 8th Inniskillings, in which service five died at Hulluch: three of their families in time 'boycotted' the CWGC. Similarly, of the six men who had been transferred from the Rangers and who died serving with the Skins, three families declined to give information to the CWGC.

These are dry statistics, composed of living people. If there was an informal boycott of the proceedings of the CWGC in Belfast, it was quite likely to be broken by a widowed parent: CWGC details of five of the 7th Inniskillings were supplied by such a single mother or father, for whom the power of bereavement was presumably greater than whatever social pressures that emerged after Partition to forget the now apparently futile sacrifices of war.

And there are stories that touch the heart even a century on, such as that of James Woods from Dungannon. He is listed, aged one, in the 1901 Census as being an only child of middle-aged Catholic parents, but in the 1911 Census he appears merely as an eleven-year-old 'boarder' in the family home. Presumably some kind of rift had occurred amongst the Woods, one that finally resolved itself with his premature recruitment into a fighting battalion of the Inniskillings, and ended with his death in action aged sixteen on 22 May 1916. Whatever had occurred in life, in death his parents, Catherine and James, claimed their only child, and the end of their line.

And what of Robert Boggs, born in Tyrone, whose parents in 1901 declared themselves to be non-denominational Christians, and his father a farmer? In the 1911 Census they simply refused to answer the question concerning religion. The family moved to Greencastle, County Antrim, from where Robert joined the Connaught Rangers, and presumably not coming from West Belfast where most recruits were being consecutive numbers, he was given the recycled number of a soldier previously killed in Salonika. Later transferred to the Leinsters, Robert Boggs was killed in action in March 1918. I suspect the Boggs were Protestant nationalists attempting to disavow the quasi-religious passions that were to define Irish politics, and divide the island. For this alone they deserve to be remembered.

And just to clarify matters for those who know about loyalist Belfast's intimate relationship with the Royal Irish Rifles; this was not really mirrored in the sole battalion of the regiment that belonged to the 16th Irish Division, the 7th. In 1916 the 160 dead of the battalion included twenty-five Dubliners, thirty-one Belfastmen, one West Indian and twenty-seven Channel Islanders, the Jersey Militia having sent a detachment 250 men to the 7th in 1915, plus men from Waterford, Cork, Louth, Leitrim and Mayo. In other words, it seems to have been a makeshift catch-all battalion from which it is difficult to create a coherent narrative.

During the 16th's attacks on the Somme in September 1916, twelve Belfast men who had originally enlisted with southern regiments died in the service of northern ones to which they had been transferred: another thirty-two died with southern battalions. In all, therefore, forty-four Belfastmen who had initially joined southern battalions were killed during the attacks of the 16th Irish Division on the Somme. Another sixty-seven Belfastmen died in the northern regiments they had initially joined. In all, 111 Belfast-enlisted men died at Ginchy and Guillemont – but it is significant that some 40 per cent of these had chosen to join regiments of other provinces, each based well over one hundred miles from Belfast.

This surely was not just an expression of Irish nationalism, but also an implicit rejection of any notion of brothers-in-arms with their immediate unionist neighbours. There are political and cultural implications in such choices that merit further analysis, for they precede Partition. Was there, for example, some atavistic identification with these two rural regiments, the Connaughts and the Royal Irish, so far removed from the chimneys and mills of Belfast, Portadown and Lurgan? For the very industry of Ulster, with those crowded, terraced houses gathered round the factories and smokestacks, at some level, be it only subliminal, must have emblematized the province's close cultural and economic ties with the north of England and the Lowlands of Scotland. Whereas Irish nationalism, both constitutional and violent, found its inspirational imagery in a pre-industrial, pre-Plantation, pre-Reformation, pre-Norman Gaelic idyll, and that seemed to be particularly embodied in the peat-fires and thatched homesteads of Connemara.

Whatever cultural separatism existed amongst northern nationalists during the recruitment surge in 1914–15, in which the notion of military identification with their unionist and Protestant neighbours was clearly and explicitly rejected, must surely have been intensified after Partition. For a Northern Ireland state was most emphatically not what the nationalist volunteers had fought for. A huge sense of injustice and betrayal amongst the nationalist community seems to have devoured all memory of its war-losses: in such circumstances, forgetfulness can be a sovereign analgesic.

So, post-war, within a span of some 300 regimental numbers that covers the most coherent group of some twenty Belfast deaths in the Leinsters, just four families submitted family details. However, the addresses from which all the dead came are themselves significant, and these can be found by cross-referencing Soldiers Died in the Great War with the 1911 Census: most were from the Falls Road, McDonnell Street, New Lodge Road, Roden Street, Divis Street, North Queen Street and Benares Street. These very streets, which had once supplied large numbers of soldiers to the King, would in a later generation provide many volunteers to the Provisional IRA. It takes no genius to see how gravely wrong matters were allowed to go.

So over time two co-existent quasi-narratives emerged; one loudly unionist and state-endorsed, marked by bands and public commemoration; and from nationalists, a wounded non-narrative of consensual muteness and amnesia.

Is there a common ground between the two?

Well, there could be, and it is not the now well-known tale of Messines. For ninety-seven years ago this morning, the men of the 36th Ulster Division and of the 16th Irish Division rose together from their flooded trenches and side by side and limb by limb crawled through the evil swamp that was Frezenberg Ridge. For this was now a fortnight into the Third Battle of Ypres, and contrary to all the usages of war the two divisions had not been held back in reserve before they mounted their attack, but were holding the front-line trenches that had become linear connecting pools in the dire, mid-winter weather of that Flanders August.

They were exhausted before they left their trenches, and by the time this dreadful day was done, our two divisions, north and south, Catholic and Protestant, Irish and British, had lost 1100 dead, including some 80 men from Dublin and 160 men from Belfast, from both sides of the divide. Most of them have no known graves, but simply vanished forever in the mud. I say British, not merely in recognition of the passionate identity of many Ulster unionists, and the sizeable British component each division had contained from the outset, but because casualties during the dreadful battles of 1916 had been so great as to be beyond replacement by Irish recruits. In their stead came British soldiers, including the first of the conscripts.

And since their common sacrifice about a common purpose must surely strike a common chord across the many divides of this cathedral city, this county, this province, this island and these islands, is there any

reason why, each 16th August, the two communities should not henceforth reach out, *together* to mourn the eleven hundred forgotten men of
Frezenberg Ridge, who died ninety-seven years ago today? To be sure,
the war was one of the most unspeakable events in human history, but
finding the right way to end the evil of violence is never easy, as we here
know. Moreover, the Irish veterans I spoke to in the 1970s and 1980s,
without exception, unionist and nationalist, passionately believed they
were fighting for the freedom of Europe.

Which is perhaps why in October 1918 Irish troops – volunteers,
every one – were, once again, advancing alongside one another over the
bloodied plains of Flanders, in the final fight for Belgian freedom. The
36th Division, still fundamentally unionist but now, after the absorption
of some of the battalions of the 16th, included many Irish nationalists, plus
also reinforcements from Britain, remained an elite unit, and the incomparable 29th Division had two southern Irish battalions, the Dublin Fusiliers
and the Leinsters, who had been re-trained as specialized shock-troops,
were to win two Victoria Crosses in the liberation of the Flemish town
of Ledegem. Among the Leinsters were many Belfast nationalists, some
recruited by direct enlistment, others via the Connaught Rangers, whose
6th battalion had in the spring of 1918 been absorbed by the 2nd Leinsters.
We need not dwell here on how in later years Belfast nationalist-soldiers
viewed their martial efforts in that final, victorious campaign of the war
to free the people of Belgium from foreign oppression. Imagination will
suffice.

When the war was over, and after much unnecessary bloodshed, two
states finally emerged on this island. Did Northern Ireland seek for all
of its peoples the qualities of justice and fairness that were seen as being
quintessentially the reason for staying 'British'? Did independent Ireland
give to its citizens the republican virtues of universal and individual free-
doms, regardless of religion? Did Britain honour its own much-vaunted
values in its dealings with *all* the peoples of Ireland?

Or did all three states fail the fallen of the war, and shirk their historic
obligations to both the living and the dead? And, if they did, with all that
we have since learnt should we not really now be doing far, far better?

7. The Mound

Four thousand metres south of Ypres lay the small mining village of St Eloi, whose primary distinction in the winter of 1914–15 was an artificial mound of spoil, ten metres high and a tennis court in area. Along a front of over a thousand miles, it was this tiny pimple, with the battles for its ownership and the apparent sovereignty this conferred over the densely peopled marshes that it oversaw, which perhaps best encapsulate the tragic lunacy of the war.

St Eloi has a secondary characteristic. It lies on a 'ridge', a word that probably excites unwarranted expectations of altitude. No other suitable word exists in English, though perhaps the Flemish have a multitude of terms to cover any slight departure from utter horizontality. A cyclist approaching St Eloi would not have any sense of a hostile gravity pulling them backwards: it is only when they reach the village that they might realize the extent of the view: and how this is dramatically enhanced by The Mound!

Such visual enhancement, and the contest it provoked, would together cost an ocean of blood, first shed by the French Zouaves, who had initially held it against German encroachment in 1914. No history that I have read records the relief that the French must have felt on surrendering these squalid and mildly altitudinous few acres to their British allies: but if such a gift come from a friend, what might an enemy proffer?

Three Irish battalions of the 27th Division were soon to find out: the 1st Royal Irish Regiment, the 1st Leinsters and the 2nd Royal Irish Fusiliers: one from three of the four provinces, with lucky Connaught excluded. What unites all accounts by these occupants of St Eloi is their bitter loathing of their tenancy, not least because they had all arrived there in midwinter, fresh from the stunning heat of India. Nowhere in the empire would have provided an adequate preparation for service in this abysmal corner of the front but, of all places, India ...

Many of the newcomers that January 1915 had to march twenty-five kilometres to their new positions in lightweight tropical boots, designed for the dust of the Punjab, and wholly unsuited for the unyielding cobbled roads of Belgium. Others were equipped with the new-issue boots, which were so badly made and so crippling that many soldiers preferred to take them off, marching instead in stockinged feet – on Flanders cobbles, in midwinter.

Entering the line of trenches adjoining The Mound for the first time, it took an hour for the men of 1st Leinsters to cross a mere twenty-yard freezing morass, in which some men were up to their armpits in corpse-infested mud, the smaller soldiers having to be pulled through by main force. They soon discovered that there were no front-line trenches, merely connecting ice-pools. In the forward fire-trench, the primary line of defence that had to be held, the water was waist-deep. In some extension 'trenches', the water was five feet deep, and in one that connected with what was known as Trench 19, the Leinsters were warned, two men had simply vanished, presumed drowned. Alongside this network of a connecting mud-system were two large ponds, the underground channels of which dutifully refilled any hollow that its valiant occupants might try to empty of water.

So narrow was the front-line trench that there was no possibility of movement, while over the edge of the parapet oozed an endless slime from the corpse-covered plain of no man's land. There was nowhere dry to put a rifle down, so every soldier had to hold his weapon in his bare hands throughout his entire forty-eight-hour duty. There were, at this stage, no gloves, Sleep was impossible. Rest, if there was any, was achieved by a soldier lying on the back of the 'trench', rifle trigger and chamber held above the waist-high water. And just as there were no gloves, there were no sandbags, no entrenching tools and no shovels. Corpses of previous tenants arose regularly in the mud. One dead Frenchman, as if driven by the underground tides of Flanders, with rifle in hand, regularly climbed up a nearby mudbank, and thereupon kept a posthumous watch, before sliding down again, his vigil done, until the next time.

From early on, life for the Irish battalions at the Mound was made even more uncertain by the complex of tunnels that the two sides soon began to dig beneath one another. Miners were imported from suitable parts of Britain, and the clay that they removed – because it was a different colour from topsoil and could be spotted by aerial reconnaissance – had to be carried far away and disposed of secretly. All this took much patience and many men.

Personal sanitation in this latrineless swamp consisted of men finding a trench whose water was shallow enough to allow them to squat over a bully-beef tin, which was then hurled towards the German lines. There was of course no paper. Men used their shirt tails or their imaginations. Dysentery was common. One Irish officer wrote: 'It was purgatory to me … I had diarrhoea very badly … fourteen times during daylight.'

And if he had raised his head once during his repeated ordeals, a patient sniper would almost certainly have shattered it.

Trench-foot took a terrible toll, especially amongst those Irishmen still equipped with tropical boots. A badly afflicted soldier would have been unable to walk or stand, and so would have had to be borne backwards through the connecting pools to the rear. Each journey would take six-bearers: four for each stretcher, plus two reliefs, dangerous work that was deservedly detested. And the end of a full forty-eight hours in the frontline brought its own special agony. The Leinsters' historian (himself a veteran) wrote: 'Bent double with cold, streaming with water from the waist down, and caked with mud from the waist up, the condition of the soldiers was terrible. Some strong men would sob like children on this painful journey back.'

Once in the rear, exhausting labour awaited the 'resting' soldiers, digging trenches and mending roads, with little or no opportunity to dry their clothes before they returned to the front-line trenches beneath The Mound. These were numbered from 19 to 22, and because they were low-lying, offered little or no view to the occupants, who were overlooked throughout by the Germans on the ridgeline, on a landscape where an added foot in altitude allowed a perfect headshot on the enemy below. The tactical and literal nadir was achieved by Trench 19A, from which virtually nothing was visible, save the joints with 19 and 20. Trench 21 had no forward view at all. Trench 22 could see to its left, but nothing at all in front of Trench 21, which was thus blind to itself and to its neighbours. History does not relate why most of these were occupied at all, but unquestioned habit in war is perhaps one of its most pernicious and deadly afflictions. Mud taken was mud held, regardless of reason. That was the rule, in this, the most abysmal small corner of the entire Western Front, in which three Irish regiments were to hold the line.

On Sunday, 14 February, a systematic German bombardment began on The Mound and the remains of St Eloi, as a prelude to a sudden infantry attack at 1 p.m. The hapless defenders of 21, unseeing until the Germans actually arrived, were overwhelmed, its ranking officer, a forty-year old Captain Taylor, was killed while bending down and opening a box of ammunition. In 19, Lieutenant Murray, aided by a long periscope, saw a line of bayonets moving above a German communications trench. He called 'Stand To'. Abandoning the periscope he put his head over the parapet, in time to see one hundred Germans advancing along a miraculously navigable trail that snaked through no man's land. He fired all six rounds from his rifle and managed to put a fresh clip in before the Germans were upon him. He bayoneted one, and it remained stuck inside its host. He shot the German off. Murray next saw the Leinsters' machine-gun crew being surrounded by fiercely stabbing Germans. He 'fought his way back' is the official description of his exit, though 'fled' would perhaps be more accurate and more human. Either way, a British Vickers had been captured, most of its crew disposed of. However, one of them, a Private Courtney, though wounded in five places, managed to take off with some vital parts of the gun. He appears not to have been decorated for this feat of considerable valour, perhaps in punishment for his loss of a machine-gun in an utterly blind and indefensible trench to overwhelming numbers of enemy. (He survived The Mound, but not the war: he appears to have died of wounds in Salonika in 1916.)

The Leinsters were thus driven back.

The men of the 1st Royal Irish Regiment were hurried up from the reserves with orders to retake the worthless Trench 19. With B Company in reserve under Captain Roche-Kelly, whose grandfather had been national-ist MP for Clare, Major White went ahead to reconnoitre the ground. He reported back that across the ground leading to Trench 19 was a deep ditch with a plank bridge. He proposed to storm it. At 8.45 p.m. he led about eighty-five men towards the bridge, and about half had got across when the Germans fired star-shells and flares, illuminating the advancing soldiers. Of the forty men in C Company making the attack, thirteen were killed instantly and twenty-one wounded: a quite shocking slaughter in a tiny area, with the dead all clustered together. Captain Roche-Kelly led the shattered survivors to the rear. Amongst the dead were Major White, aged forty-two, and twenty-six year old 2nd Lieutenant Philip Anderson, both from Dublin. Of the total of seventeen dead, all of them Irish, the bodies of fifteen men were not recovered, and were duly subsumed into the battlefield.

The Royal Irish Fusiliers were next drawn into the battle, and lost one officer and fourteen men killed or fatally wounded. Of their fifteen dead, fourteen have no known graves, and their corpses remained in the vicinity of Trench 19, and the fifteenth, nineteen-year-old Charles Wright of Monaghan, died of his wounds in hospital. Of the total of thirty-six Leinster dead, fifteen simply vanished in the ooze. So, after this single brisk engagement, across about one hundred yards of trenches, the bodies of forty-four Irish human beings simply slid into the mud.

Many of these men, who had had to endure the most appalling priva-tions before they were killed, were not young. Of the officers, Captain White of the Royal Irish Regiment was forty-two. The oldest of the thirty-two enlisted Leinster's men and four officers killed was a forty-six-year-old veteran of the Boer War who had freely re-enlisted on the outbreak of this war, Captain Moffatt, from Finglas. Captain George Whalley Robinson from Shinrone, County Laois, was thirty-eight. The youngest officer to die was Frederick Younge, a farmer's son, from Oldtown, County Offaly, aged twenty-two.

The area around The Mound soon reverted to its usual, swampy abomination, and so unsustainable was life there that the Germans with-drew from the recently captured Trench 19 and its evil, conjoined sibling, 19A. The regimental histories make light of the following month, though life around the The Mound was acutely uncomfortable and often short. Snipers potted the unwary, and outbreaks of 'hate' – unprovoked German shellfire – took a regular toll. In one single day, for example, the 1st Leinsters lost twenty-seven men killed and wounded. Of the six dead, four have no known graves. At this time German ammunition seemed both limitless and accurate. British guns were allowed three rounds each, usually badly aimed. To improve the British accuracy, there being no periscopes, Lieutenant Mackenzie peered over the trench to spot the shellfall, and was shot between the eyes. The regimental history mentions him, but not the other eight who died that same day. Three of the dead were from Cork, and six of the dead have no known grave. Michael Hallissey, aged twenty-one, was in either mortal category, and by the time his name was put on the Menin Gate Memorial his parents and his widow were dead also.

From the three Irish battalions going in melancholy rotation into the trenches in the weeks after the German attack on The Mound, forty-three officers and men were killed during what would be called a 'quiet' period, thirty-two of their bodies being disposed of, or lost, or vanishing near where they had fallen. Not one of the regimental histories even records any of these deaths: only a close-scrutiny of casualty-records brings back to life the forgotten dead. The conditions for the undead remained the same: a freezing swamp, in which connecting pools served as trenches, while men kept sleepless, forty-eight-hour vigils and tried simultaneously to stay awake, not to drown and to keep their rifles dry. No doubt they were sustained throughout by the primary recreation of hurling the contents of their bully-beef tins into the sewer between themselves and their often notional enemy.

The one attempt to alleviate the troops' conditions consisted of the British raising, by great efforts over night after night, a protective earthen rampart between St Eloi and The Mound, which soon earned the rather grandiose title The Breastwork. At 5 p.m., on 14 March, the Germans made a concerted artillery attack on St Eloi and the liquid trench network around it. Two mines were fired beneath The Mound and Trenches 17 and 18, and a major German assault fell on the 2 Royal Irish Fusiliers, 2 Kings Shropshire Light Infantry and 4th Rifle Brigade. The Mound was taken, and so were many of the evil, suppurating trenches alongside it, though in an unusual stroke of military prudence the low-lying follies that were 19 and 19A, having already been abandoned by the Germans, had not been re-occupied by the British. By nightfall 17, 18, 19 and 19A, plus The Breastwork, were in German hands.

In the early hours of the next morning the Royal Irish Regiment and the Leinsters in reserve were hurled into a counter-attack to retake what no sane person could possibly want. In the utter dark the Leinsters marched in fours over the broken ground, much impeded by British telephone wires ensnaring already encumbered feet. That any narrative was ever assembled in the battalion histories about how men fought in the pitch-black night across the ponds and swamps surrounding The Mound is surely more a testament to the writers' imaginations than to any empirical skills. In the confusion the Royal Irish apparently attempted to retrieve trenches 21 to 23, which were believed lost, but were actually still held by the Royal Irish Fusiliers. One company of Leinsters moved towards Trench 20, and once illuminated by star-shells, gave a roar and charged the enemy without firing a shot, taking their objective by bayonet. Or so it is said: but who can testify to the truth, when deep mud meets with ink-black night, bedlam, blood and utter confusion?

The Royal Irish joined in the attack, to retake 19 and 19A; those excavations had previously been regarded as worthless, indefensible and expendable, but now the German had them, they were suddenly precious beyond all measure. The Breastwork was retaken, though the Royal Irish attack on The Mound was held up by 'three machine-guns and heavy rifle fire', or so the official account relates, but without indicating how such numerical certainty was achieved in the total dark. The Royal Irish attack having petered out, a German counter-attack followed on the Leinsters in Trench 22, and the officer, Captain Herbert Radcliffe from County Meath, who had joined the battalion only the day before, was killed.

An attempt by the Germans to strengthen their newly taken positions on The Mound was foiled by Lieutenant Ireland – from Borrisokane, County Tipperary – who came out in the open with his machine-gun and, lying utterly exposed lengthwise along the top of the trench, started firing on them from just fifty yards away. He was hit by return fire from The Mound, and was grievously wounded. Lying there, in the lee of The Mound, he wondered was it possible, before stretcher-bearers took him away, to have something to eat? He recovered, was awarded a Military Cross, and three years later, as a lieutenant colonel, was killed in the great German offensive of March 1918.

After The Breastwork was taken by the Germans and then retaken by the British, at 7 a.m., it – plus the Irish tenants of Trenches 20, 21 and 22

– came under fire from the artillery of both the Germans, who knew the identity of the men they were firing at, and also the British, who didn't. This ecumenical slaughter continued while three runners tried to alert the British guns to their fratricide, all British telephone lines having been cut. Two of the runners vanished forever amid the swamp and pond and lagoon that lay between the trenches and the artillery liaison officer. The third succeeded in getting through, but his message did not immediately convince the gunners to alter either their convictions or their coordinates.

Some men from the Royal Irish meanwhile took over the ruins of a house outside St Eloi, near The Mound. Second Lieutenant Royster Forde led an attack by five men to retake the nearest portion of The Breastwork. The officer was killed, as were four others: Sergeant Browne was shot in the head, but survived. Elsewhere, the battalion commander, Colonel Forbes, whose ancestor had first raised the regiment, was fatally injured.

The duty of defending St Eloi now fell to the remaining men of the Royal Irish, which lasted the day, and of which no detail survives. The next day, the 16th, two men of the Royal Irish, CSM Kelsey from Ipswich and Lance Corporal Carroll from Dublin, walked from their trench towards The Breastwork to gather in their wounded. A German officer called out to them to come forward and surrender. Kelsey replied that they had already helped two Germans to their (German) lines, and now they wanted to get their own men. The German consulted someone beside him, and then waved the two men away. They left, taking their wounded with them: two blinding acts of civility in a saga of insanity, which would earn them both a DCM.

Peace of a sort came to this particular section of the front on St Patrick's Day, and the three Irish battalions gratefully withdrew, with their brigade soon being posted elsewhere on the Front. In the three months that they had been in the St Eloi area, the three Irish battalions had suffered 209 deaths. Only thirty-one of the dead were buried in cemeteries behind the lines. The rest – 178 – were interred or lost where they fell, as entrail, lung, brain tissue and bone became one with the Flanders mud. That is of the Irish alone. The death-toll of the British battalions that served at The Mound through January-March 1915, was at least 450: over four hundred of these men had no known graves. German casualties during their two frenzied attacks in mid-February and mid-March, with much sniping in between, would have been no less, and of course, they rather inconsiderately left their dead behind in the British lines when they retreated. Thus, perhaps well over a thousand corpses were shallowly interred, or scattered in body-parts, over a few hundred square yards, but mostly around a few narrow trenches beneath and around The Mound. It was if an ocean liner had sunk, and its floundering passengers and crew had then been instantly embalmed in a layer of mud. These cadavers were then left to be slowly digested by the salient, though with much subsequent regurgitation, and occasionally projectile vomiting.

Meanwhile The Mound itself remained in German hands, while the pestilential paddy-fields around it rested in those of the British. The future homes of successive battalions of soldiers at St Eloi through 1915 were walled with human flesh, and as regimental historians were to observe with a strange, and almost stricken nostalgia, those who survived and returned back home, for the rest of their lives could never thereafter smell rotting meat without being immediately transported back to their days in the Ypres salient. One such group of later visitors came from the 2nd battalion Leinsters, (as opposed to the 1st), with the great Francis Hitchcock of Birr as their chronicler. By this time the iconic object of quite obsessive dementia had been slightly renamed; now it was called The Mound of Death, and as we have seen, not wrongly. Nor had ground conditions improved in the least that November night in 1915 as the 2nd battalion forded the expanse of mud to their front-line trench, to find no trench at all. Heavily laden bombers were engulfed by the mud, and had to be rescued.

The topography of the battlefield had been altered by three mine craters in No Man's Land. Each side, German and British, held the crater-lips closest to their trenches, which were connected to the craters by saps (connecting trenches). Hitchcock rapidly found all movement along his sector of the front, to check on his men, was made almost impossible by the mud and wire entanglements. Progress through one water-filled trench could be achieved only by using the foot of a German, sticking out of the side of the trench, as a handhold. During the night a parapet fell on one of the Leinsters, and he had to be dug out.

At dawn Hitchcock was told by his NCO, Sergeant Ginn, that the Germans were out of their trenches and strolling about in full sight, swinging coke braziers to keep them alight. The Leinsters, being below both the ridge and The Mound of Death, and open therefore to annihilation should the German so choose, prudently did nothing. The weather, though, was of a different frame of mind, changing from the downpour of all night to a stark and bitter cold. Gum boots were issued to the men, but these were soon sucked off in the glutinous mud, and so the soldiers stood in their socks, ten months after their colleagues in 1st Leinsters had hobbled to these very trenches in their stockinged feet along the frozen cobbled pave.

A bizarre game of belligerent pacifism seemed to be underway. The Saxons opposite occasionally fired a 'Little Willie' at them, with no real intent and certainly no real effect, and remained visible, calling out 'good morning' to Hitchcock as he emerged, and bidding him 'goodbye' later. During the night sniping followed, and Private George Levis, the twenty-year-old son of a Church of Ireland bank-clerk from Cootehill, was shot dead: his brother had recently been commissioned into the 1st battalion. C.S.M. Brereton shot two Germans in reply. What was real in this insane place, where civil greetings were a prelude to murder?

At dawn Hitchcock went around his men with the restorative tot of rum. He later wrote that the old sweats would take it gratefully, then holding out their ration, would murmur, 'Best respects.'

Private Kelly, who appears to be Bernard Kelly, from Dublin, sighed happily after downing his tot: 'Begorra, 'tis wonderful, sorr. 'tis trickling yet.'

That, anyway, is how Hitchcock rendered the man's speech: Bernard Kelly, of Taylor's Lane, Dublin, had just eleven months to live. At least he has a grave, and is buried in Menin Road North Cemetery, outside leper.

Not long afterwards, perhaps in revenge for Brereton's bagging a brace of Germans, the Leinster's line was straddled with whiz-bangs, and a group of soldiers just making some tea was hit. Drummer Spencer of Northamptonshire was killed. Private Farrell lost an eye. In the three days since they had arrived, the Leinsters had suffered seven casualties. Death came and went, and left the men largely unperturbed.

Later that morning General Capper – whose brother, also a general, had been shot dead by a sniper in Loos while visiting frontline troops: clearly the family had no intention of being seen as 'Chateau-Red Tabs' – came to see the Leinsters at The Mound. He encountered a frost-bitten, unnamed soldier of D Company, lying half-submerged in a sea of mud, and asked him how he was.

'Grand entirely, sir.'

Perhaps not incorrectly, Capper took that as a fair reflection of the Leinsters' morale.

Later, Hitchcock and two fellow officers went over to one of the communal craters so perversely shared by the two sides. One of them, Drummond, a German-speaker, started to talk to a group of the enemy, and threw them a small flask of whiskey – this, the very day that had begun with whizz-bangs blowing apart a group of Leinsters brewing up some tea.

At night the two sides wired their front lines, often no more than fifteen yards apart, and by tacit agreement, without interfering with one another. Soon afterwards the 2nd Leinsters left The Mound and their dead there, never to return.

In February 1916 the British army's General Plumer decided to end this chronic, repetitive purgatory. This entire German 'salient' within the Ypres salient was still, after two years of war, only one hundred yards deep and six hundred yards wide, beneath which a network of tunnels and counter-tunnels had been sunk. In 1915 alone the British had fired thirteen mines and twenty-nine 'camouflets' – countermining explosions – and the Germans, perhaps less skilled at detecting British tunnels, twenty mines and two camouflets. Plumer ordered General Haldane to arrange nothing less than the complete destruction of The Mound, with a combined assault on it by mines and artillery. Meanwhile, as the plans for its extinction proceeded underground and in gun-parks, The Mound continued to exact further, but now microbiological, punishment on the soldiery gathered in its shadow: some six hundred men from one division had to be evacuated suffering from trench-feet as they prepared for the final, once-and-for-all assault on St Eloi.

At 4.15 a.m. on 27 March six mines were exploded under the complex, the largest containing fifteen tons – 15,272 kg – of ammonal. British troops, Northumberland Fusiliers and soldiers from London regiments, who had been waiting all night in the open in sub-zero temperatures, and meanwhile suffering terribly, rose with relief to advance. But the complete destruction of the surface of the battlefield meant that the attacking troops could no longer recognize their objectives. German artillery rained down on the baffled infantry scrabbling around No Man's land, unable to differentiate between new craters and old ones: and The Mound began, once again, to claim corpses: 34 from the Scots Fusiliers, 12 West Yorks, 118 from three Fusiliers battalions, all to join the thousands who had already entered the food-chain. Moreover, the mines had damaged the elaborate drainage system, and the few trenches that the British had managed to have taken then rapidly became uninhabitable. An entire brigade was withdrawn, exhausted and nearly broken.

Meanwhile the Germans had, as was their wont, captured two of the new craters. Wave upon wave of allied troops fought their way to reclaim these newly created, newly lost pits, only to be repulsed, until finally, on 3 April, the work that should have been complete on 27 March came to an end. German defenders south of St Eloi, exhausted, began to surrender. The Mound as a mound was no more: instead, a crater lay there, and now, finally, British-held. Canadian troops were sent to replace the exhausted British Division. They found their new trenches uninhabitable, and the broken terrain behind them meant that they could not be re-supplied. In their muddy holes, they hungered and went thirsty.

Then, unbelievably, the evil and repetitive spell of St Eloi was once again invoked, for the Germans counter-attacked, and with their artillery annihilating the defending Canadians, they retook craters 2 and 3 (the latter being formerly The Mound, but now inverted) and 4. A rocket-signal then brought devastating artillery down on the British support trenches. Where was the vital rocket fired from? From Crater 3, namely, the still-haunted, subterranean remains of The Mound, of course.

Now it was the Canadian's turn to hurl themselves futilely at the British-made, German-held craters 2, 3 – The Mound – 4 and 5. Soon Canadian corpses were lying in layers over the generations of cadavers of those that had gone before, many, many times. And the Germans then counter-attacked one more time, which was their way, of course, and recaptured craters 6 and 6.

Mutual exhaustion set in, the Canadians in their holes, the Germans in theirs. Battles for The Mound had cost the Canadian Army Corps, in these, its opening days as a corps, 640 lives, 210 of them with no known graves, which could only mean one thing.

By now The Mound, which was the same area as the fountain and pavements in the centre of St Stephen's Green, and the area adjacent to it, far smaller than the Green itself, had become a mud sarcophagus containing at least 2000 bodies, many barely covered, most just a hand-reach below the mud.

Logically this could go on forever, provided each side had enough men to funnel into the charnel-sea of St Eloi. The question that remained for anyone who wanted to occupy and hold The Mound was: how to take a small enough amount of land to ensure success, but large enough to prevent the enemy's artillery from making it impossible to retain tenancy of the captured ground? There was no answer to this conundrum in such material terms. The only solution was nihilism, with the complete elimination of everything around St Eloi. If there was nothing left to fight over, maybe the two sides could cease this insanity. So, in August 1916, teams of miners started digging well behind British lines, going 125 feet vertically and then moving horizontally, directly underneath St Eloi and Crater 3, formerly The Mound.

At 3.10 a.m., on 7 June, nineteen mines exploded beneath German positions south of Ypres. That beneath St Eloi/The Mound was the biggest-ever conventional explosive charge in human history: 95,000 lbs, or 40 kilograms, or 42 tons of ammonal. When that mine detonated, the result was the largest man-made explosion the world had ever known – even London heard the bang. It was finally exceeded only by the first atom bomb test on 16 July 1945, in New Mexico, and remained the largest explosion directed at human beings until Little Boy was dropped on Hiroshima. When Surrey, Kentish and Royal Fusilier battalions of the 124th Brigade of the 41st Division arrived at the village of St Eloi, there was absolutely nothing on the surface other than wide smoldering wasteland, with at its heart a crater one hundred feet deep and ninety yards in diameter. The Mound and the trenches around it and the last fragments of St Eloi were as totally erased as had been the mountain that had made Krakatoa. The graves of thousands of men had been turned into billions of molecules, and their DNA scattered like meadow-pollen across the Flanders plain.

Not far away two other divisions were seizing the main road from Messines into St Eloi. They were the 16th (Irish) Division and the 36th (Ulster) Division. When men of the Dublin Fusiliers were waiting to take part in the assault, they were fully aware, through the meticulous training that was now commonplace before a major assault, that a huge mine was about to explode beneath the Germans. And what did they do as they prepared to attack? They said a decade of the rosary for their German enemy, or so Major Standish Smithwick of the Dublins was later to report. Such was the cosmic madness of The Mound, that the story is more than possible.

Major Willie Redmond MP at fifty-six was far too old to be in the front-line for this final battle, which would decide the ultimate fate of The Mound, but he was determined to be there. He sought permission from his senior officer, and very much his junior in years, Major Edmond Roche-Kelly – naturally, a veteran of The Mound – to be allowed to lead his men into action. He was granted it, and duly passed to his doom. His seat, and long previously also that of Major Roche-Kelly's grandfather, was then won by Eamon de Valera, whose political victory in the coming decades was a prime reason why so much of the history of this time was duly forgotten. Indeed this, if only symbolically, could be said to be The Mound's lasting triumph.

As for Edmond Roche-Kelly, who gave this vital permission, he finished the war as Lieutenant Colonel Edmund Roche-Kelly DSO MC Legion d'Honneur. And it was well that he survived, for his wife Kitty, originally of the Shine family from Dungarvan, County Waterford, was to lose all three of her brothers on the Western Front. For the truth is that The Mound did not just stand at St Eloi: it stood wherever man fought his fellow man during these terrible years. Take John Leo Whitty, a Castleknock-educated Catholic boy who had been awarded the MC for his gallantry at St Eloi, whose bloody exactions he managed to survive. Enough of The Mound having been enough, he then sought the sanctuary of the clouds and joined the Royal Flying Corps, in whose service he was shot down and killed in 1916.

A round tower stands at Messines today to mark the achievement of the two Irish divisions in June 1917. However, there is nothing whatever to mark the ghastly travails of the battalions of men who waded back and forth through the bacterial lagoons of St Eloi, who dwelt in those conjoined hellholes trenches 19 and 19A, and who later had to endure the enduring, unendurable sink of iniquity that was Crater 3. Not merely is all trace of The Mound now gone; so too is any public memory of almost three years of torment, and the thousands of dead, many hundreds of them Irish, it had begotten.

8. Gallipoli

It was one of the enduring images of Ireland at war that didn't endure: the picture of the hundreds of volunteers gathered at Lansdowne Road under the watchful eye of the president of the Irish Rugby Football Union, Mr F.H. Browning. He had called for the footballers of Dublin to join, as he would doubtless have put it, the cause of civilization against the violator of little Belgium – and there they stood in lines, chests clumsily out, stoutly imitating soldiery. In large part they were representative of Protestant commercial Dublin, and unionist Trinity – but not completely. There stands Paddy Tobin, handsome, Rupert-Brooke-like, the son of a Catholic doctor and former army officer. And there too stands Michael Fitzgibbbon, son of an Irish Parliamentary Party MP and former Land Leaguer. They couldn't possibly have known that the enemy they would be fighting was not the enemy they had joined to fight, but one that had done no wrong to justify a war. For the first casualty of war is not truth, as is so often proclaimed; it is the cause for which it is declared, as these young men were to discover.

Eight months later, while they were still in training, their minds fixed on Germany, another image of the war captivated the world. It was of troops landing from the *River Clyde* at Sed El Barrh on the Gallipoli peninsula.

Here was myth in the making, at the very home of myth, for this was where the great southern waterways of Asia and Europe debouched into the Mediterranean, and the perfect place for new and enduring myths to be minted.

The basic idea was beautiful. It was that a collier, whose iron-plate would be impervious to bullets, was to be rammed ashore on the beach at Sed Ed Barrh. Wide holes had been cut in the sides of the vessel, from which specially-built gangways led to the ship's prow. Upon impact, lines of men from the Dublin and the Munster Fusiliers could emerge from each side of the collier and storm ashore, aided in their final few yards by extensions that had been thrown out after the ship had beached. Meanwhile, landing before the *River Clyde,* rowing boats would disgorge some five hundred Dublin Fusiliers who would provide covering fire for the troops emerging from the collier.

The soldiers' adage is *train hard; fight easy.* The men doing the landings had never once seriously rehearsed this operation, though precise timing was key to everything. The planners behind this operation were all classically trained, and it was if they had been hypnotized by the mythologies borne on the waters of Dardanelles. They knew of Hero in her tower, of Leander swimming to her and thereby to his doom. And maybe, in some deep psychic sense, that was the key to Gallipoli: that crooning siren upon the waters of the Hellespont was the midwife of a strategic madness. This would make it a Greek tragedy in its purest sense; maybe, within the collective and unconscious will of those who ordained it, a tragic myth was intended from the outset.

For there was no way that the British intention – to seize one side of the Dardanelle's Straits, force a naval flotilla up through the sixty kilometres of waterway across the Sea of Marmora, and then, by arriving on Istanbul's shores, force Turkey out of the war – could be realized. This absurd concept could only be hatched by young men whose mythic-inclined brains been further deluded by the grand schemes of Winston Churchill, First Lord of the Admiralty. They should have known better. Their minds were hard-wired with the stories of Troy, of the abduction of Helen, the wife of Meneleus, by Paris, and the endless war that resulted.

The Hellespont had repeatedly been the home of vain wars. Determined on the conquest of Athens, the Persian Emperor Xerxes had built a pontoon bridge to get his army over the Straits, and when the bridge was destroyed in a storm, he had his engineers executed, while his soldiers flogged the water three hundred times in punishment. Byzantium, later Constantinople, the second Rome, flourished here until the city fell to the Ottomans, who turned it into a Muslim capital. Mehmed II's fortresses still dominate much of the straits, and at Chanak no vessel is more than 500 metres from the Ottoman cannon that still gazes across the Narrows. The tsars of Russia grew huge palaces from the revenue raised by the grain on Ukraine's vast prairies that reached the wide world through those waters. These waters, and the rights and the rites of passage through them, continue to dominate the world's headlines.

That ruthless narcissist, Winston Churchill, the primary architect of the Dardanelles adventure, was seduced by the mythic possibilities of a campaign there. Could he be another Xerxes, though this time triumphant? Certainly, his reputation needed rescuing after his opening foray of the war, in which, as First Lord of the Admiralty, in the autumn of 1914, he assembled an improvised force of untrained recruits and middle-aged naval reservists at Antwerp, which he intended to turn into an army, with himself at their command. He even telegraphed Prime Minister Asquith, demanding to be allowed to resign the Admiralty, and instead to be instantly made Lieutenant General Winston Churchill, Commanding Officer of the Antwerp Expeditionary Force. Instead of being sacked, he was brought back to London, and his force of five thousand passed into captivity, with some two hundred deaths (over which he never expressed any contrition).

That was not his first fiasco of 1914. The war between Britain and the Ottoman empire was in part due to him. Upon the outbreak of hostilities with Germany he had personally cancelled the delivery of two warships built in Britain for the Ottoman Empire, and without compensation: *Sultan Osman I*, the largest battleship in the world, and her smaller sister ship, the *Reshdaih*. This was a needless insult to the Turkish people, who had themselves paid for the vessels, an astounding £7.5 million, by public subscription, in advance. To be sure, Berlin already had a military mission in Istanbul, and had been grooming the Sultan with ivory, peacocks and Krupps howitzers, but nonetheless much of Turkish opinion was pro-British, an opinion that needed to be groomed. But Churchill could seldom see a china-shop without enquiring within, and thereupon proving, by means of his shapely horns and his flailing hooves, the abject pusillanimity of the porcelain cup and the utter spinelessness of its saucer.

Churchill was determined to force the Dardanelles, to put Turkey out of the war (as if that were an inevitable consequence of a few ships standing off Istanbul) and thereby force Germany to abandon the occupation of Belgium and France. There was no logic at work, just the intoxication of myth. The full strategic background of how the men arrived on the *River Clyde* on the beach at Sed El Barrh need not detain us here but all that followed was largely of Churchill's doing.

The landings themselves were from the outset the very stuff of legend, as on that Sunday morning the *River Clyde* journeyed to what the British were now calling 'V Beach' – one of an alphabetic series of code names – and the Munsters' chaplain Father Finn said Mass in the hold. Meanwhile, rowing boats with half a battalion of Dublin Fusiliers neared the shore. But then they were caught in a ripcurrent, against which their blue-jacket rowers had trouble making any headway. So the *River Clyde* had to loop backwards and make a second approach, but now she was going too slowly, and so was grounded too far out from the beach.

Everything that happened then belongs to myth, and this is how the myth unfolded. The *River Clyde*'s Commander Unwin struggled ashore to manhandle some lighters together, and he and some ratings physically held them in place while the Dublins and Munsters poured out of the large portholes on each side of the vessel, to be met by swathes of machine-gun and pom-pom fire, which sent the first waves of men tumbling into the water. Heavily encumbered, those not already dead, drowned in their scores. On the beach, the few survivors huddled in the lee of a sandbank, while Father Finn, his right arm broken, blessed the wounded and the dying, steadying the fractured limb with his left hand, until he too fell down dead. Inside the boat was hell itself, as the waiting soldiers listened, appalled, to the thunder of machine-gun and pom-pom fire hitting the metal sides, and sending thunderous echoes booming through the hold.

In the bows of the *River Clyde,* Joshiah Wedgewood MP was firing his machine-gun at the unseen Turks. 'The wounded cried out all day in every boat, lighter and hopper and along the shore. It was horrible.'

'I never knew blood smelt so strong before,' later said Midshipman Drury, coping with the turbulent lighters in the waters (he was to win the VC for his gallantry that morning).

Meanwhile, a parallel slaughter was engulfing the rowing boats struggling against the unexpected current. One boat was reported to have made it ashore with just three men, all wounded, out of a complement of forty. In another, Lieutenant Maffett of the Dublin Fusiliers was later quoted: '... just before we grounded, the boat was hit with incendiary shells and we began to go on fire. She was half full of water. Several of the men who hit fell to the bottom of the boat and were drowned there or suffocated by other men falling on them. Many, to add to their death agonies, were burnt as well.'

Their boats began to drift broadside on, with desperate Dublin Fusiliers trying to manhandle the oars. Major David French, cousin of the famous song-writer Percy French, and uncomfortably the tallest man in the battalion, later said, 'I realized that having practically wiped out those in the three boats ahead, they were concentrating their fire on us. I jumped out at once, into the sea up to my chest, yelling for the men to make a rush for it. But the poor devils, loaded like sardines in a tin and carrying those damnable weights on their backs, could scarcely clamber over the sides of the boat, and only two of them reached the shore unhit.'

Overhead, Lieutenant Commander Sampson of the Royal Naval Air Service was watching from his seaplane; it was he who described the sea as red, and images of this scimitar of crimson reaching from the line surf to the boats in the water became fixed in the popular imagination, invoking Macbeth: 'Now, will all great Neptune's ocean wash this blood from my hand? No, this my hand will rather the multitudinous seas incarnadine'.

Thus the story of the Irish being slaughtered as they emerged from the sides of the *River Clyde,* or being massacred in their rowing boats, was widely believed at the time. Indeed, I have myself repeated it on many occasions, and it is still the preferred narrative today; one recent best-selling account declared 'within a few minutes, 50 per cent of the 700 men who had just landed were dead'.

In fact, no such slaughter of men emerging from the collier occurred, for the simple reason that the landings had been stopped quite early on. The intrepid Lieutenant Guy Nightingale of the Munsters was one of the first ashore, only to find that the soldiers on the beach were being picked off with ease. So he returned up the gangway, and halted further disembarkations. Contrary to myth, the Turks had no pom-poms, no incendiary bullets and probably no machine-guns that could actually be brought to bear on the portholes or the gangways. The pom-poms existed only in the imaginations of veterans of the war in South Africa, where the Boers had used them to fearsome effect. (But where the myth is truthful is in the tale of the gallant Father Finn, who had certainly gone out to tend to the early wave of soldiers seeking shelter on the seashore, and who died a heroic death while ministering to them.)

The vital timetable of events – not repeated in any of the popular books on the landings at the time, nor in the more recent ones now that the First World War is fashionable again, but quoted in the regimental history of the Munster Fusiliers – tells us that the *River Clyde* grounded at 6.25 a.m. Movement out was impossible for a while, because the vessel was too far from the shore. When the seamen had finally fixed the lighters, they clearly took the Turks by surprise, because most got ashore. But then the lighter bearing the gangway broke free, and some men fell into the water, and almost certainly drowned. Contrary to the myth – that word again – of men pouring out of the sides and all being slaughtered, parties of men not merely continued to get ashore, but some soldiers, including a few injured, even returned to the vessel. The injured and dead on the lighters and on the shore certainly presented a grisly picture, but then all battle-fields do; the real difference was that this one had so many witnesses who could view the appalling proceedings from positions of relative safety, and just as importantly, live to tell the tale.

Here is one account, always cited as fact (twice by myself) from Private Timothy Buckley from Macroom, County Cork. 'The captain led the way, but fell immediately at the foot of the gangway. The next man charged over him and kept going till he fell, on the pontoon bridge. Altogether out of 200 men, 149 men were killed outright and 30 wounded.'

Here is a quite different account from a Captain Lane, which of course is never used, perhaps because it lacks the tragic drama that myth requires: 'Henderson led Z company, ordering me to follow at the end of the first platoon. One by one they popped out, and then my turn. All the way down the side of the ship bullets crashed against the side. On reaching the first barge I found that some men had collected and were firing. … I led them over the side. … *None of us were hit* [my italics], and we gained the bank.'

It was while he was on the beach that Lane was shot in the leg by a sniper; it was at this point that the gallant Guy Nightingale returned aboard to stop the landings. So the real slaughter was not occurring as men rushed along the side of the vessel, where they would have been diffi-cult moving targets for Turkish riflemen, but once they were stationary on land. The disembarkation proper only really started after nightfall, and the last men out, Dublin Fusiliers, led by twenty-three-year-old Henry Desmond O'Hara, left the vessel at 12.30 a.m. on 26 April, after waiting aboard for eighteen hours.

However, the myth had begun, and was reinforced by the claim that on V Beach alone some 440 bodies (by implication, all Irish) were buried the next day. Here are the facts. On 25 April 1915, during the landings at V Beach, and during the day-long gunfight on the sands, essentially until nightfall, just fifty-three enlisted soldiers and five officers of the Dublin Fusiliers and fifty-five men and one officer of the Munster Fusiliers were killed. (So much for Timothy Buckley and his oft- and lovingly-quoted '149 men killed outright', as if such certain knowledge would ever be possible.) In addition, just twelve sailors were killed during *all* the landings (and not just V Beach), one of them Henry Kenny, from Courtown, Wexford. What about Sampson's crimson sea? He saw what he saw, to be sure, yet how much arterial bleeding does it take to turn the pellucid Aegean red? Have you ever had a nose bleed into a basin, and seen the effect of a single humble capillary within even a minute?

But what is both mythic and true is the proportion of officers killed or injured among the Dublins: just about 100 per cent, O'Hara being the exception. In trying circumstances, officers usually have to expose them-selves to danger – which explains the high proportion of casualties among senior officers above battalion level, with one brigadier general and three brigade majors down. For V Beach was theatre, and the tragedy unfolding there had so many witnesses, it seemed to be worse than other military disasters, but it wasn't. Thus was the myth born, and it is unlikely to be damaged by anything said here.

To put the Irish losses on V Beach into perspective: during their land-ings at 'W Beach' a few miles away, the 1st battalion alone, the Lancashire Fusiliers, lost 183 men (including four Irishmen) and had six officers killed, a death rate three times greater than that of either the Dublins or the Munsters. Since the Commonwealth War Graves Commission records that in all, some 524 British soldiers and sailors in total died in the landings on 25 April, the losses on W Beach alone mean that there cannot have been 440 burials on V Beach. Moreover, in Flanders the next day, the Dublin's 2nd battalion lost seventy-two men killed during the dreadful gas attacks, with no mythic status attached to this tragedy at all.

Indeed, only after the landings did the real slaughter at Gallipoli really began, invisibly, untheatrically, and most of all, quite unmythically. The two battalions, now joined by the 1st Inniskillings, then embarked on some terrible fighting. By 1 May the Dublins had lost another 207 enlisted soldiers; that is, 260 killed in six days. The Munsters had got off rather more lightly – another eighty-one to add to the original fifty-five.

The day after the landings, 26 April (the same day that the Dublin Fusiliers' 2nd battalion was being gassed in Ypres), Lieutenant Henry Desmond O'Hara took the 1st battalion, under the command of a staff officer, Charles Doughty-Wylie, to assault and take the fort at Sed El Barrh. Doughty-Wylie had previously lived in Turkey, and went armed with only a cane, as a measure of the love he felt for the Turkish people. He was mortally wounded in the attack and won a posthumous Victoria Cross; Henry Desmond O'Hara got an immediate DSO in the field. Nine hundred Dublin Fusiliers from three battalions were to die in Gallipoli; he was the first and last to be so decorated.

Certainly, Henry Desmond O'Hara DSO, the son of a former policer officer and now Resident Magistrate, is a mythic hero who never became a myth. After so many officers had become casualties, he, aged twenty-three, was effectively in charge of his battalion. He was also, by default, the battalion censor, which meant that he had to censor his own letters, which (as we now know) he didn't. So he wrote to his fiancée the most extraordinarily injudicious accounts of the battles through which the Dublins toiled in their fight northward from V Beach. At one stage, he said, the men were gibbering like lunatics – the kind of line for which army censors would have burnt a letter.

The surviving Dublins and Munsters – together once 2000 strong, but now reduced to a total of 770 men – were combined into a single battalion, the Dubsters. Under O'Hara's command, on 30 April–1 May, they parried a fierce counter-attack from the Turks, in which 150 Dubsters were killed. This was evil, barbaric, bayonet-and-boot, eye-gouging killing that has no place in myth. Far better the men running alongside the steel plates of a merchantman, the sea turning red, or a dying priest kneeling decorously in the roseate surf, pronouncing extreme unction.

Henry Desmond O'Hara was fatally wounded in August, and died in hospital in Gibraltar on 29 August 1915. His fiancée was in due course sent the letters that she had sent him. It's hard to believe now, but fifty years ago, in 1964, the First World War was all but forgotten, and when Robert Rhodes James, a clerk in the House of Commons, proposed a book about Gallipoli to the publisher B.T. Basford, the company was rather dubious: Galli-*what?*. However, Batsford finally agreed, and James wrote to various newspapers asking for readers to let him know of material relevant to the Gallipoli campaign.

One day a bashful woman in her seventies turned up at the House with a bundle of letters wrapped in a ribbon. Her name was Mrs A. Bruce – I still don't know her first name – and what she had brought was the correspondence between herself and Henry Desmond O'Hara. The letters were deeply moving, and were in their own way personally injudicious, for it was quite clear that the couple had been sexually intimate, but they also provided a searing insight into how young O'Hara had felt in battle. But Rhodes James had a big canvas to paint, far greater than the thoughts and feelings of an Irish infantry subaltern; moreover, Mrs Bruce's husband had apparently thought she was a virgin when they married, so the more intimate aspects of her relationship with Henry would have to wait until her husband had joined him in that Valhalla that apparently awaited Mrs A. Bruce's former lovers. (I note that a Captain Bruce joined the 1st Dublin Fusiliers in May, and was shot and wounded on 23 June: is he the same man? Did he bring her letters to Henry back from Gallipoli? Is that how they met?) She and Robert agreed to put the archive into the safekeeping of the Imperial War Museum, with James intending one day to make a full book about Henry and his time in Gallipoli, and his love affair with A.

As it happens, Rhodes James's Gallipoli book was a great success, and remains the standard work on the campaign. However, he had other more pressing projects on his plate, and so Henry Desmond and Miss A. were put on the back burner, so to speak, but at least their letters were safe. In 1969, after a demonstration against the Vietnam War, some hero threw a bomb into the Imperial War Museum, completely destroying the O'Hara Archive. Robert told me about this, shortly before his own death in 1999.

'How many people have you told this story to?' I asked.

'No one, until now. You're the first person ever to show an interest in Henry Desmond O'Hara.'

And that is how frail the narrative of human life can sometimes be, for even a tale as heroic as Henry Desmond O'Hara's can vanish overnight, unless it has been consecrated at its outset in that holy chalice wherein

myth is born, and then passed on from lip to lip by people who are dedicated to keeping the myth alive. The truth about Henry is almost all gone,
but the untruths of V Beach live on.

(How apt that the young Henry had a French governess whose name
was Julia Cherfils, which means 'dear son'. The O'Haras never got over
the death of their only boy, and his mother Cecilia appears to have died
soon afterwards. His father William moved to Shropshire, where he lived
out the rest of his days, quite alone. In Kilkenny, meanwhile, Henry's
grandfather James Hercules Connellan was able to weigh his losses in the
war: four grandsons by four different children.)

Days of astonishing awfulness lay ahead, with the Dubs losing another
59 dead on 29 June, 105 dead between 7–9 August, fifty-seven dead on 16
August, and twelve on 21 August. Meanwhile, the Inniskillings, who didn't
land on V Beach, and who accordingly are ignored by all myth, lost 48
men dead on 22 May, ninety dead on 15 August, and 129 on 21 August.
The very worst day for Ireland was this last day, with 497 men of the Irish
regiments (though not all of them Irish), and Brigadier General Thomas
Pakenham, 5th Earl of Longford, being killed.

This was the nadir of the Gallipoli campaign, most particularly in the
assault on Scimitar Hill, with the men charging in lines abreast, and being
threshed like standing wheat by cleverly-sited machine-gun fire, with
another deadly weapon poised overhead. In August, the Turkish sun is
quite African in its pitilessness, and soon the desiccated grasslands and
the tinder-dry scrub, under which many wounded soldiers had crawled
as cover from the equally ubiquitous sun and Turkish snipers, had caught
fire. The flames spread with astonishing speed right across the battlefield,
as the helpless wounded were burnt alive, the explosions of their ammunition pouches and their grenades marking their final resting places. Those
who tried to run from the wildfire were systematically bowled over by
snipers, and if they were lucky, killed. Try making a myth out of that.

Suvla is where the second part of Ireland's Gallipoli story began, a
couple of weeks before this disaster, and after it had become clear that the
landings in Helles and in Anzac were not going to take anyone anywhere
close to Istanbul. The 10th (Irish) Division was one of the new divisions,
but even before it arrived on the peninsula, its failure was foreordained, for
it was broken up, and one brigade, including the 5th Connaught Rangers
and the 6th Leinsters, was sent to assist the hard-pressed troops at Anzac.

The Divisional Commander, General Mahon, proceeded to pass into a monumental sulk, leaving his two brigades that had landed on the wide bay at Suvla to their own devices, and in due course, their own deaths.

Suvla enters the myth by accident; the 10th Irish were not meant to be landing there at all, but farther north. Difficulties at that intended beach caused the two brigades of the 10th to land at Suvla, and at different times. The division was no longer a division, but a disconnection of molecules. The absurdities soon became grotesque. Two discoveries had been made after the April landings: hand grenades were vital in a war fought over ravines and gullies, and as precious as life itself was water. Entire battles around Krithia, just north of V Beach, had been fought, with hundreds of British soldiers dying, and all in vain, merely to get access to its wells.

So, naturally, the two commodities that the August landings lacked were hand grenades and water carriers. Yet not merely did men lose huge of amounts of liquid through normal respiration and sweat, most of them had severe and often uncontrollable diarrhoea. From early on the flies in Gallipoli had been an unbearable curse but now they became an insufferable plague, feasting on the pools of excrement, settling on faces and hands, and instantly covering all food the moment it was laid out. Men were unshaven, filthy, bloody and soiled. The sun's rays were lethal. A kilted Scotsman was pinned down on the battlefield and unable to move because of snipers, and with flies crawling all over his blistering skin, sepsis and gangrene rapidly set in. After he was finally retrieved, both legs had to be amputated.

The details of the peregrinations of the 10th Division's component parts around the salt lake landscape of the northern part of the peninsula make tiresome reading, both for their futility and for the mind-numbing ineptitude of those in command. Let us focus, therefore, on the ultimate objective of the 10th: the whaleback ridge of Kiritch Tepe Sirt, 600 feet high and several miles long. This was not held by regular soldiers, but by Turkish 'gendarmerie', part-time policemen who, unlike the invaders, had water and grenades galore. They were also defending their country, and in their own minds, their religion. And most of all, they occupied the high ground, which is an ideal circumstance for the one weapon they had in plentiful supply: remove the pin and leave the rest to gravity.

Readers interested in the details of the sorry and foredoomed assault on Kiritch Tepe Sirt may find them in Bryan Cooper's *The Tenth Irish*

Division in Gallipoli (the writing of which, within a year of the campaign, was no mean achievement for a chronic alcoholic who returned home to Sligo to find that in his absence, his wife had contrived both to become pregnant and to have given birth to a son, but not quite his heir). We have already met the most famous body of soldiers in the 10th: D Company of the 7th Dublin Fusiliers. These men now found themselves fighting an enemy not of their choosing, and that had not even been an enemy when they had first enlisted. They were also waterless, grenadeless, guileless and almost helpless against the defenders holding the ridge. Horizontal rifle fire was perfectly useless in that landscape of flint and granite boulders, and which was dominated by the Turks above. The only available weapon for the Irish was the bayonet.

So that August dawn the Dublins left cover and charged. There is something desperately forlorn about these boys and men, thirsty, filthy, soiled with their own waste, rising from amid the rocks and advancing with agonizing slowness up the ridge and along the ridge, merely making targets of themselves for the Turkish machine-gunners far away, and above them, the gendarmes with their grenades. The footballers were chopped to pieces.

The survivors then lay motionless among those rocks alongside the lifeless bodies of their friends. The sun rose, and the flies began to feast on the dead, and the wounded groaned as the broiling granite became too hot to lie on, and men would have to move, and then be shot for doing so. And all over the ridge, the cowering Irish, both the wounded and the hale, grew mad with thirst, while their skin burnt and blistered, and the hillside echoed with the tortured supplications of the dying. Meanwhile, the Turks continued to snipe at and lob bombs down on the invaders of their homeland. With night, finally, came retreat, and defeat.

Some names have survived from that iron hillside. Fred Heuston, a medical student at Trinity, won a Military Cross for his courage in this fight, even though he was dead when it was awarded to him, and since this particular medal could not be issued posthumously, in the interim the fiction was promulgated that he was merely 'missing'. There were no 'missing' on the peninsula, and no prisoners, just the living and the dead. His fellow Trinity medical students, the Catholic lads, Michael Fitzgibbon and Paddy Tobin, and Edward Weatherill, son of a prosperous English-born ship-owner living in Dublin – they had all perished. Daniel Clery, son of a Catholic commercial traveller from Maryborough (Portlaoise) also vanished here, as did Robert Stanton, a former Trinity student who had left his law practice in Cork to join up. Other illustrious sons to leave their bones on the unforgiving granite of the ridge were Ernest Julian, Reid Professor of Law at TCD, Charles Ball, chief botanist at the Botanical Gardens in Dublin, and most spectacularly Albert Wilkin, a shop manager from Clontarf, who – it may safely be presumed – was not of ardently nationalist sympathies: his sister was called Victoria Jubilee. The shop-keeper Albert caught and threw back grenades on five occasions; the sixth and final one exploded before he could return it. By these fearless deeds, he gave his life for his comrades, and is certainly worth remembering for that alone.

There were other, less illustrious Irishmen who died on Gallipoli – such as the brothers Billy and Sam Smyth, of Glendermott, County Derry, who were killed four months apart, or John and James Garrity, from an Irish family in Hamilton, Scotland, who were killed on the same day: 9 August. In tragedy, we can sometimes glimpse hints of other stories. The Lamberts, for example, were a religiously mixed family, in which the boys were raised as Protestants, the girls as Catholics. Two Lambert brothers, John and Thomas, seem to have enlisted in 1914, and were posted to the regular, 1st Battalion to make up numbers on its return from India. John, aged thirty-nine, was killed just four days after the V Beach landing, but his mother did not claim him in death. However, Thomas was killed, in October, and the cemetery register declares him to be the 'stepson of Mary Lambert, Bridge House Milltown' and thereby hangs a family-tale whose mystery remains forever buried in the graves of a son apparently disowned and a stepson specifically claimed.

The Finnerty brothers, Mark, and Matthew, a gardener, from Granagh, Galway, had signed up together at a recruiting office in Warrington to join the Dublin Fusiliers. Mark was killed shortly after the landings at Suvla, and his botanist brother was killed the following year fighting the Bulgarians – and if it is difficult to explain why the Irish were fighting the Turks, it is virtually impossible to give a plausible account of why they were fighting Bulgarians, other than by resorting to that central truism: *The first casualty of war is the cause for which it is fought.*

Anzac was the name given to a foothold on a long, almost vertical ridge that ran from near Krithia in the south (an hour's walk from V Beach, a walk that the entire invasion force never once managed to make) almost to Suvla in the north. But the word 'ridge' doesn't even begin to describe Anzac, whose almost vertical slopes are cleft in three dimensions, as if at the moment of creation, a mad axeman had repeatedly swung his blade in all directions and at all angles deep into the ridge's sides, and here deep thorn thickets grew, man-tall and higher, impenetrable. The Australians had lost 613 men dead here on the first day alone, the New Zealanders 124 – on the same day that Ireland's 100 or so dead of the *River Clyde* briefly embarked on the wings of myth. The key of this myth, repeated by almost all Australian historians, is 'whatiffery': had this battalion broken through here, or that company advanced there, victory was at hand.

No, it wasn't; the only consequence would have been another step deeper into a more terrible military quicksand, which would probably have ended in midwinter trench warfare in Anatolia, a remote and Artcic Ypres. The absurdities of the entire venture had already been comprehensively exposed by Lieutenant Commander Otto Hershing in *U21* (which in 1914 had pioneered the new form of underwater warfare when it sank the HMS *Pathfinder*; see the chapter on Kerry). Making its way from Wilhelmshaven on 25 April, the first day of the landings, it arrived in Gallipoli waters on 25 May, and promptly sank the battleships HMS *Triumph* and HMS *Majestic*, taking with them (among others) John Cotter and Jeremiah Cronin, both from Whitegate, County Cork; this tiny community was to lose 23 men killed with the Royal Navy alone during the war. Thus one U-boat, one raid, one harbour, and the supply line to any British fleet that managed to make it up the Narrows would have been some 2000 miles long. This is a strategic insanity that could only have been composed under the influence of an utterly intoxicating myth.

The 6th Leinsters and 5th Connaughts had been dispatched to Anzac, and the former were perched high on the wrongly-named Rhododendron Ridge – Charles Ball or Matthew Finnerty not being with the Anzacs, as they had misidentified wild oleanders – on the night of 9 August 1915. Ahead of them lay the dominant mountain in the entire chain, Chunuk Bair, which they expected soon to attack, and from whose high point they would then be able to see – but not take – the waterway for which all this fighting occurred. However, the Turks struck first. Shortly after 4 a.m. on 10 August, the Turks erupted downwards, no rounds in their chambers, using the bayonet and rifle butt only. A thousand British soldiers were killed in minutes, beaten and bayonetted to death. Among them were many men of the Leinsters, soldiers like John Carr of Carrick-on-Shannon, Patrick Casey of Ardee, and James Purcell and John O'Toole of Dublin.

On only one occasion did a group I was with ever explore the deep, vertiginous, thorn-clad gullies and ravines of Rhododendron Ridge. It was the most shocking landscape I have ever encountered – as wicked as it had been when the invaders, the New Zealanders and the Australians, had first fought their way up through almost the impenetrable briar thickets. After several hours of travail, one of us spotted a glimpse of blue beneath a spine-covered bush – the colour of the British water-bottles before they were clad in camouflaged fabric.

Gingerly, with our bare hands, we cleared the soil away, fully aware that swift gangrene and tetanus could be the price of a cut in such a toxic bacteria farm. A white, sutured edge appeared beneath our digital excavations: part of a skull. Now using sticks, we dug some more. The whole skull appeared. And then alongside it, a second skull, and as a suitable warning, rusting coils of barbed wire – then some vertebrae, and a femur, and ribs. In time, we revealed the skeletal remains of two men, one of whom appeared to have been killed by a shocking blow to the head, perhaps a rifle-butt, as he struggled from his sleep while the Turks were upon him, defending their homeland against the infidel invader. Or had he been caught in the barbed wire that still held him, and thus helpless, been easily killed?

There it was on the high ridge that that the Turks call Sazli Dere, the pathetic debris of life, that no one had seen since that August dawn in 1915. These men were not officially dead for years, merely 'missing'. All these decades later, we had held these loved ones in our hands, touched their mortal remains, and felt a deep grief for men we had never met.

What should we do with these bodies? No identification had survived. The policy of the Commonwealth War Graves Commission on the peninsula – certainly at that time – was that unidentified remains should simply be left where they were found. Moreover, we didn't have the means to retrieve the bones, and we should never be able to find our way to this place again. And so we re-assembled the skeletal detritus with as much dignity as possible, and then covered it all with the dry red clay of Sazli Dere.

Then we, believers and otherwise, stood in a small semi-circle, and every one of us prayed, and tears fell as we thought of all the good lives lost here. For we had within our hands a secret that their families would have probably given all they owned to have had. And those two men stood for all the dead of this terrible war: the peasant Turks from Anatolia and the sophisticated polyglots of Istanbul, and the Arab levies from Mesopotamia and Palestine, the New Zealanders and the Australians, the Scots, the Welsh, the English and even the Newfoundlanders – and of course, our own dead, the dead of Ireland, ruthlessly abandoned and forgotten by their own land and people for so long.

Anzacs who survived this peninsula became heroes in Australia and New Zealand; rather less so the British in Britain, but the Irish simply became invisible, their story untold. Only the mythic image of a ship disgorging troops survived dimly in popular memory. For within a year, events in Dublin were to rob V Beach of all the mythic grandeur that had seemed so eternal at the time. The far smaller drama at the GPO in Dublin not merely overwhelmed the myth of Gallipoli, but in time subsumed it, and even cannibalized it: *'Twas better to die 'neath an Irish sky than in Suvla or Sed El Bahr,* went one of the first – and probably the best – of the ballads about the 1916 Rising, called 'The Foggy Dew'. And so successfully was all memory of the landings eradicated that generations of ballad-singers would later bawl out those Turkish place-names, without having a clue what they referred to.

All memory of the Pals of the Footballers' Company, of Paddy Tobin and Michael Fitzgibbon and Charles Ball and Albert Wilkin, perished with the Rising. So too did F. H. Browning, he who had raised the Footballers' Company at Lansdowne Road, for on Easter Monday 1916 he was ruthlessly shot down in an ambush at Mount Street Bridge, just as he and other unarmed members of the Volunteer Corps, the Georgius Rex, were finishing their annual bank-holiday route march. Of his fate, even the IRFU would in time fall silent.

And so too did all the other people in this story vanish, just like poor Henry Desmond O'Hara, the dear son and the dear fiancé, who led his men safely ashore from the *River Clyde* and in time to a common ruin on Gallipoli's iron shores. Shortly before Henry's death, the real hero of the landings – *the man who had managed to stop them* – Lieutenant Guy Nightingale wrote home: 'I've never seen fellows getting old so quickly.

This morning, I saw a fellow called O'Hara in the Dublins who I hadn't seen in a fortnight, and I barely recognized him.'

Unlike Henry Desmond O'Hara, Guy Nightingale led a charmed life throughout the war. Three of his batmen were killed beside him, but he nonetheless survived, and went on to serve on the Western Front, from the battle of the Somme right to the Armistice Day, remaining unscathed throughout. On 25 April 1935, on the twentieth anniversary of the landings, Major Guy Nightingale MC took out his old service revolver, put it to his temples, and blew out his brains.

9. Business in Great Waters: Jutland

Contrary to what people believe about Ireland's involvement in the Great War, the first Irish casualties were at sea just three days after war had been declared. The British vessel HMS *Amphion* chased and sank the German minelayer the *Konigin Luise* off the Heligoland Bight. The *Amphion* took twenty German survivors aboard. She then ran into one of her victim's minefields, blew up and with her forward-section gone was clearly doomed. Rescue ships took on further survivors, including some of the already-rescued Germans. Then the *Amphion* detonated a second mine, causing an already-loaded but abandoned gun to fire, killing several of the men just taken from the waters, including two twice-rescued Germans. Among the 170 dead were at least sixteen Irish crewmen, our first victims of the war. One was Signaller Joseph Pierce Murphy. A fortnight later a neighbour of his, Stephen Corri, from Thorncastle Place, Ringsend, a dead-end street of just seven houses, was killed in the first land-engagement between the British and Germans outside Mons.

The dead of the *Ampion* were the first of at least 2000 Irishmen who died serving with the Royal Navy as what, to modern Irish perceptions, was to be a great maritime struggle across the oceans of the world. This was the outcome of a pre-war naval arms race between Britain and

Germany leading to the emergence of the 'dreadnought' class of battle-ship, the most complex and formidable fighting machine then known. By July 1914, with British shipyards turning out five 'super-dreadnoughts' a year, and with a standing fleet of twenty-nine battleships and battle-cruisers, the Royal Navy estimates stood at £50 million. The Germans had built twenty such vessel. Von Tirpitz, founder of the modern German navy, had told the Kaiser that war with Britain would be out of the question until the Kiel Canal had been widened and deepened to allow the rapid passage of dreadnoughts between the Baltic and the North Sea. The canal was completed in July 1914. Germany was now ready for war.

The first encounter in European waters between the two fleets, the battle of the Dogger Bank in January 1915, was certainly a British victory – only fifteen British dead, including Boy Patrick O'Mahony, compared to nearly a thousand Germans – but in defeat the Germans learnt a vital lesson. Their battlecruiser, SMS *Seydlitz,* had been hit by a 12.5-inch shell from the battlecruiser HMS *Lion,* piercing the armour of the aftermost turret and entering the working-chamber. The explosive propellant-charges being brought up from below for the guns above were ignited by the shell, the flash shooting upward into the gunhouse and downwards into the maga-zine, setting fire to charges there. The magazine-crew – naturally – tried to escape by opening the doors into the turret next door, enabling the flash-fire to leap turrets and causing a huge, widespread explosion, killing almost everyone there. The ship would have been lost but for the swift reaction from the *Seydlitz's* Executive Officer, who flooded both turrets, drowning any survivors but saving the ship. The navy can be a very hard service.

What the super-dreadnought design had inadvertently done was to create a lymphatic system within the ship that could spread the violent cancer of explosive gases from the point of impact to its very heart, trans-forming the entire vessel into a bomb on the very point of detonation. The German post-mortem on what happened was decisive. Until the ships could be completely redesigned, all doors between turrets and magazines, in all directions, must be padlocked, with the keys held by an officer outside the turret. The padlocked exits ensured that turrets and their magazines were crematoria for anyone trapped on the wrong side of a fire.

As the war unfolded, each navy looked at a way of luring the enemy into a trap in which it would have the advantage. A fleet action, if only in theory, was of epochal importance, for it drew into conflict the manufacturing and research resources of each nation's entire industrial base over the previous decade, and its crews totalling tens of thousands of men. The maritime fate of Germany or Britain, and even the war, could be decided in a matter of hours.

The British had one superb secret advantage over the Germans: Room 40, a code-breaking unit that could read German radio traffic. German naval headquarters in Wilhelmshaven could not use its wireless without the Admiralty knowing; but no ointment being complete without a fly, the Royal Naval Director of Operations, Thomas Jackson, the primary conduit for the signals intelligence, did not like or trust the boffins (though the word is of a later vintage) in Room 40. They had not been before the mast at the age of fourteen; how could they possibly know *anything*? His use of Room 40 intelligence was intermittent; sometimes he listened, sometimes he didn't. The constistency of his inconsistency made him a poor director of operations.

Consistency of another kind was at work here. German acts of terrorism against civilians had been a feature of the war from the outset. The massacres of civilians in Belgium and Northern France in the autumn of 1914 were a deliberate terror-policy, and a studied violation of the Geneva and Hague Conventions on war. The sinking of the *Lusitania* in May 1915 fell into the same category, as did the bombardments of English coastal towns such Scarborough and Hartlepool in December 1914, with nearly 600 civilian casualties, and 177 dead. The only intention was, by perpetrating such a massacre, to lure the British Home Fleet into a trap of awaiting U-boats, and even more spectacularly, into the iron arms of the German High Seas Fleet.

The Easter Rising in Dublin was the first step towards the battle of Jutland. As a form of inexpensive but provocative solidarity, the German fleet was going to bombard the fishing towns of Lowestoft and Yarmouth. However, the unfortunate *Seydlitz*, just recovered from her near-death experience at Dogger Bank, ran into a mine as she put to sea on 24 April. The attacking admiral, Boedicker, had to switch his flag to the SMS *Lutzow*, and the resulting signals alerted Room 40: the High Seas Fleet was on the move. Where to? The signals didn't say. At 4 a.m. on 25 April the considerably diminished German force unleashed a bombardment that destroyed two hundred houses, yet killing no-one. The absence of the *Seydlitz* had been vital in not generating a bloodlust in Britain. The Grand Fleet had already been mobilized, but the two armadas – with confused intentions – managed to miss one another.

However, each side was now anxious for a decisive fleet action, naturally on its own terms. The British were confident that their ace in the hole were their battle-cruisers, faster than battleships, more heavily armoured than other vessels: their battle-cruiser admiral was David Beatty, from a Wexford family that had recently moved to England but kept lands in the county, and contacts. When young David Beatty was about to be transferred to the China station, his mother – formerly a Sadleir of Dunboyne Castle, County Meath, promptly pulled the strings available to Hibernian gentry by contacting Lord Charles Beresford to ensure her son's career stayed close to England, and to power. Beatty came of hunting stock, and his father made a good living selling Irish hunters to the English county set. The field guided everything Beatty did at sea: his analogies were usually those of the more tempestuous Irish hunts. However implausible it might seem to modern ears, perhaps jaundiced by racial stereotypes of what is *not* Irish, he certainly regarded himself as Irish.

In May the German Admiral Scheer decided to lure his prime adversary, Admiral Jellicoe, Commander of the Grand Fleet, into action by attacks on merchant shipping west of the Skagerrak. Room 40 noted something was afoot when it intercepted orders from Admiral Scheer that the High Seas Fleet was to assemble off The Jade Bight, home of the German navy. Thus the British Grand Fleet was at sea four hours before the German High Seas Fleet. It was considerably more powerful – 264 guns of between 12 and 15 inches in calibre, the latter firing shells of nearly 2000 pounds in weight some ten miles: that is, firing a shell weighing the same as a small car from Bray into O'Connell Street in Dublin. The Germans had just 200 guns, of smaller calibre. Moreover, Beatty's battle-cruisers not merely outgunned the battlecruisers of his adversary Hipper, but they were faster. On paper and by metal, the British could bring to bear twice the weight of gunfire than the Germans, and had six more dreadnoughts not engaged in this dispute, with seven building. The Germans, on the other hand, had no more ships; this was it, the first and last throw of the dice.

The Germans had an unwitting ally in DO Admiral Thomas Jackson, who asked Room 40 where it placed DK, the German Commander-in-Chief's call-sign. It replied in The Jade, namely, 'in harbour'. Jackson didn't trust Room 40's ability to interpret naval information, nor ask what 'in harbour' for DK meant: whereas Room 40 knew that whenever Scheer went to sea, his call-sign was always transferred to the harbour-station. So in a state of almost contrived ignorance. Jackson told Jellicoe and Beatty that if any of the German Fleet was out, it did not include Scheer's battle-fleet.

A game of chess in a maritime fog of war now began, which later analysis of radio orders and flag signals has elucidated, though that eluci- dation itself confers a false clarity as confusing as any fog, as different parts of these two huge fleets were moved about the vast board that was the North Sea. Neither knew where the other was, but almost by chance their two outlaying flanks blundered into one another, and fire was opened. The battle had begun. In the subsequent account all major vessels mentioned are battle-cruisers, which to modern eyes are battle- ships, a distinction instantly understood by connoisseurs of the genre, of which, happily, few breathe today.

Only those few could describe a naval battle in which there were hundreds of decision makers, spread across an ocean, communicating by radio (or Wireless-Telegraphy, WT, as it was then called), flags and searchlights, often transmitting incorrect or misleading information. Two hundred warships, most of them still coal-burning, generate more smoke and steam than anyone alive today has seen. A single broadside would generate pollutants that could stay in the air for hours, and since only one in twenty shells struck its intended target, vast amounts of gunfire was needed to fight a battle.

A new age was also begun at Jutland. When HMS *Engadine* put into the air its Short seaplane, it was the first time that a heavier-than-air machine had been used in naval war. Pearl Harbour, if you like, began here. So undeveloped was aerial terminology that the pilot's observer Trewin had the rank of 'Assistant Paymaster'. Meanwhile, as the twentieth century unfolded in the skies, on the mastheads of the British ships flew signal flags familiar to Nelson: *Assume complete readiness for action,* with battle ensigns fluttering from the yard-arms of HMS *Indefatigable,* carrying the largest Irish crew in the entire fleet, and HMS *New Zealand,* in which Rear Admiral W.C. Pakenham of Longford had hoisted his ensign. Across the North Sea marines' drums beat the crews to quarters, just as they had done at Trafalgar.

Firing in earnest began. Beatty's ship HMS *Lion* was hit once, and then again. A blood-stained, hatless sergeant of marines appeared on the bridge, reporting that Q turret had gone and the men in it had been killed. Lieutenant Chalmers looked aft and saw that the armoured roof of the turret had been folded back like an open sardine tin, thick yellow smoke was billowing upwards, the guns were pointing drunkenly at the sky.

It was a re-run of the *Seydlitz*. The shell had actually ignited the cordite charges in the working-chamber, the flash leaping down the channel up which shells were hoist, into the magazine handling-room. The officer in charge, Major Harvey, Royal Marine Light Infantry, realized that unless the disaster was confined, the magazine would blow up, and with it the entire ship. He instantly ordered the connecting chambers, from the powder-keg at the bottom, to the turrets at the top, to be sealed. He was sentencing himself and everyone else in the great artillery-complex, which reached from the bowels of the ship up to its battery of four 13.5-inch guns, to certain death. It was here that the first Irish fatalities at Jutland occurred.

Stoker First Class Christopher McCarthy was eighteen, the son of John, an agricultural labourer, and Margaret, from Cloyne in Cork. He'd enlisted as a boy and was barely more than that when his life ended. Jeremiah Fitzgerald, twenty-two, was also from Cork; his father Jeremiah was a commission agent, and his mother a shopkeeper in Kinsale. He was probably part of medical team standing by to deal with casualties, of which he became among the first. Royal Marine Artillery Gunner Murlagh Hennesssey, the twenty-seven year son of a coachman from Bagnalstown, would certainly have been inside the turret complex, and so would prob-ably have helped lock the steel-doors in place, sealing his own doom and that of ninety-two others. By their selfless action the Royal Marine gunners gave their lives not merely for their crewmates but for the fleet commander. It is impossible to imagine what would have happened had Admiral Beatty been killed in the opening engagement of the battle.

Four minutes later the HMS *Indefatigable* was hit by two shells from the *Von der Tann,* one of them on the fore-turret. Nothing *visible* occurred for thirty seconds. The hit on the turret penetrated the casemate, and sent a flash-flame into the working-chamber below, where the shells and their propellant charges were married for the first time, causing a secondary explosion within the confined space. With nowhere to go, the blast would seek the only aperture available, to the magazine below, the tempest of white hot gases moving nearly as fast as the speed of sound, racing hundreds of feet through all open hoists and hatches, in microseconds heating everything that was combustible past its ignition-temperature to its point of explosion. Almost instantly, the entire ship had been transformed into a massive bomb.

Thirty seconds after the first hit on the forward turret, the bomb that was HMS *Indefatigable* blew up, with a vast sheet of flame and huge upward explosion, sending a fifty-foot long steamboat over a hundred feet in the air. Only one man of the thousand inside the vessel survived — the skipper, Captain Sowerby. Two others, lookouts on the mainmast, also survived and found Sowerby alive, but missing an arm and a leg; they kept him afloat until they grew exhausted, then perhaps mercifully let him go.

The destruction of this ship was a minor disaster for Cork, home to at least thirty-seven of the dead. Most of them were from small coastal towns: three — stokers Maurice Loudon, twenty-one, Jeremiah Dhuig, Tim Buckley, eighteen, Thomas Connell, were all from Whitegate. Twenty-two of the Cork dead were stokers, the least skilled men in a man'o war, reflecting the poor educational standards of the time. The other Cork deaths were of seamen. Just two of them were commissioned: Surgeon Sidney Punch of Cork City and Sub Lieutenant Cecil Law from Glanmire.

Dublin's eleven dead in the *Indefatigable* included Boy First Class Henry Mills and Boy Telegraphist, Robert Fegan, both seventeen, Artificer-Engineer Michael Lambe, forty-one, and Chief Petty Officer Patrick Carroll, forty-four. Wexford lost Patrick Cahill, twenty-three. Waterford lost Seaman James Daly, thirty-one, and James Coughlan, thirty-four. Galway lost James Founds, twenty-five. Derry lost George Callaghan, twenty-nine and George Robinson, twenty-four. Newry lost Royal Marine Artillery Gunner James Mallon, twenty, and Marine Private William McCausland, nineteen.

Belfast lost twelve dead on the *Indefatigable,* including Able Seaman James Patrick Reilly, twenty-three, and Cooper Hugh Malone, forty-one. Two teenagers from Mayo perished on the *Indefatigable*: Thomas Morley, eighteen, a private in the Royal Marine Light Infantry, from Claremorris. The second was Boy First Class Thomas O'Toole, aged just fourteen, from Castlebar, the youngest Irish serviceman to killed during the war.

Thirty-one of these men were stokers. They serviced their cruel and implacable furnaces beneath the waves; they messed beneath the waves; they slept beneath the waves. And in the final moments of their lives they entered the seventh circle of Dante's Inferno, as plummeting shells and the flash-fire of cordite turning the bowels of their ship into the heart of a volcano, with steel-plate becoming boiling lava and the contents of boilers turned into lethal jets of superheated steam. These were the first human beings in the world to know what it was like to be fried alive in the hull of a super-dreadnought, ingesting the fires that would cause it to explode, and in that fragment of a second taking 995 lives, 67 of them Irish. The time was 16.04.

Now it was the *Queen Mary's* turn to come under German bombardment from the *Derfflinger* and the *Seydlitz*. The Germans had managed to outmanoeuvre the British, and were able to concentrate their fire on this isolated British ship. So, at 16.26, just twenty-two minutes after the *Indefatigable* catastrophe, the *Queen Mary* was hit in the turret-complex. The resulting magazine-fires instantly raced through her passageways and chutes, until she became a single connected explosive organism; moments later she detonated, taking with her another thousand lives. Irish losses here were far smaller; from Cork there were Signal Arthur Kidney, nineteen, of Courmacsharry, and Stoker Michael Dwyer, from Blackpool.

Dublin was in the *Queen Mary's* recruitment division, and it lost more heavily. Its dead included Able Seaman Felix Kelly, twenty-one, Major Gerald Rooney, RMLI, thirty-nine, Stoker William Bolton, forty-six, Midshipman Kildare Burrowes, sixteen, Stoker Michael Doherty, twenty-seven, Stoker John Shields, fifty-three, and Stoker John Mangan, sixty-two. Officers' Steward Frank Miller, twenty-two, was from Mayo, and Fred McLaughlin, nineteen, from Derry. Stokers Robert Fletcher, James Rodgers, twenty-nine, and Peter Kennedy, thirty-three, came from Belfast.

A handful of survivors were found, almost unbelievably, cheering in the sea, and taken aboard by the destroyer HMS *Petard*. In that brief but shocking double-engagement some two thousand British lives had been lost – and as ominous for the Royal Navy, German marksmanship proved to be considerably superior to that of the British – the latter had landed only ten hits compared to the Germans' forty. British battle-cruisers and destroyers then entered the fray, bringing some balance to the fight. Having rescued a handful of *Queen Mary* sailors, *Petard* fired a torpedo at the *Seydlitz*, holing her and causing her to flood.

All this time, thanks to Jackson's dogmatic ineptitude, Beatty had thought that the main German battle-fleet – with the battleships that could easily outgun his battle-cruisers if allowed remotely within range

– was still standing in the Jade harbour, safely beyond the Helligoland Bight. And then, majestic and awful, the entire German fleet suddenly appeared out of the mist before the astonished eyes of the watch on HMS *Southampton,* with Jellicoe's main battle-fleet fully fifty miles away.

When Commander The Honourable E.S. Bingham, from Bangor, County Down, caught sight of the German ships, he was elated, assuming they were Jellicoe's coming to the rescue. When he realized that the enemy was upon both him and the British battle-cruiser fleet, he turned and launched his destroyer *Nestor* in a headlong torpedo attack. She fired off all her torpedoes at the advancing German ships, and his vessel having been repeatedly hit and now sinking, Bingham gave the order for the crew to abandon ship. They took to the boats, and as their ship slipped beneath the waves, the survivors gave three cheers, and sang 'God save the King' and 'Tipperary'. Bingham and most of his crew were rescued by Germans, and they spent the rest of the war as POWs. For his deeds he won a Victoria Cross, and having looked at the many actions of that day I'm confident that his aristocratic connections did not in the least harm his medal prospects.

Jellicoe had been warned by radio of the serious threat to Beatty's battle-cruisers, and the two forces raced towards one another, with the Germans pursuing Beatty, not knowing that they were sailing into the arms of the main British fleet. The first of Jellicoe's ships made contact with Beatty's battlecruisers at around 18.00 hours, and general battle with the Germans was then joined. At 18.15 a salvo of German shells hit HMS *Defence* abaft the after-turret. The fate of the *Indefatigable* and the *Queen Mary* would probably at this point have consumed her anyhow, but she was then hit again by a salvo that straddled both the forecastle turret and her foremost funnel. She disappeared behind a cloud of smoke, and when it cleared there was absolutely no trace, not a spar or a length of rigging, nor any mortal remains from her complement of 892 men.

Vanished in that second or so were twenty-eight men from Cork, such as stokers Daniel Cronin, thirty-nine, Maurice Riordain, nineteen and Timothy O'Mahony, eighteen. From Whitegate there were another two deaths, stokers John Coleman, twenty-four, and John Broderick, twenty- two. Other Cork deaths were of Petty Officer John Howes, thirty-five, from Kinsale, and Chief Writer Thomas Reynolds, thirty-four, from Courtmacsharry.

Four Dubliners vanished in the fireball that had consumed *Defence*:

Cook's Mate Gordon Veitch, twenty-three; Able Seaman Michael Hart, twenty-two, Petty Officer Telegraphist Daniel Hogan, thirty-four, and RMA Gunner Laurence Brown, nineteen. This last death was the second for Phoenix Park in barely more than a month: he was the son of a gardener who lived in the Lodge. One of the first victims of the Rising, which had indirectly led to this battle, had been an unarmed youngster called Playfair, son of the officer in charge of the Magazine in the Park, who had been coldly shot down by Volunteer Gary Holohan.

From Wexford were RMA Gunner William Furlong, twenty-four, Stoker James Kehoe, and Stoker John Sunderland, nineteen. Waterford had at least five deaths on the *Defence:* stokers Joseph Hogan, twenty-four, William Ryan, forty-one, and Edward Wallace, sixteen, plus Ordinary Seamen Thomas Carlton, twenty-six, and Stephen Power, seventeen.

Galway lost one man on the *Defence,* Martin Bury, twenty-four, of Clifden; Mayo two, Officers' Steward Frank Millar, twenty-two, and Stoker John Loughney, thirty-seven. Donegal lost three: RMLI Lieutenant Alexander Hamilton, twenty, Stoker John Todd, forty-seven. Belfast lost ten, including RMLI privates Joseph Glover, twenty-two, Thomas Crossan, twenty-two, John Montgomery, twenty-three and Leading Seaman Patrick McAuley, twenty-nine. Stoker John Prendergast came from Dundalk.

Alongside her, HMS *Warrior* was in dire straits. She had been hit fifteen times, she had over one hundred dead and wounded, she was on fire aft, and her upper deck was a slaughterhouse. Three of the sixty-three dead were Irish, all Cork: Chief Petty Officer Michael Daly, forty, from Castletownshend: Petty Officer Stoker George Patterson, of Queenstown; and Stoker 1st Class David Courtney from Courtmacsherry.

At 18.31, as the mist of battle cleared, the German dreadnought *Derfflinger* saw HMS *Invincible* silhouetted against the sky, and fired off her last salvo. One shell hit Q turret in the aft of the ship, and the same appalling train of incendiary events seems to have raced through her innards, like a complex, perfectly synchronized firework. The ship wobbled briefly and then righted itself, like a drunk emerging from a pub. A second latter, shortly after 18.31, the 690-foot long vessel exploded from deep inside her hull, cutting her in two amidships. Her two ends sank separately, taking with them over a thousand lives. These included near-neighbours from Bloomfield in Belfast, Engineer Artificer Hugh Sloan, twenty-six, and

Engineer Sub-Lieutenant Hubert Unsworth. The other Irish victims were Ordinary Seaman Robert McKenna, eighteen, and Boy First Class John McCullough, seventeen; RMLI Private Thomas Wilson, twenty-nine; stokers William Hughes, thirty and William Rea, thirty-seven. From Dublin there was Able Seaman Moses Caulfield, twenty-two. From Donegal came Stoker Patrick Brennan, thirty-five, from Derry Stoker George McGrath, and from Drogheda, Patrick Curran, twenty-three. Boatswain William Donovan, thirty-two, was from Skibbereen, and Chief Engine Room Artificer Robert Broughton, fifty-three, was from Cork City. Midshipman John Henry Grattan Esmonde, seventeen, was the best connected to die on the vessel, the son of Sir Henry Grattan Esmonde (Bart) MP. Twenty-six years later his cousin, Lieutenant Commander Eugene Esmonde, Fleet Air Arm, was to win a posthumous Victoria Cross leading a torpedo-attack on a German fleet breaking through the English Channel.

Now that Jellicoe had brought his forces to bear, this was the time that the Germans should have been slaughtered, for a turn away from an approaching flotilla of battleships would have placed them beam-on towards the British guns, but unable to bring their own guns to bear. But the Germans had secretly mastered an elegant turn, the *Gefechtskehrtwendung,* which began at the rear, and instead of the ships moving in a wide and vulnerable arc before hostile guns, in a trice they had all turned about, and with German torpedo-boats making smoke the High Seas Fleet disappeared from beneath the very guns of the British battleships. It was a stroke of extraordinary brilliance. The British did manage to catch up with and maul elements of the German navy, but matters soon dissolved into chaos as night fell.

The *Kaiserliche Marine* had trained its sailors for night-actions. Many warships were equipped with powerful searchlights linked, with typical ingenuity, directly to the look-outs' binoculars: what the men on watch were viewing, so too were the searchlights. In night-fighting mode these lights remained on, concealed and cooled behind iris-shutters, which could instantly open to enable any German vessel to blind their British enemy. The Germans also had star-shells that could create near-daylight conditions many miles away. Conversely, Admiral Jackson was creating his own areas of darkness, as he received information from Room 40 about movements of the German fleet, much of which he chose not to pass on to the admirals at sea.

In the general and encompassing dark, there was more blundering than certainty. At one point some British destroyers fired a couple of torpedoes at a group of German vessels. A German ship turned to avoid a torpedo, ramming a second German vessel, which itself had just been hit by a torpedo. In the heart of the melee HMS *Tipperary* was hit by shells and caught fire, later sinking. HMS *Spitfire* collided with the German SMS *Nassau,* and both ships were seriously damaged and put out of the fray. HMS *Broke* was then hit by shellfire that killed some fifty of the crew outright. The helmsman, wounded and dying, fell, bringing the helm down, causing the *Broke* to ram HMS *Sparrowhawk,* violently jamming the two ships together. Some of the crew of the *Sparrowhawk* ended up on the *Broke,* and vice versa. Then another destroyer, HMS *Contest,* sailed into the rear of *Broke,* shearing six feet off her stern. The three ships were then frantically disentangled before a hungry German battle-cruiser arrived like a hyena on the Serengeti, and *Broke* managed to limp homeward. On the way she encountered some German destroyers, who put more rounds into her, but unbelievably failed to sink her. She made it back to the Tyne three days after the battle. Among her dead was Surgeon-Probationer David Ferris, from Rostrevor, County Down.

A line of German battleships came across the isolated destroyer, HMS *Turbulent,* and fixed her with their floodlights, while the battleship *Westfalen* rammed her, cutting her in two; then the slayers vanished on the wide dark sea, leaving all ninety of *Turbulent's* crew to perish on this, the first day of June. Two of them were from Belfast: twenty-seven year old Petty Officer Robert Elder, and Able Seaman John Thompson

Meanwhile HMS *Black Prince* had found herself stranded in the middle of the German battle-fleet. No friend saw what became of her; only enemy accounts, collected after the war, tell of her last minutes. In the most shocking act of slaughter of the entire battle, six German battleships, their searchlights fixing her in the sea and blinding her crew, gathered to fire at her from point-blank range, their guns not even elevated. Her return fire was ineffectual, then non-existent. The German battleships continued to pour shells into the brightly illuminated hulk until finally she blew up, taking all her crew of some nine hundred souls with her. The most eminent Irishman aboard, and perhaps the most eminent person to die, not merely in this unspeakable hell but in the entire battle, was Herbert Lyne Geoghegan, surgeon, polymath and linguist, and a graduate of both

Queens College Galway and Trinity College, Dublin, who had translated the seminal work *Bacteria* by Schottelius from German into English. Also aboard were these other Irishmen: Engineer Lieutenant Commander James Niven, thirty-four, of Dublin; Petty Officer P.J. Archdeacon, thirty-three, of Queenstown; Jeremiah Buitchart, nineteen, of Lady's Well, Cork; Edward O'Leary, twenty-four, of Wexford, and five men from Belfast: Boy 1st Class Allan Henry, fifteen; Able Seaman George Smiley, twenty-seven; Private Isaac Stewart, RMLI, twenty-one; Able Seaman John Morgan; and Stoker James Shanks, thirty-five.

With dawn, the German navy retired to The Jade, half a dozen of its vessels battered beyond fighting-condition. Nine of its battle-cruisers had been hit in the turrets, but thanks to new fire-control regulations, unlike the four Royal Navy vessels so hit, damage had been confined to the turrets. On 2 June the North Sea was once again in British hands, but in those few hours at Jutland, which the Germans call 'Skaggerak', nearly ten thousand men had died; probably around three hundred were Irish – and at least eight of these were from the small inlet of Whitegate near Queenstown. How did that tiny community cope with such a catastrophe, and how does it remember it today? The oldest Irishman to perish at Jutland was John Mangan, sixty-two, making him one of the oldest Irish servicemen to be killed in the war; and on the *Indefatigable* Thomas O'Toole from Castlebar, aged just fourteen, was probably the youngest soldier or sailor in the British service to be killed in action. This Irish lad was duly and completely forgotten, as were all those other thousands of Irishmen and boys, from Joseph Pierce Murphy in the first days of 1914, to Trimmer Denis O'Connor, nineteen, of Burnt Lane, Cork, who was lost four days after Armistice when his vessel hit a mine in the Aegean.

All these men went down to the sea in ships, and they never returned.

10. 'Billy Gray, Billy Gray, will you not come to me?' Ireland and the Somme

Nightfall, 1 July 1916, and 899 Belfast men who that morning had risen from their trenches as soldiers and non-commissioned officers of the British army, lay dead on the single hillside of Thiepval Ridge, over-looking the River Ancre in the greater Somme Valley. One hundred and ninety-one of them were from the Shankill Road, among them forty-six officers. Another hundred officers and men of the Belfast battalions of the 36th Ulster Division were to die of their wounds in the coming week.

Philip Orr, in his memorable and ground-breaking book on the 36th Ulster Division, has reported hauntingly of the aftermath of the battle. 'In one part of the B Line,' one survivor remembered, 'the trenches near the river, there was a carpet of dead and dying Ulstermen and Germans. Blood lay like a layer of mud, and do you know, you couldn't tell one blood from another ...'

Another spoke of 'a 9th Inniskilling lying at the top [of a trench] has a bullet through his steel hat. He rolls over into the trenches at my feet. He is an awful sight. His brain was oozing out of the side of his head, and he is calling for his pal. An occasional cry of "Billy Gray, Billy Gray, will you not come to me?" In a short time all is quiet, he is dead. He's the servant to an officer who is lying on the trench with a fractured thigh, and won't let anyone touch him, and he is bleeding badly. They die together.'

Private Robb of the Mid-Antrim Volunteers remarked after seeing a clergyman bury a German and two of his fellow riflemen of the 12th Royal Irish Rifles: 'It still sticks in my mind that a Protestant pastor said the same burial service over the three men. I wondered what in hell we were doing fighting one another. After all, we were all men, only the uniforms were different' – the refrain of fighting soldiers through the ages.

That night there was a glorious sunset, and the guns fell silent. 'I heard someone in the reserve trenches start to sing, "Abide with Me". Then slowly all down the line the men took up the hymn ..."

Reality defeats fiction every time, which is perhaps why we have literature in the first place, to remind us that our imaginations will not permit art to match life, because if it did it would put us on a par with the creator. We are not creators. We are created, and not created all that well, to judge from the horrors that Picardy was to bear witness to that July day, and every other day thereafter for three months. Certainly no writer of fiction would ever dare to create a figure like Henry Gallaugher, a farmer who before the war had been a company commander of the Ulster Volunteer Force in Manorcunningham, County Donegal. As an example of who is a planter and who is not, the Gallaugher household provides a useful insight: the family with a Gaelic name was Presbyterian, while their Catholic labourer was called 'Robert Porter'.

Henry was commissioned into the Donegal and Fermanagh Volunteers battalion of the Inniskilling Fusiliers in 1914. On 1 July, after a bombardment that was expected to annihilate all the German defences, the infantry were expected to capture all the German positions in depth, enabling the cavalry to break through deep into their territory and even bring about a complete collapse of the German army. And that is how naïve army commanders were at that point. As we know now, the advancing British infantry was met by intense machine-gun fire, which annihilated wave after wave of them. However, the Ulsters, having left their trenches early before the German machine-gunners were able to emerge from their bunkers, were quickly in the enemy trenches and fighting through. Despite this element of surprise, casualties rapidly mounted, and soon Henry Gallaugher found that he was the only officer of his company still in action. Noticing German snipers firing on his wounded, he took a rifle and shot six of them. By the time he reached his tactical objective, the Crucifix (for a Presbyterian inappropriately-named), only nine of his platoon were still with him. He erected a barricade, and went out to No Man's Land to collect his wounded men. He came across several parties of Germans and was able to kill or capture them all, bringing back the prisoners and the wounded to safety.

He was relieved at the Crucifix by a senior officer, Major Peacocke, from Cork, and by an officer from Belfast, Major Gaffikin – whose contribution that day proved to be more potent as myth-maker than as a soldier – though, as it turned out, he was no slouch at the latter either. With the Germans counterattacking the divisions on either side of them, and worse, making serious headway, the Ulstermen were soon isolated and outflanked on the Schwaben Redoubt/Crucifix complex, and had to retreat. Henry Gallaugher did so while carrying a wounded officer, right through the German wire and to his own lines. A night later he led a small party of volunteers into the butcher's field of No Man's Land, the Shankill Road writ in blood and marrow, from which he rescued a total of twenty-eight wounded men.

But beyond all mortal salvation was Major Gaffikin, even as a wave of his arm was about to achieve immortality. The identifying colour of his 250-strong company had happened to be orange, and like a tourist guide keeping their pack together, he had waved a large orange cloth to keep his men visibly in touch with him as he crossed the bullet-laced chaos towards the German trenches. None of the men on that evil morning of larksong and slaughter were aware that the first of July, before the (yes, papistical) calendar changes, was the 'real' date of the battle of Boyne. Gaffikin's orange pennant was later transubstantiated by the myth-machine into a sash, and then someone realized that 12 July = 1 July. Who? No one knows. And so the binary elements to the birth of myth met, to create a legend that was thereafter proclaimed as The Word to a Bible-folk for whom The Word is, so to speak, Gospel. A single non-sash orange cloth was mythologized into hundreds or even thousands of sashes, creating the legend of how the besashed men of the 36th Ulster Division proudly went to their deaths for God, King and Ulster. The province needed another myth like it needed more rain, but of course an addiction to mythology is like a weather system: the more cloud there is, the more rain, and more rain, the more cloud. So the tale of the Orange Somme was born, was whispered at the hearth and crooned over the cradle, and proclaimed by murals on gable-ends in Belfast. It is even depicted to this day in a painting in the visitors' centre in the Ulster Tower at Thiepval, which shows an Orangeman, complete with his lodge's decorative cuffs, heroically leaping into a German trench and shooting one of the defenders with his officer's pistol.

The myth has even leapt so far as the works of respected historians such as John Keegan and Martin Middlebrook. Keegan, former senior lecturer at the Royal Military Academy at Sandhurst, wrote in the *The Face of Battle*: 'The 36th ... was the most close-knit of all British Divisions, its infantry having been wholly raised in Ulster. Its very existence testified to the extreme militancy ... of the Protestant people from which it exclusively sprang ... there were not Catholics in the 36th.'

Middlebrook's otherwise magisterial *The First Day on the Somme* is no more discriminating. The Ulstermen, he wrote, were pleased at the proposed date of the impending battle, 'the anniversary of the Battle of the Boyne'. In that same vein he wrote: 'The Ulstermen awaited the attack in a state of religious fervour ... some had sent for the Orange sashes of their order and wore these.' And of some Ulstermen wavering during the actual attack, he wrote, 'Major Gaffikin took off his Orange sash, held it high and roared the traditional battle cry of the Boyne: "Come on boys. No surrender." This action drew a whole crowd of men after him onto No Man's Land.'

Yet – as Philip Orr reminded us – as long ago as 1966 the 36th veteran Malcom McKee wrote: 'What nonsense is stuck onto the story ... Certainly Major Gaffikin waved an orange handkerchief, but orange was the colour of our battalion ... If he had said, "Come on boys, this is the first of July", how many would have known the Boyne was fought on the first day of July? I don't know why they plaster such incidents on our battle. Nothing was further from my mind than the Boyne on the Somme.'

Henry Gallaugher had borne witness to the untruth of this legend from its outset. Asked about it in a letter from home, he wrote to his family in Manorhamilton that he certainly had not seen any sashes, and if anybody had been wearing them, he would certainly have known about it. Then he, the Irish farmer, asked about the Donegal fields, and wondered how the crops were coming on. He made no mention of what he had done, of his journeys into No Man's Land to rescue dozens of wounded. He should have had a Victoria Cross. He didn't, though any one of his deeds, never mind the full range of them, matched or exceeded in bravery anything known during that battle or even that war.

Even as he was rebutting the myth, it was taking on a life of its own – a life that endures, regardless. The beauty of myth is that it can co-exist with knowledge that reveals its fundamental falsehoods, but does not all religion not do the same? Even some loyalists now admit the 36th Ulster Division was never entirely Protestant, or entirely Ulster. Its officers came from every part of Ireland, and 140 men of the Dublin and Wicklow Loyal Volunteers (oh how forgotten they!) had marched to the recruiting office in Dublin to offer their services when war broke out in 1914. They ended up in the 9th Inniskilling Fusiliers, with the 'Ulster' Division. And some Catholics joined up with their mates, like Peter Rooney, originally from County Down but living in Belfast, and so found himself in the 36th, and as was the case for a thousand of his fellow Belfast-recruits, Peter Rooney was to die on 1 July.

For every single death, there was the aftermath. One member of an Ulster family remembered: 'My mother and I was lapping a field of hay beyond Bleary school … My mother saw the minister up at the house … She just looked steady at him without blinking and said, "Is it Ted (her brother) or Willie (my father)?" He said, "I'm so sorry to say it's Willie." She walked along the head – right back to the house, her back as straight as that of a girl of nineteen.'

One may repeat that vignette in different forms, with different names, in hundreds of Irish communities after that first, shocking day. Banbridge town lost thirty-three men killed on 1 July, as did Lisburn. In Donegal, Raphoe lost eight, and little Burt lost three. However, comparable tales could be told of other communities across the United Kingdom. For the Ulsters were not alone in their bravery or their losses: four British battalions and the unfortunate Newfoundlanders suffered even more casualties than the worst-hit Irish battalion on 1 July. One thousand and one hundred men who had enlisted in Newcastle-on-Tyne died on 1 July – some with the Tyneside Irish, some with the Tyneside Scottish, and some sixty, a little confusingly, with the Inniskilling Fusiliers of the 36th Division.

Even Dublin had its now long forgotten first of July. Not far from the 36th Ulsers, the 1st Battalion Dublin Fusiliers were attacking. One of their number was Eugene Riordain. In 1986 he told me why. 'I was a political soldier. I want you to understand that. I was a political soldier. I joined because I felt sorry for Belgium, yes, but I joined because I believed in John Redmond and Home Rule. And I should have been in the 8th Battalion of the Royal Dublin Fusiliers, which was all Redmond's men. But when that battalion was sent to France I was left behind because I had flu.'

As it happened, the 8th was to have its tryst on the Somme in September. Eugene's personal appointment was, however, being moved forward. For when he recovered, he was sent as a replacement to the 1st Dublin Fusiliers, attached to the 29th Division. He arrived with the battalion the day before the offensive began, and was appalled when it was proposed that because of his splendid physique he should be immediately made a lance-corporal. 'You can't expect me to go around with veterans, telling them what to do,' he protested to his commanding officer, who replied, laconically: 'Don't take any notice of them. They won't take any notice of you either. They certainly don't take any notice of me.'

Next morning, after a sleepless night, he watched the British bombardment hitting the German trenches. 'Nobody could live out there,' he said to his officer.

'You're probably right,' came the reply. 'Nobody could possibly be alive.'

The Dublins left their trenches at 8 a.m. 'Our men were very professional, and when the Germans opened fire on us the army training came back. They assumed a prone position, and started skirmishing.' (The men of the nearby Ulster Division, amateurs almost to a man, did no such thing, and their casualties reflected that.) So Eugene, though untrained in such matters, followed the example of the men around him as they crawled in the vague direction of an abomination called Trones Wood. 'But anyone who tried to get through the German wire got stuck there. They were sitting targets. The Germans shot them.'

Out of the thousand men of 1st Dublin Fusiliers who started the advance, some two hundred fell, fifty-five of them dead – and about 90 per cent of those were Irish. These were perhaps the lightest casualties of any of the twenty-four Irish battalions in action on that dreadful morning. Six of these Irish battalions had lost more than five hundred men each, and the 1st Tyneside Irish had lost more than six hundred men.

Eugene Riordain was not the only Dublin Fusilier to have arrived on the Somme battlefield earlier than he might have expected. Another Dub, Thomas Curley, had been transferred from the regiment to the Royal

Berkshires, I suspect because of his possible involvement in the shooting of a British army officer named Algernon Lucas during the Easter Rising. At all events, he was one of the 150 men of the 2nd Battalion of the Royal Berkshire Regiment to be killed on 1 July 1916 – along with another Irishman serving with them, Samuel Winters from Drumcree, one of the local Orangemen whom the famous (or infamous) march would later honour. Of course, no one remembered the Catholic named Curley who died alongside him.

Such neglect – we all now know – was to be the fate that awaited the nationalist, Catholic volunteers of the war, most unfairly the men of the 16th Irish Division, so many of whom, like Eugene Riordain, were political soldiers, who had joined as a statement of good faith that self-governing Ireland could be trusted. In the year of 1916 alone, the 16th lost nearly 2700 dead, compared to the 2000 of the 36th. Rather like the 36th in their own particular way, the 16th were distinctly different from the other British army division.

An English officer with the Connaught Rangers, Rowland Feilding, said of his men that they would do nothing if ordered; if asked, they would do anything. 'I can never express in writing what I feel about [them],' he said in a letter home. 'Freezing or snowing, or drenching rain; always smothered with mud; you may ask any one of them, any moment of night or day, 'Are you cold?' or 'Are you wet?' and you will always get but one answer. The Irishman will reply – always with a smile – "Not too cold, sir," or "Not too wet, sir."'

He was as much impressed by his Irish officers: cheery, friendly, open towards outsiders, the star of whom was his trench mortar officer. A former law-clerk, James Patrick Roche, born in Kerry, but then resident in Monasterevin, was, Feilding felt, the wittiest raconteur he had ever met. Whenever Roche was about to utter one of his quips, a small grin would settle on his face, lingering afterward when the jest was complete, while around all collapsed with laughter. But most importantly of all, Roche was a superb soldier: 'As brigade mortar officer, a genius.'

One of the many deplorable aspects to the ideologically driven amnesia that initially obscured and then eradicated any public memory of the 16th Irish Division is the paucity of Irish nationalist voices to describe life in the division. Feilding of course was English; so was Lieutenant J.F.B O'Sullivan, and Connaught Rangers, though his Irish surname has allowed some observers to claim he was Irish. The other voices that were heard about the 16th in later years were largely from people of unionist loyalties. I interviewed three Irish Catholic nationalist volunteers attached to the 16th – I do not include Jack Moyney VC, Irish Guards, in this category, because he was largely unmoved by political interests. Three others, Denis O'Toole, Michael Tierney and Eugene Riordain, were enormously proud of their war records, and of the achievements of Irish nationalists in the colours of the British. The proof of their kidney was the VC won by Lieutenant John Vincent Holland at Ginchy on the Somme (more details are briefly given in the chapter on the Leinsters). These men testified to the religious fervour of the Division, as did Feilding: 'The fortitude that the men draw from their faith is great and marked.' Just before a big attack, he observed: 'For hours that evening the priests were engaged, the men crowding up silently, passing one by one to the canvas confessionals … dimly lighted by a candle or two for the occasion.'

It would be as wrong to paint the 16th Irish as uniformly 'nationalist' as to declare the 36th thoroughly orange. The 6th battalion of the Royal Irish Regiment included one quarter from the Guernsey Militia, some of whom could not speak English. The battalion was brigaded with the 6th Connaught Rangers, and the presence of two nationalist MPs in the ranks of each – Willie Redmond in the Royal Irish and Stephen Gwynne in the Rangers – had a remarkably beneficial effect on morale and identity. The officers messed together each evening, and their men belonged more to the division than they did to their regiments, making their basic association with Ireland all the greater.

When the division moved to northern France, religion, including that of the Normans amongst them, brought them into close contact with the people there. After the terrible gas attacks at Hulluch near Loos in April 1916, and in honour of the 500 of their comrades who had been killed, the men of the 16th subscribed to the erection of a statue of Our Lady of Victories in the church at Noeux-les-Mines, where they had regularly worshipped.

The 16th was an unusually experienced New Army Division when it arrived on the Somme Front. It would be need to be. Unusually, it would be expected to make a two-stage attack on the Ginchy-Guillemont area, six days apart. This, if nothing else, marked out the respect in which the Division was held by high command.

But the Division's great achievement was the attack on Ginchy, not the first assault on Guillemont (see the chapter on the Leinsters), because by the time the second offensive went in, the troops had been in the front-line battle area for a week. The 8th and 9th battalion Royal Dublin Fusiliers lost 89 NCOs and enlisted men killed in that period of waiting, with probably 190 men injured. That was at least one quarter of their combined strength.

Tom Kettle, the former MP, of the Dublin Fusiliers, was deeply apprehensive about the outcome of the battle. As is now well-known, but was once completely forgotten, he had volunteered for service on the front after the murder of his brother-in-law Francis Sheehy Skeffington by a deranged British army officer (for more on this, see the introduction). In his letters home he barely mentioned the casualties the Fusiliers were suffering, though they must have been weighing on all the soldiers who waited for the next big push, not least Kettle himself, for he was overweight, and enjoying a brief respite from the alcoholism that had wrecked much of his professional and private life. Only his political influence in Irish nationalist society could have justified him holding a commission at all. But that said, he was loved and he was witty – he called his gait after drinking, 'his roll of honour'. A senior officer, enraged to find him drunk again, expostulated: 'This can't go on, Kettle. There's no place for you in this army while I'm in it.'

'We'll be very sorry to lose you, sir,' replied Kettle

Before the battle, he wrote this now-famous sonnet to his daughter Betty:

In wiser days, my darling rosebud, blown
To beauty proud as was your mother's prime,
In that desired, delayed, incredible time,
You'll ask why I abandoned you, my own,
And the dear heart that was your baby throne,
To dice with death. And oh! they'll give you rhyme
And reason; some will call the thing sublime,
And some decry it in a knowing tone.
So here, while the mad guns curse overhead
And tired men sigh, with mud for couch and floor,
Know that we fools, now with the foolish dead,

> *Died not for flag, nor King, nor Emperor,*
> *But for a dream, born in a herdsmen's shed,*
> *And for the secret Scriptures of the poor.*

So tired were the Irish by the night of 8 September that Brigadier General Ramsay reported that his men would have to be relieved directly after they took their objectives. Feilding wrote of his men that they were completely exhausted on the eve of the battle, more suited for a rest camp than for attack. After a general absolution from the divisional padre, the men were led through the evil remains of Trones Wood, before which Eugene Riordain had crouched for two months and nine days previously. The division next passed the wasteland that was Guillemont: 'Not a brick or stone is to be seen, except it has been churned up by a bursting shell. Not a tree stands. Not a square foot has escaped.'

Feilding was told of the 'empty' German trench before Ginchy. 'We shall know more about this tomorrow,' he wrote home dryly.

The artillery bombardment before the assault on the morning of 9 September he regarded as dismal, and the assembly points for the attacking infantry even worse: 'From a tactical point of view, nothing could have been worse for launching an attack. The 8th Munsters [were] in a front trench where two men could not pass without exposing themselves to machine-guns and snipers.'

The 8th Munsters and the 6th Royal Irish Regiment then rose to cross No Man's Land, and the 'unmanned' trench, which was the downfall of the officers of the 7th Leinsters (as outlined elsewhere in this volume) did considerable damage to these two battalions also, but in contrasting ways. The Munsters lost only twenty-one men killed, and three officers, suggesting they were (prudently) reluctant to move against a heavily manned trench later reported to contain 300 Germans and five machine-guns. The solidarity within the common mess doesn't seem to have extended its benedictions to the front, for the Royal Irish lost 61 men killed and only five officers, including their CO, Lieutenant Colonel Curzon. Seven of the dead were Guernsey men; twelve were northern nationalists.

The night before the battle, Lieutenant Tom Kettle was writing his last letter home. 'The bombardment, destruction and bloodshed are beyond all imagination, nor did I ever think that the valour of simple men could be as beautiful as that of my Dublin Fusiliers. The big guns are coughing and smacking their shells … The men are grubbing [eating] and an odd one is writing a letter home. Somewhere the Choosers of the Slain are touching, as in our Norse story they used to touch, with invisible wands those who are about to die.'

So determined was Tom Kettle not to be in their number that he had made a steel plate to put on his chest, which he fitted that morning, and rose with his men to advance on the field beside the Ginchy sucrerie. Meanwhile, the 7th Royal Irish Rifles had been fought to a standstill, and the 7th Royal Irish Fusiliers sent to reinforce them. 'The bombardment was now intense,' wrote Captain Young later. 'Our shells were bursting in the village of Ginchy and made it belch forth smoke like a volcano … We advanced at a steady walking pace, stumbling here and there. [A shell] landed in the midst of a bunch of men. … I have the most vivid recollection of seeing a tremendous burst of clay and earth go shooting up into the air – yes, and even parts of human bodies – and when the smoke cleared there was nothing left. … I remember men lying in shell-holes, beseeching water. I remember men crawling about, coughing up blood, as they searched for some place in which they could shelter…'

Yet the 16th Irish, despite some bloody setbacks, took Ginchy, with the 8th and 9th Dublin Fusiliers in the van. The senior officer of the 8th Dublins, Sir Edward Bellingham, had as his second-in-command Captain Jack Hunt, a working class Catholic from the northside of Dublin who had been commissioned from the ranks. Both men survived the battle and the war. The CO of the 9th Dublins was in his own way as extraordinary as any officer on that day. Captain William Joseph Murphy, thirty-six, was the son of a farmer from Tullow. A first class athlete, outstanding at rugby, cricket and golf, he initially had emigrated to Australia, and did well there. He then returned to Ireland – presumably to run the family farm. However, having seen at first hand the freedom conferred by Dominion status, he was a convinced Redmondite. He joined up in 1914, aged thirty-two, as a private soldier, and rapidly made it to sergeant major in the 7th Leinsters, from which he was commissioned into the Dublin Fusiliers and soon promoted to captain. To be leading a battalion after just two years in the army was by any standards a remarkable achievement. Tragically, he was killed leading his men into Ginchy.

Another of the Dublins' officers who did not survive the field was poor portly Tom Kettle. After he fell, shot through the chest, eighteen-year-old

2nd Lieutenant Emmet Dalton briefly cradled his head, before rising again and leading the remnants of his platoon through Ginchy, for which he was later to be awarded a Military Cross. Five years after this deathbed solicitude, Dalton – who in boyhood had changed his name from 'Ernest' to the more patriotic 'Emmet', and who was now an officer in the new Free State Army – was to perform the same melancholy office for the dying Michael Collins at Bael na mBlath.

However, the visitation of the 8th and 9th battalions of the Dublin Fusiliers to Ginchy was not to be the last time the regiment fought in the Somme battle, for the 10th battalion, attached to the 63rd (Naval) Division was there for the very last day of this campaign. Its very divisional attachment says something about it: army recruiting officers in Dublin felt that they were still not getting enough of the clerical and shop-assistant class in Ireland that had proved to be so patriotic in Britain. Presumably, the 16th Division was held to be a little working-class or nationalistic for these recruits, and a quite different identity was initially established, though not retained.

Nearly one hundred men of the 10th Battalion of the Royal Dublin Fusliers were killed or fatally wounded in the final assault of the Somme on 13 November 1916, though in the process, they managed to take the village of Beaumont Hamel – which had been the objective of the 1st battalion on 1 July. The dead, where their bodies could be identified, were buried in the cemeteries around the village – a couple of these house men from the 1st Battalion from 1 July and the 10th Battalion from 13 November: a posthumous companionship that suitably bookends the battle of the Somme.

The slightly different status of the men of the 10th is clear from what we can discover from the cemetery registers. Leo Holland, twenty-five, a former clerk in the Land Commission, the son of a former soldier, was born in India; both his brother and his sister were telegraphists in the GPO. (How had their Rising been?) He had been wounded in Gallipoli. Another post-office employee was John Cobbledick, from the centre of Dublin, a father of four, and aged forty-two at the time of his death. Dominick Kearney from Sligo was also a post-office employee. Albert Victor Lea had been a clerk in the Land Commission. Hugh Stamper, a Wicklow farmer, was the son of a clergyman, and like Leo Holland, had been born in India. Of their officers Lieutenant St John Guisani, a former Clongowes boy, was the son of a Cork doctor, and Lieutenant P.J. McCusker, from

Dromore, County Tyrone, was probably one of the last Catholics from the county to seek a commission in the British army. Harold Mansfield, who does not appear on the 1911 or 1910 censuses, was the son of a Church of Ireland leather-goods dealer, and though it's not clear what he did before he enlisted, his brother was precisely of the right class: a stockbroker's clerk. Two of the names are striking for their youth – John Fellows of Dublin and William O'Riordan were just seventeen when they died, and though army records state that they were born and enlisted in Dublin, neither appears in the 1901 or 1911 Census. Charles Findlater, who had been injured in Gallipoli where his brother had been killed, was aged forty-six. He had been living with his elderly – and apparently somewhat tyrannical – mother when he had enlisted, and perhaps army life was an escape from life with her, which he managed finally to make permanent on the last day of the battle of the Somme.

This was the first and last time the 10th Dublins fought in the 63rd Division (a somewhat preposterous confection created by Churchill to have a naval presence on the battlefield; its soldiers even had naval ranks). Soon the 10th would be attached to the 16th Irish Division, to create – briefly – an all Dublin Fusilier Brigade. But by the time of the Second Battle of the Somme, in March 1918, there were just two Dublin Fusliers battalions on the Western Front, the 1st and 2nd, which incorporated the survivors of what had been five battalions.

The 16th and the 36th divisions were once again alongside one another, for the third time: the first occasion had been a victory, the second a ruinous defeat, and the third was going to prove to be the worst of them all. The two divisions were aligned near the villages of Ronssoy and Epehy, and the German attack, the *Kaiserschlact*, came in the morning fog of early spring. (Some of this is dealt with in the chapter on the Leinsters.)

The 16th Division on that first day of the German offensive – and mostly in the first hour of a truly stupendous bombardment – lost 572 men killed, the highest death rate for any of the divisions in Gough's Fifth Army. The Ulster Division, to their north, lost 267 men killed. And this was just the first day of battle; it was to last nearly two weeks more, with the broken, reeling battalions, sleepless and shell-shocked, retreating before the German onslaught.

On the first day, the 1st battalion, the Royal Dublin Fusiliers, lost forty-three men killed, the second lost 108 killed, and between them they lost fifteen officers. Thirteen more officers and 120 other Dubliners were to die over the next week. Even after the attrition of three years of war, with no recruiting at all in the last two years, the two battalions of the Dublin Fusiliers were 70 per cent Irish, as the three day-death toll of 163 reveals, with forty-eight of the deaths being British by birth.

A similar fate awaited the newly formed 7/8th Inniskillings, which had large numbers of northern nationalists in its ranks. Its losses came to nearly two hundred dead. Most of the Irishmen who died in this offensive did so anonymously. Such was the weight of the artillery fire, and the follow-up with flamethrowers, that their bodies were effectively vapor-ized from the face of the earth.

Others did not disappear quite so conveniently. Lieutenant Edmond De Wind of the 15th Royal Irish Rifles, who a few years previously had been a bank clerk in Cavan, refused to surrender to besieging German forces at Race Course Redoubt near Cambrai, resisting for two days until he was fatally wounded. De Wind won a posthumous VC.

The stand of the Munsters at Malassisse Farm, when surrender was an option, is similarly striking. The defence of the farm was led by Captain Kidd MC, a religious Unitarian from Fitzwilliam Square in Dublin. After he had been killed, and the Germans finally managed to take the farm, a rear-guard action was still fought. Under Major J.J. Hartigan, South African-Irish, the 2nd battalion had formed a defensive line beyond the farm, and fought against the besieging and numerous Germans, retreating from one defensive bay to the next. Hartigan ultimately was taken pris-oner, surviving the war and his heroics. Lieutenant Whelan MC, another South African-Irishman, contested each yard of the trench until mortally wounded at noon on 22 March, dying as a POW three weeks later.

Two Chandlers were officers in the Fusiliers' battalions, holding the line there. George, a lieutenant with the Dublin Fusiliers, was captured, and was released only in January 1919, suggesting that he was still very unwell. Lieutenant Cecil Chandler MC had just returned to active service after marrying Bridget Josephine McSharry, in Meath, and was injured in the fight near Malassise, dying on 30 March. She would not hear of his fate for weeks. Finally, the news began to trickle through: Lieutenant P.L. Cahill, of Ballyragget, Kilkenny, killed near Malassise Farm with the Munsters, whose brother had been killed the year before while leading a battalion of the Royal Irish Rifles with the 36th Division on Frezenberg

Ridge; of Lieutenant-Colonel John Ireland, of Borrisokane, last surviving offspring of Mrs de Courcy Ireland, killed near Malassisse (whose earlier exploits as a lieutenant feature in the chapter 'The Mound'); of Lieutenant J.A. Donnelly, a Protestant working-class lad from Willowbank Street, Belfast, commissioned from the ranks; and of his Catholic namesake, Lieutenant Gilbert Donnelly, twenty, from Glastonbury Avenue; of Lieutenant Hugh Moore, Connaught Rangers, also commissioned from the ranks, thirty-one, a trench-mortar battery specialist and only son of Mr and Mrs J. Moore, Auburn Terrace, Athlone.

Tragedy achieved quite gothic dimensions with the death of 2nd Lieutenant Thompson, of Gobnascale House, Derry, killed in action with the Inniskilling Fusiliers. He was the third Thompson brother to be killed. A fourth had lost a leg, a fifth lay wounded in hospital, and a sixth was reported 'missing in the present fighting'. Second Lieutenant Clarke, of Whitworth Road, Dublin, and serving with the Dublins, died the same day, his eldest brother having been killed the previous December. Captain Fenton Cummins, aged twenty, from Cork, serving with the Connaught Rangers, was also a fatal victim of the March offensive; his brother, Harry, had been killed at Gallipoli. He had four other brothers and five uncles serving.

One man for whom the German offensive was the final proof of his mettle was Jack Hunt. As the British line collapsed, he formed an improvised unit of odds and sods, 'Huntforce', which fought a methodical but superb rearguard retreat. Unbroken, it held out for the best part of a week before making it back to British lines. Hunt was recommended for a Victoria Cross; he got a DSO instead – a poor return for such extraordinary gallantry. Nonetheless, by the end of the war this working-class Catholic from the centre of Dublin was an acting Brigadier General with the DSO and bar and a DCM for gallantry in the field. He had also formed an improbable and lifelong friendship with his fellow officer, Sir Edward Bellingham (Bart).

Not all the Irish dead of the Second Somme were infantrymen. Lieutenant Edwin Talbot, from Sandycove, Captain Marcus O'Keeffe, of Cork, and Major David Nelson, of Monaghan (who had won one of the earliest Victoria Crosses in the war) were all gunners who died in the Second Somme. Captain Robert Gerald McElney, Royal Army Medical Corps, was killed tending the wounded. He was the son of a County

Down Presbyterian clergyman. (And there is surely a thesis to be written on casualties suffered amongst the sons of clergy in this war.)

According to Terence Denman (*Ireland's Forgotten Soldiers*), the 16th Division suffered 7149 casualties (killed, wounded and missing) between 21 March and 3 April. This was to be the end of the 16th. Widely but wrongly perceived to be Sinn Féin, it was broken up, its battalions posted to other divisions, where they continued to serve well. Many men of the 16th now found themselves in the 36th Division, which saw out the last days of the war on the Ypres front.

Yet despite the drama and the colossal battles in which the Irish were involved during the year, every single aspect of 1918 – both the defeats and the final victory in October-November – are completely absent from the mythology that has emerged about the war. In its own way, though lacking the ferocious and visible slaughter that characterized the first day on the Somme, the casualties of the *Kaiserschlact* and the open warfare over the months that followed were every bit as bloody as 1916. Eight hundred and ninety-five men who had enlisted in the city of Belfast (not counting its suburbs) were killed or died in first week of the Somme. The figure for 21 March 1918 to the end of the war was 960 (though not all these were killed on the Somme). Dublin's dead for the three occasions its battalions went to the Somme in 1916 was 341 dead. For the final months of the war, there were 812 dead.

Incredibly, the story of the 16th Division on the Somme simply vanished: in the coming decades no one spoke of the drama of Tom Kettle, the heroism of William Murphy, the courage of Dalton, and the extraordinary tale of Jack Hunt. They were, quite simply, all to be forgotten, as if they and their deeds had never existed. By 1980 not even Tom Kettle's name retained any popular resonances, and all that was known of Emmet Dalton was his later services for the IRA and in the Free State Army. When I wrote about the curiously congruent Kettle-Dalton-Collins deathbed sagas in *The Irish Times* in 1980, an assistant editor came to me in the newsroom, waving the galleys (pre-print pages) indignantly in his hand, and asked: 'This can't be true? Are you making it all up?'

And of course, 1916 is the defining year for the narratives that were to emerge in Ireland: one battle, two divisions, two kinds of Irishness, and two completely different kinds of myth: one glorious and orange, and the other – until very recently – the myth of silence, drawn curtains and untold stories. Perhaps the most telling footnote concerns the memory of the great William Joseph Murphy, whose brief career – from being a completely untrained civilian to being battalion commander, with a mention in dispatches, in just two years – marked him out as one of the finest Irish soldiers of the war. When the war was over, his now childless, widowed mother Mary decided to endow money to erect a memorial hall in his name in Tullow, County Carlow. I enquired about it from a highly intelligent and usually well-informed local man, and was told that Tullow's 'Captain Murphy Hall' was named after a hero of the 1798 Rising – an elegant piece of populist and creative reshaping that thereby slots the brave life and gallant death of this hero of the Great War neatly into the nationalist template that governed the mythology of independent Ireland throughout the twentieth century.

11. *Verdun: Where No Birds Sing*

I have walked the field before Ginchy where Tom Kettle died and where thousands of Irishmen fell during the battle of the Somme; and on the bleak plain of Flanders I have stood where in August 1917 hundreds of Dublin Fusiliers set out in the mud to seize Beck Farm and Borry Farm, never to be seen again. But in neither place, steep with horror though they are, did I encounter the poisoned atmosphere that is gathered about Verdun three-quarters of a century after it first achieved its dismal celebrity.

A stranger arriving in complete ignorance of the events of Verdun would sense that this is an evil place. After visiting those sites in Picardy and near Ypres where so many Irishmen so forgettably perished, we were moved and sorrowful. There is a peculiarly touching beauty about the British Commonwealth War cemeteries, and in both places the sun had shone and skylarks had shrieked their giddy little anthem, and there was a sort of consoling beauty that to revisit either location would offer no great burden to the spirit.

Verdun, though, is different. We felt contaminated there. No birds sang in that spring air. No crops grow in that corrupted landscape. Tangled shrubs cover a soil that teems with ancient and implacable foes of men, sinister vectors that transport gangrene and rabies and tetanus and sepsis to feed off young flesh. Verdun is a terrible place; other than the death camps of the Third Reich, there could be nowhere in Europe where the reek of human corruption is as strong.

What makes Verdun so terrible is that it serves as an axis in history, a most uncomfortable place to be, for it provides a unique conjunction between medieval forms of war – of fort casemate and the subtle brutalities of laying a siege – and of modern warfare with its poison gas, flamethrowers, machine-guns, and its huge artillery shells, conscript armies and the most evil weapon of all enunciated as policy for the first time in military history in the preparations for Verdun, *attrition*.

Verdun was the first battle in history that had no strategic objective other than mass killing. In his memorandum to the Kaiser, Field Marshal Falkenhayn stated: 'Within our reach behind the French sector of the Western Front there are objectives for the retention of which the French General Staff would be compelled to throw in every man they have. If they do so the forces of France will bleed to death ... whether or not we reach our goal.'

Yet another factor ensured the ghastliness of Verdun: the mythical culture that existed in French High Command stating that every inch of French territory must be defended to the death; if lost, it must be regained by counter-attacks, in which, according to the philosophy of the time, 'imprudence is the best of assurances'. This nonsense was made doubly lethal by the magical belief in the potency of the bayonet over heavy artillery. 'Thank God we have no heavy artillery,' a general staff officer once remarked.

Verdun, a curiously German place where they speak an improbable French and devour sauerkraut and sausage, was chosen as the place for the German offensive because it was the centre of the French defences, and because the Kaiser's son the Crown Prince was local commander. The German code for the operation was '*Gericht*', which can mean 'place of execution'. Verdun was that and more. The Romans called it the true fort, '*verum dunum*', the fort of forts that would still be there when all others had fallen. Its purpose was to stand astride the Meuse, commanding the last great river protecting Gaul, and its capital, against invasion from the east. It was to be the epicentre of the worst battle of the Great War.

German preparations for the offensive were germanically meticulous; a vast array of artillery was assembled for the reduction of the trench works, but most of all the huge forts that defended the town of Verdun. The seizure of Verdun was secondary; the primary aim was to take the French in a mortal embrace; but Falkenhayn made a fatal error. The embrace was mortal in each direction.

The German offensive began 21 February 1916, and the ensuing battle lasted until 18 December, some ten full months, with an intensity that defies all human understanding. What made Verdun so terrible was that relative to the Somme and Third Ypres, it was fought over a small area.

Hundreds of thousands of men were funnelled into a killing zone the size of Phoenix Park or of Dublin city centre from the Mater to Rathmines. The concentration of artillery fire in that zone was incomparably horrific. On the first day alone, 80,000 shells are calculated to have fallen not on the entire battlefield but on one corner 500 yards by 1000.

Henri Barbusse wrote of what such shelling did to men: 'Men squashed, cut in two, or divided top to bottom, blown into a shower by an ordinary shell, bellies turned inside out and scattered anywhere, skulls forced bodily into the chest as by a blow with a club.'

James McConnell, an Irish-American volunteer with the French Air Force, saw the results from above: 'There is only a sinister brown belt, a strip of murdered nature. The woods and the villages have vanished like chalk from a blackboard; of the villages nothing remains but grey smears.'

Fighting took place inside the vast concrete fortifications that the Germans managed to penetrate and on occasion seize. It was uniquely ghastly. At Fort Vaux in June the garrison was trapped waterless in the lower chambers; their wounded lay in the dark in their own excrement and blood, their injuries untended and gangrenous for days, while in neighbouring galleries their fellow Frenchmen were being gassed and charred alive by flamethrowers. Shocking, unseen encounters took place at every corner, leaving no witnesses, just corpses. In the heat, the stench and the putrefaction caused men to yearn for the relative sweetness of poison gas.

But the inside of the forts conferred some protection from the artillery. The infantry outside had no shelter from the ceaselessly probing guns that explored every inch of the battlefield time and time again – so that by summer, quite literally, every single foot of it consisted of compressed soil and human flesh and bone and tooth and tissue; and men desperate to escape the endless attentions of the guns dug through human remains.

Human flesh was parapet and fire-step. Men slept on it and rats gorged on it. The smell was unbelievable.

Men never became inured to the horror. 'To die from a bullet seems to be nothing,' wrote a young Frenchman. 'Part of your being remains intact. But to be dismembered, torn to pieces, reduced to pulp, this is a fear that flesh cannot support.' Medical conditions were of almost Crimean primitiveness. Operations were conducted without anaesthetic upon the wounded French; if their wounds were too complicated or too terminal, they were labelled 'untransportable' and left out in the winter cold, untroubled or untouched by further medical attention.

'Humanity is mad!' wrote a young French officer who had arrived at the front to strains of 'Tipperary': 'It must be mad to do what it is doing! What scenes of horror and carnage! I cannot find words to convey my impressions. Hell cannot be so terrible. Men are mad!'

Those who passed through this Golgotha of human slime, of dispersed eyelids and entrails and sundered skulls, joined a unique fellowship. 'Whoever floundered through this morass full of the shrieking and the dying, whoever shivered in those nights, had passed the last frontier of life, and henceforth bore deep within him the leaden memory of a place that lies between Life and Death, or perhaps beyond either,' wrote one German of Verdun.

The daytime battlefield was permanently covered by a sinister half-light and the ground resembled a vast rubbish dump of equipment and bleached bones and rummaging rats. Men burrowed into this, hardly ever seeing their human adversary at any stage, waiting sleeplessly for days on end for death, dismemberment, or relief.

The two military machines remorselessly fed men, tens of thousands a week, into this mincing machine; there could be no respite. The French supply line was a single road, *La Voie Sacrée*, along which lorries trundled, one every fourteen seconds, with no stopping. If a lorry in front was hit by artillery, the one behind had to keep going, even if it meant driving over the wounded. Water supplies were one with the medical for the French. 'I saw a man drinking avidly from a green scum-covered marsh where lay, his black face down in the water, a dead man lying on his stomach and swollen as if he had not stopped filling himself with water for days.'

Forts were taken and retaken; for days the French garrison of Fort Vaux pleaded in vain for reinforcements. None arrived, and finally the besieged, starved and bloodied survivors surrendered. At the point the French High Command decided to reinforce a fort they did not know they had lost.

A regiment of Zouaves from North Africa was wiped out by artillery before it even started its attack. But another regiment of fellow North Africans, Moroccans, went ahead with their attack; 75 per cent were killed or wounded before they reached the fort they were to relieve; but inside that fort the embrasures were held by German machine-gunners who held their fire until the innocent Moroccans were at point-blank range.

Moroccan and Algerian, French and German, entered the food chain of those few fields around Verdun; 420,000 men died there and another 800,000 were gassed or wounded. There is not a tree or an animal in those bleak acres, there is not a lump of soil that is not composed of something which was human a lifetime ago.

Helmut Kohl and Francois Mitterrand joined hands in reconciliation at Verdun and perhaps the dead now rest more easily. But I cannot believe that they curse they have left on this dreadful place will ever be lifted. It is the vilest place in Western Europe. The great ossuary at Douaumont alone contains the skeletal remains of 150,000 men, a generation who in the lives of people still living today, loved and were loved, and were in their youth reduced to a jumble of bones, a calciferous layer, like an army of archaeological mollusc remains, a modest Carrera of humanity.

The ferocity of Verdun destroyed the French army, not just for the duration of that war but for a generation. Moreover, it probably consumed the best of the rising political classes of Germany, with the direst consequences possible.

After Verdun the French army became obsessed with defence, with retreating behind stone walls of Maginot. France forgot General Ducrot's words about that other earlier fortress, Sedan: 'Nous sommes dans un pot de chamber et nous y serons emmerdé.' The Nazis broke through in 1940 at Sedan, and the French defences divided, like the Red Sea before Moses. Within hours the Germans had taken Verdun in its entirety.

Verdun, though, did not vanish from history with that swift defeat. If the EU is a vast political and economic device to restrain German appetites for war, as many believe, then the anvil upon which that contrivance was first hammered was Verdun. The least that the Eurpopean Union can do is to remember and honour the men who unwillingly were that anvil.

12. *The Leinster Regiment*

'To hell with them bloody French anyway,' bawled a former Connaught Ranger at the doors of the Marborough (Portlaoise) depot of the Leinsters, demanding to be allowed to rejoin the Colours. Aside from offering perhaps the most lucidly incomprehensible explanation of the catastrophe that was to engulf Europe, he also became the town's first new recruit of the war. History doesn't relate whether he survived: 122 men who joined the Leinsters in Maryborough didn't, including fifteen who were later transferred to other regiments.

That August, as were so many regiments, the 2nd Leinsters were suddenly and rudely mobilized for war, their numbers soon to be boosted with unfit reservists called up from sedentary lives, without serious retraining, and the chance to get muscles fit or their feet used to heavy boots. Amongst the additions to bring the 2nd Leinsters up to full strength were draughts from the 5th (Extra Reserve) Royal Meath Militia, with which the Farrell family of Moynalty, County Meath, had long been associated. The battalion was commanded by Lieutenant Colonel E.F. Farrell, and its initially part-time officers included Cecil, Valentine, J.A. (as he was always known) and Gerald. However, the ambitions of the Royal Meaths (as they preferred to call themselves) to serve as a fighting battalion were not to be realized. Instead, they were fated to supply draughts to the battalions in the field – initially, the 7th battalion, and later the 2nd. No single regiment can tell the story of the Irish in the Great War, but certainly for southern Ireland, the Leinsters come closest.

After the 2nd battalion arrived in France, in a touching scene that would in retrospect seem naïve, when finding the bread in the port of disembarkation rather expensive, Lieutenant Louis Daly took his section inland in the search for cheaper loaves; he smilingly led his section back to his approving battalion with baguettes smartly set at the slopes of their shoulders. (Daly was one of the few officers of the BEF to survive the war.)

Soon the 2nd battalion was sent in pursuit of an evasive enemy, crossing the Marne battlefield without even knowing it, the newly called-up reservists hobbling in agony on their blistered feet. Across the BEF, boots were nearly as great a threat to a man's health as the German army.

When orders finally came that they were soon go into action, the men broke into 'Tipperary' as they marched through the small town of Chateau Thierry. It would be four years before allied troops would walk its streets again, by which time 'Tipperary' was a memory as ancient as Thermopylae. The Leinsters' first real experience of the war came on 22 September 1914, in the opening shots of the battle of the Aisne. A skirmish before the rudimentary trenches that they had just dug ended in the death of a soldier of C Company: Matthew Costello, aged twenty-eight, from Borrisokane, County Tipperary; and the fatal wounding of two others, William Mills from Huntingdon and Joseph Fitzgibbon from Dublin. Their officer, Lieutenant Morrogh, was injured. He recovered and returned to duty to become a company commander, and survived the war. The first decoration to the battalion, the newly inaugurated Military Cross, was won by George Young of Donegal for staying with the wounded of his patrol while under fire, and bringing them all in (carrying one) at nightfall.

After the battle of the Aisne the British army was swiftly redeployed to the left of the allied line. The 2nd Leinsters accordingly found themselves near the French-Belgian border, at Strazeele, where the Abbé Bogeart had been shot the day before for failing to give the key to the church tower quickly enough to a German officer. Such a charming episode indicated that this was now war to the utmost, and when four years later the 2nd Leinsters marched into Cologne, the stern old ghost of the Abbé clearly marched with them as a corporate, if rather incorporeal memory.

On 2 October the Leinsters was ordered to assist in the attack by the 6th Division near Lille, their objective being the village of Premesque. As they advanced in open order, snipers hidden in haystacks opened up from behind them. The snipers were hunted down and killed. But the village, once taken, had to be held. Two days later the Germans unleashed a devastating barrage on the exposed Leinsters, whose still-shallow trenches were barely covered against rifle fire, never mind the rain of high explosives that fell on them. One officer, a Captain Maffett from Finglas, Dublin, began to scribble a note to Lieutenant Daly, asking for covering fire against German machine-guns from the artillery (of which there actually was none). A shell-splinter killed him outright, and soon the note was being read by a German officer, who wrote in his diary: 'I have kept the message as well as the addressed envelope. Perhaps I shall have the opportunity after the war to forward the last words by a fallen English comrade to his relations. I have his wrist compass, which I shall send too.'

In the slaughter that befell the Leinsters, a vignette endures: Captain G. Orpen-Palmer was blinded and Captain Frederick Whitton had his leg shattered by German fire, and both were captured by Saxon troops. Made exposed and insecure by the very success of their initial attack and unable to hold a position, yet still unbarbarized by years of war, the Saxons withdrew, leaving the two wounded Irish officers alive. They both then made it back to British lines, the blinded Orpen Palmer carrying the crippled Whitton, who issued instructions, rather like a talking guide dog. Both men survived the war. Orpen recovered sight in one eye, and Whitton wrote a history of the Leinsters – one of the finest regimental histories of the time, and a primary source for this account.

No lesson is quite so thoroughly learnt as the one provided by evil experience, and now the 2nd Leinsters had discovered what countless other battalions had learnt since the opening shots of the war: exposed infantry is doomed when faced by the massed weight of magazine rifles, machine-gun fire and rapid-fire field artillery. In this single engagement 137 Leinsters rank and file were killed, and their deaths at least give us a chance to analyze the composition of the battalion. Of the dead, seventeen men, or 12 per cent, were British-born. Irish regiments had enjoyed a high prestige since their relative successes in the Boer War, which might explain why some Englishmen seemed to have chosen the Leinsters. An examination of names – a fraught and imprecise science at best – suggests that recruits from Irish emigrant families were opting for the Leinsters.

It was very much an Irish rather than Leinster regiment. Some forty-four of the dead, or 32 per cent, were from Munster, and sixteen were from Dublin. Lieutenant Edward Cormac-Walshe was from Crossmolina, County Mayo. (His brother Harry would be killed with the Royal Horse Artillery three years later, just two days after the anniversary of the death of his brother.) Another two years would pass before allied boots entered Premesque again.

The 2nd Leinster were to find themselves in the front line just outside Lille, near the hamlet of L'Epinette, for much of the winter of 1914. A stream passing through No Man's Land into the trenches had been dammed, but on 12 December the dam burst, and a wave of water filled the trenches and flooded battalion HQ. By Christmas Eve the 2nd Leinsters had been in the front line and awash for three weeks. Even by the louche standards that were set over much of the Western Front during Christmas 1914, the 2nd Leinsters and their German opponents achieved levels of civility that would have graced any peacetime community. Aside from the many obvious explanations, one largely unmentioned reason for the fraternization at Christmas was the truly appalling conditions borne by the troops. No army had equipped its soldiers for winter fighting, never mind trench warfare across thousands of miles of flooded countryside where the drainage had been toally destroyed by shellfire, and where men were always wet and cold, and often, at the very least, up to their knees in water. The conditions were of a severity that would be unexampled despite all the now-legendary horrors of trench warfare in Flanders during the future, better-known years.

The truce began with the enemy. On Christmas Eve 1914 some Saxon soldiers opposite the Leinster trenches outside Lille hoisted lanterns, and began to chant: 'Play the game! Play the game! If you don't shoot, we won't shoot. If you don't shoot, we won't shoot.'

Captain John Markes, commander of C Company, a thirty-four-year-old Boer War veteran whose experience had been extensively deployed in raising and training new bodies of troops in Ireland, ordered all aggressive action to cease, but to open fire on any advancing Germans. Later, some unarmed Germans carrying shovels were seen openly walking around No Man's Land, burying their dead. Men of the Leinsters emerged from cover to assist them in disposing of the rotting corpses. Fraternization became widespread, with 'cognac' – more probably Schnapps – being exchanged for Christmas pudding, the fortifying effects of which in trench warfare are probably beyond all medical calculation. Gossip was exchanged, during the course of which an officer – probably Captain Markes, a Londoner married to a Philomena Ryan from Tipperary – had his official claim of two Germans sniped unofficially confirmed. The Saxons believed that Ireland was at war with England, a delusion that even some relatively current Irish newspapers were able to confound. Both sides openly repaired their trenches, both sides used the same house for firewood ('the enemy even lent us mallets to put down pegs'), and both sides fastened their wire to the same row of pickets, reported Whitten. 'It has been said that opposing snipers used the same loophole, but this is an exaggeration.'

Thus it was before the C Company, but in the area of front controlled by D Company, apparently under the command of Captain Orpen-Palmer or 'OP2' (brother of OP1, the half-blinded officer, and both the doughty sons of a Kerry clergyman), in which sniping continued until St Stephen's Day, when the battalion completed their tour of duties in the front line. During the three months that the battalion had been in action, in what was to become a forgotten year, 172 officers and men of the 2nd Leinsters were killed.

That winter, between 1 December and 28 February 1915, of the 9560 British soldiers who lost their lives, 2114, or 22 per cent, are recorded as just 'dying' – that is, they perished from tuberculosis, heart strain, pneumonia, cold, exhaustion or drowning. During the equivalent period three years later, 1917–18, though the total death toll rose by 30 per cent to 12,323, non-violent deaths caused by illness and disease on the Western Front fell by 32 per cent to 1455, or 11.8 per cent of the total death toll. Behind these bare statistics, of course, lies infinite individual human suffering that renders such percentile calculations almost meaningless.

The two regular battalions of the Leinsters shortly thereafter began a common trial that is covered elsewhere in this volume, entitled 'The Mound'. But they had another, even more enduring impact on the parlance of the landscape and of history: the 1st battalion gave the name 'Birr Crossroads' to the much-shelled road junction outside Ypres, a title that it carries to this day for hundreds of thousands of strangers who have no idea what or who Birr was. The 2nd battalion also named a notorious death-trap of a rural house 'Leinster Farm', the melancholy resonances of which would ring through countless regimental histories that knew nothing of either the province or the etymology of those deadly addresses.

The officers of the Leinsters in these early days tended to be Protestant, and often sons of clergymen (as was Francis Hitchcock, the author of another prime source for this essay, *Stand To*, which I recommend for all students of the Irish in the war). The first young officer to whom Hitchcock answered was George Young, a St Columba's boy and the son of a land agent. Young was very much of an imperial family: staying with them during the 1901 Census were a governess, five guests born in India, and a Scottish cook. But the changing demographics of Ireland were becoming clear with young men from the emerging Catholic middle class seeking opportunities in military life, as represented in this account by Louis Daly, the son of a Cork coal-merchant, and Paddy Lynch, the son of a Waterford draper.

At home, by spring 1915, war-fever recruitment had dried up; whatever indignation was felt at the fate of little Belgium had exhausted itself against the concrete abutments of the casualty figures and the realization that Home Rule was no longer on the horizon. So the 5th Leinsters, which between December 1914 and the summer of 1915 had managed to find just four recruits, began a recruitment drive conducted on normal lines around counties Meath, Westmeath and Louth, with resulting enlistments being registered in Mullingar and Drogheda. This campaign brought in 600 new soldiers, at a cost of 117 pounds, or three shillings and ninepence (twenty cent) a man. Their graves were presumably to cost rather more. From 1 January 1916, 121 men who enlisted in Mullingar and 139 men who enlisted in Drogheda were killed in action. I cannot say how many of each group were in that 600, but it must have been a majority for both.

Let me restrict myself to the observation that the diplomatic provocations offered to the Ottoman empire before the war, and the assault on the Dardanelles – once Britain had been lured into hostilities by more astute statecraft in Berlin than London could manage – was the UK's greatest strategic and moral disaster of the entire war. Initially, one battalion of Leinsters was drawn to the second stage of this monumental folly: the 6th. Contrary to Whitton's assertions about the battalion being predominantly English, a majority of its casualties in Gallipoli were Irish. Of the foreign intake, 43 per cent were transferred from English West Country regiments, and 11 per cent were West Country recruits taken directly into the regiment. This does not seem to be accidental: someone in the war office seems to have decided that Irish countrymen would get on better with emphatically rural recruits from the West Country.

From the outset, this was not a happy battalion. Whitton admits to problems between the English and the Irish, and religion is unlikely to have been an absent factor: after all, the Monmouth Rebellion against the Catholic King James had occurred in the West Country. Along with a battalion of the Connaught Rangers, the 6th Leinsters had been detached from the 10th Irish Division and attached to the Australian and New Zealand forces in the Anzac beach-head. This separation from the rest of the Irish Division cannot have had a good impact on Irish morale, but the travails of the battalion – if such there were – are largely invisible in the battalion diaries, which are more than usually economical in their coverage of the fighting alongside the New Zealanders on Rhododendron Ridge.

Perhaps the best one can say of the 10th is that it might have been a goodish division if allowed to fight together, but it wasn't. Moreover, its commander – the headstrong, egotistical General Mahon – even absented himself from command, once he had been overlooked for a promotion. Assessing the performance of the division, and its component battalions, on the strength of how it and they were mishandled, is not fruitful. Out of a batch of 300 Wiltshires put into the Leinsters between 1914–15, twenty-six were killed in Gallipoli, or one quarter of the battalion's death-toll there, with overall totals of fifty-five Irish dead and forty-eight British.

The battalion was clearly in poor shape when it arrived with the re-assembled 10th Irish Division in Salonika. Six men, all of whom appear to have been Irish, were involved in a series of incidents in which direct orders from NCOs were disobeyed. Patrick Downey, who had enlisted at the age of seventeen in September 1914, firstly had disobeyed an order to fall in, and then to put on his hat. He was initially charged with disobeying a lawful order, which is a non-capital offence. This was then amended, with an addition of 'wilful disobedience of authority personally given by his superior officer,' which transformed the alleged offence into a capital crime. Not having a clue about what he was doing, Downey, aged nineteen years and nine months, pleaded guilty at his court martial, where, worse still, he was not even represented. Evidence against him was given by an NCO, a warrant officer and a captain, and he was sentenced to death by a panel of three officers, two of whom were from Irish regiments.

The sentence was passed to General Mahon, now commanding British forces in Greece, and he wrote to the theatre commander, General Monro. 'Under ordinary circumstances I would have hesitated to recommend that the Capital Sentence awarded be put into effect as a plea of guilty had been erroneously accepted by the Court, but the conditions of discipline in the battalion is (*sic*) such as to render an exemplary punishment highly desirable and I therefore hope that the Commander in Chief will see fit to approve the sentence of death in this instance.'

Comment on such murderous advice, about a harmless, hapless teenager, being superfluous, I shall merely add that the boy was shot by firing squad at Eurenijk outside Salonika at 8 a.m. on 27 December under the command of Captain Charles Villiers. (See also 'Shot at Dawn', p, 221.)

A slightly different case had already occurred in France, involving Thomas Hope, from Mullingar, whose family appear to have been broken up by the time of the 1911 Census, with his tinsmith father – that is, a tinker – dead and his mother apparently in jail. Tinkers were usually regarded as good, cheerful and reliable soldiers, and their service welcomed. Thomas, however, was an incorrigible if cunning deserter, who had fled the 2nd battalion of the Leinsters in December 1914 after two months' service. He was captured two months later, in the uniform of a corporal of the Royal Military Police. He told the court he had deserted after hearing his two brothers had been killed (he had none). A damning letter from his commanding officer Major (later Brigadier General) Bullen-Smith – a veteran of the slaughter of Premesques, and possibly thereafter somewhat unhinged – asserted that Hope was determined not to serve. And that sealed his fate. Thomas Hope, Traveller, was shot on 2 March 1915.

However shocking such sentences are, we should resist the instant temptation to presume anti-Irish motives, in this case at least. For example, Bullen-Smith's adjutant, Alfred Durham Murphy, was both Irish and a Catholic, and moreover much loved by his men, and he might possibly have had an input into Bullen-Smith's decision. Furthermore, nothing that happened to any Irish regiment remotely compared with the quite barbaric execution of five men of 3rd Worcestershires, shot together on a single day in 1915. That said, the high number of Irishmen executed with the 29th Division (five out of six, when only three, *at most*, of the twelve divisional infantry battalions were Irish), does demand answers.

Meanwhile, the 7th battalion, an intentionally all-Irish unit (though it never actually managed to be one) was being formed around the nucleus of the quarter-master Lieutenant P.J. Ahern, a Thurles man who had settled and married in Birr. One company was formed to train cadets as officers, and not merely was it an outstanding success, much of what the Leinsters were to provide in 1918, namely one of the finest infantry battalions in the British army, was due to the culture that was both patriotic and professional of the 7th Leinsters, and the inspiration its founding ranker-subaltern had had on the young soldiers who joined its ranks.

The Royal Meaths – namely the 5th battalion – had continued their routine recruiting tours of their area through 1915 into 1916. These were less affairs of noble principle than of exigency and excitement, but they largely came to a halt when the battalion was posted to the Curragh. It was from there that the Royal Meaths hastened by train to Dublin to take part in the suppression of the Easter Rising, though not quite in the spirit of the later ballad – *And from the plains of Royal Meath, Strong men came hurrying through*. The official accounts of the Leinsters' (or Royal Meath's) skirmishes in the centre of Dublin are largely unrewarding. However, one tragedy emerges. A soldier of the Meaths, Private Christopher Moore, was killed in the fighting near Trinity and was buried in the Provost's garden. He was in fact Meath-born, moving in adulthood to become a grocer's assistant in Gloucester Place in north central Dublin. He was later recruited in Mosney, which suggests that he had been one of those eager, bored young men that a Leinsters' recruiting drive had picked up while it was touring the villages of Meath. No doubt he had been visiting home when the Leinster band arrived, and oppressed by the tedium of working in a grocery shop, where he also boarded, he went for a soldier. He ended up being shot dead by a fellow-countryman, and possibly even a neighbour, half a mile from the grocer's shop from whose dispiriting, tenement drudgery he had been attempting to escape. His family did not claim him after the war, merely providing his age, twenty-eight. His body was later moved to the Blackhorse Avenue Cemetery, whereafter this unfortunate vanished from history – until now.

The 6th battalion was now engaged with the 10th Division in operations in Macedonia. These are insufficient to merit much attention: of the battalion's twenty deaths that winter, twelve were caused by disease, and seven of the deaths were of volunteers from England. The 1st battalion would in time be joining them in the 10th Division, providing it with the only regular formation in its ranks – which suggests army command believed it needed stiffening. I shall not be paying a great deal of heed to the division's toils, though in the long run, it was engaged in events of considerable and even calamitous moment: the sequestration of the Mesopomatian and Palestian provinces of the Ottoman empire. However, these events do not in themselves constitute a militarily interesting picture.

Grave matters awaited the Leinsters in France, where war had turned into a mortal grind. George Young, the battalion's first MC, had confessed to Francis Hitchcock after the two of them had been blown up by whizz-bang, though without the respite of an injury, that his nerves were getting to him, and he didn't think he could take much more. However, a tiny piece of shrapnel in the shoulder soon afterwards gave him the 'Blighty' that he had been longing for.

'Jammy one,' he said happily as he left for the dressing station. He died in hospital ten days later of gangrene.

By July 1916 the 2nd battalion were preparing to enter the battle of the Somme. They trained to advance behind the new creeping barrage system, which was only possible with the skilled gunners that time and experience alone could provide. They learnt night attacks, and entered an inter-brigade boxing competition, in which they won 'everything'. This is not the bagatelle it might seem: boxers need skill, intelligence and strength, the very qualities prized by soldiers. The men of Meath and Longford. Westmeath and Offaly were probably not fighting in the war for any other reason than they were; but they were Irish countrymen of Gaelic footballing stock, and were also professional soldiers, inured to fighting and to casualties. This is what they did; this is what defined them.

The battalion's work on the battlefield of the Somme began with a duty they all knew well: they were digging trenches, before the high ground of Guillemont, which was occupied by Germans. When within firing range of the enemy, the work was done at night. During the day, when beyond sniper range, and like all labourers of their time, they hated to be interrupted; they preferred to get the job done, regardless of whether or not they were spotted by German artillery-spotting scout-planes. The price was duly paid. Alongside the trench were the crosses of men killed by shells, and who would be lowered to earth still warm. Eleven Leinsters died digging the 1500 yards of 'Leinster Trench': one

American, two Britons, and eight Irish countrymen whose deaths were not even recorded in the regimental history.

The Leinsters were brigaded with three battalions of the New Army. Its job was to provide spine to the raw recruits of 24th Division. As such, when the division's assault on Guillement – seven times attacked, yet still German-held – occurred, the Leinsters would be in reserve to break-through after the German defences had been breached. The assaulting infantry left their trenches watched by the Leinsters, and who then watched as minutes later the bloodied youngsters came streaming back, some hideously injured: few things daunt a man so as a jaw-bone hanging off a boy's face.

Lieutenant Colonel Orpen-Palmer knew from bitter experience what would follow such a retreat: a German counter-attack. He ordered the 2nd Leinsters forward into the teeth of the artillery that was pursuing the departing soldiers. Almost immediately, half a dozen officers fell down dead or wounded, including OP himself. Unfortunately, his second in command, the incomparable Alfred Durham Murphy, had been tempo-rarily posted to command a neighbouring New Army battalion, whose CO had been wounded before the battle. So the 2nd Leinsters fought their way through to the front-line trenches, to await the advancing Germans, under the command of a captain. Soon the medical officer was hit, and then the chaplain, Father Doyle, had his leg blown off; he died shortly after-wards. Only a regiment made of the sternest material could not merely have stood firm amidst a collapsing brigade, but, though almost officer-less, have then actually advanced through a blizzard of shellfire to regain abandoned positions. Their duty done, the men of the 2nd Leinsters lay down and slept alongside the dead of their brigade. That day, just one of a hundred in the battle of the Somme, nearly two thousand British soldiers died. All things are relative.

Days later, the same battalion that had crumpled before the Leinsters did so again under another attack, surrendering a length of hard-won trench, and streaming back without arms or order. The Leinsters were again called into the breach, their padre Father Molony blessing the men of 'B' Company as they scrambled out of their trench. Few things are more difficult in battle than holding and reversing a disintegrating front, but for the second time the Leinsters did it. One platoon was ordered to retake some of the captured trench by bombs. The Leinsters' official history declared that thirteen men were killed trying to retake this trench, with more losses incurred later – 'nearly all our snipers being shot in the head'. In fact, total Leinsters losses for the day were just eleven dead, and (perhaps) forty wounded. Two of the dead were West Country recruits, and two of them were called Patrick Kelly, Irish-born but both recruited in Britain.

The position having been stabilized, on 1 September the Leinsters came under a five-hour artillery bombardment, and among the dead was Lieunenant Roderick O'Connor, from Sydney, Australia. A judge's son, he had chosen not to join the Australian army but – roots clearly calling – had journeyed to the UK, where he had joined the Leinsters in June 1915.

The three weeks on the Somme front, during which they had only ever been in reserve, had cost the Leinsters seven officers and 88 men dead and 418 wounded, and 54 'missing', with Whitton asserting that the bulk of these must be presumed dead. In fact, SDGW compiled several years later concurs with the figure 88, which means that the tallies were not being correctly kept, or that missing men stayed prudently out of the way until the battalion had left the front-line. This could reflect badly on the men's morale or well on their intelligence; or possibly well on both. Few things are quite so good for morale as survival. Either way, when inspected by the diligent General Capper after the battle, the battalion could muster only nine officers and 270 other ranks.

Now it was the turn of the 7th Leinsters to take their place in the line. When they arrived in France in late 1915, they were gravely under-trained, and so were attached to the 90th Regiment of France for improvement, before being attached to the British 47th Division. It was while the battalion stood in companies in the square of Les Brebis on 17 February 1916 that the men heard a strange whirring sound. A shell exploded amidst 'A' Company, killing three men, even before they'd reached the front-lines. They were Harold Austin, an Englishman living in Limerick, John Comiskey, a twenty-one-year old from Belfast, a former labourer and the son of a widowed 'tayloress', and Michael Walsh, from Dorset Street Dublin, the son of Annie, an illiterate charwoman and mother of ten, only five of whom had survived to adulthood. And now the figure was four. These three men, with among the shortest-ever military careers and unnamed in the official history of the regiment, lie alongside one another at Cambrin Church Cemetery.

Their misfortune seems initially to have bestowed extraordinary good luck on the 7th Leinsters, who were soon posted to Hulluch outside Loos. This was the scene of the series of catastrophic gas attacks on the 16th Irish Division in late April 1916, coinciding with the Easter Rising in Dublin. But happily (admittedly, hardly the right word) the Leinsters often happened to be out of the front-lines whenever major German attacks occurred. Somewhat later, the battalion conducted a successful and rather ruthless trench raid in June during which the Germans behaved with 'grossest treachery', whatever that might mean, leading to some Leinster deaths, and those of a considerably larger but unspecified number of Germans.

The 7th had had the good fortune to have experienced and talented officers from other Leinster regular or militia battalions, and these included Major John Markes, whose coolness had helped assure the Christmas truce with the 2nd battalion in 1914. Posted to the 7th, he became its official diarist. He was killed with the 7th in July, after which the diary – as it itself lamented – was not properly kept for much of August. And is there a worse crime for any institution than to keep no written record?

The journey of the 7th to the Somme occurred while their brothers in the 2nd battalion were already passing through such a torrid time there, near Bernafay and Delville Woods and Guillemont. The 7th arrived on the Somme front on 2 September, encountering the sorry trundling caravans of ambulances taking the maimed back down the cobbled road on which the departing had arrived not long before, whole and healthy men; and of course visible to none were those myriad others that had been left behind for ever.

The Leinsters brigade, the 47th, were to be attached to the 20th Light Division for the attack on Guillemont. The lessons of war had been learnt. The Leinsters, Munsters and Royal Irish were to leave their trenches at Zero Hour, at precisely the moment that the artillery opened its bombardment on the German positions. The Irish were to advance, at quick-time, towards the German-held quarries, with the protective artillery fire for the Connaughts ending after just three minutes, and for the Leinsters after four. While the Connaughts and the Munsters advanced beyond Guillemont, the Leinsters would stay behind and 'consolidate', which, from bitter experience, meant just one thing: to find and kill German defenders who had waited for the advance to pass through their positions, before emerging from cover and firing on the rear of the soldiers who had just passed by.

The impetuosity of the attacking Irish soldiers accorded to the cliché, for they clung on the coat-tails of the artillery barrage, and were on the Germans' positions before the defenders could emerge to offer resistance. Lieutenant J.V. Holland, from Athy, led his bombers not merely against their specified targets, but well beyond, clearing most of the village. He began with twenty-six bombers and finished with five. This suppression of the enemy's defensive positions was followed by infantrymen who shot, bayonetted or brained with rifle-butts any Germans that were slow to surrender. In such clearing-up battles, against soldiers who had chosen to stay behind and fight after both the first waves of British soldiers, and the first opportunity to surrender had passed, Germans were not usually taken prisoner, and those that were, could consider themselves very lucky indeed.

So: Guillemont had resisted seven attacks – but it had not withstood the assault by the novice soldiers of the 7th Leinsters. Of the thirty-three dead, eleven (33 per cent) were from the Six Counties, and three (9 per cent) were British-born but not necessarily of 'British' identity.

Four of the Leinsters officers were now transferred to the 6th Royal Irish Regiment, as the 16th prepared for its huge set-piece battle to take the neighbouring village of Ginchy, effectively involving all the division's battalions. Not far away from the Leinsters, the former Nationalist MP, Lieutenant Tom Kettle of the Dublin Fusiliers, was writing to his brother: 'I am calm and happy but desperately anxious to live.'

Kettle must have known the actuarial unlikelihood of his surviving, just as he knew how Irish history would view the leaders of the Rising: 'These men will go down as heroes and martyrs,' he had earlier observed. 'I will go down as a bloody fool.' All subsequent accounts would later agree: the 7th Leinsters were in for a uniquely torrid time. On 9 September men of the battalion left their positions fifteen minutes after the German positions in front of them had been flattened by a furious fifteen-minute barrage. However, one trench that was believed to have been empty, and was thus spared the softening-up attack, was actually fully manned. The result – all histories concur – was a catastrophe for the 16th Division, and for the 7th Leinsters especially; according to the regimental historian it was the worst day in the battalion's history. In addition to losing all their officers save Valentine Farrell, the four officers transferred to the Royal Irish were also killed. Perhaps the most grievous loss was that of the personification of the battalion: Lieutenant Quarter Master P.J. Ahern. Alone, Valentine Farrell survived unscathed to lead his batallion's battered remains out of battle, for which he was later to win the Military Cross.

However, there is more to all this than either official history or legend allows. Even though almost all officers were down, few enlisted men with the 7th Leinsters went the same way. Both SDGW and CWGC report eleven deaths amongst enlisted men, which is, incredibly, the same number of commissioned officers that the battalion had lost. Four of these we know were attached to the Royal Irish. A death-ratio of seven officers, plus one NCO, to eleven enlisted soldiers, suggests that the latter were killed trying to 'encourage' the former to leave the safety of their trenches. Moreover, battalion-returns are shockingly clear. On 7 September 7th Leinsters had 298 men. On 10 September battalions-returns showed 289 men: namely, nine men fewer – which probably means that a couple stragglers had come back, and that in fact there were virtually no wounded, leaving us with the melancholy conclusion that of nearly 300 soldiers, perhaps half a platoon, had braved the German fire and had been totally wiped out, both in life and in history.

So, when Whitton spoke of 'the worst day in the history of the 7th,' he clearly wasn't referring to the losses at Ginchy, but to the collapse of morale in the battalion, leading to their officers fatally exposing them-selves – in futile exhortation – to German fire. One can imagine from the two extremes of the social spectrum, Thurles-man Lieutenant Q.M. Ahern, promoted from the ranks, now settled in a nice little house in Townsend Street in the regimental town of Birr, where his daughter was to remain, unmarried, for the rest of the century, and his senior officer, Captain Lancelot Studholme, who lived with his mother and seven servants just outside the town; for them both, this encounter meant the end of the line for either family, desperately and futilely trying to get their cowering soldiers to advance – and both men thereby dying in the futile doing of their duty.

Somewhere not far away, their four former Leinster colleagues were perishing with the Royal Irish. And therein lies another metaphor. For one of the officers of the Royal Irish to die alongside those four Leinsterman was Lieutenant Eric Hackett, of Castletown, Ballycumber. All three of his brothers were to die during the war, as was a sister, Venice, a VAD nurse. By 1938 his very bereaved mother was dead, and the family lands had been requisitioned by the Land Commission. Deprived of its economic base for survival, the family home, Castletown, was no longer viable, and Edward – perhaps made witless with grief – sold it to Offaly County Council for £100. The Council demolished it, and used the rubble as core to make a new road out of Ballycumber. Now childless, landless, homeless and widowed, Edward Hackett was probably as alone as any man possibly could be; and so he was to remain, until his death in 1945.

But to return to the Leinsters: in 1979 Michael Tierney, former Irish National Volunteers, and latterly of the Leinsters, told me how pleased he was to have been transferred from the 7th Leinsters to the 2nd, and alluded to some shameful affair on the Somme that reflected badly on the regiment. He refused to go into details. I now suspect the metaphorical shambles of Ginchy, rather than the literal one of regimental myth – with which 'all accounts agree' – was what he was referring to.

There are perhaps two morals to this tale. The first is military, and it is that young soldiers cannot be exposed to the searing violence of offensive action against a well-prepared enemy twice within a week. The second – and more important – is that a hapless ignorance, as with the unwritten Leinster diaries – is usually preferable to a beguiling fiction. Unknowledge is neutral and can be undone: myth is a friend-making virus, a vast pyramid-scheme of the mind, that is far harder to displace than a blank sheet.

We now can say that the 7th battalion had fought well at Guillemont, but not, save its officers, at Ginchy. Yet all in all, it had genuinely suffered: by the end of 1916, in nine months it had lost 139 soldiers killed, thirty-seven (27 per cent) being northern nationalists. And of the twenty-five bombers who had gone in with Holland, sixteen had been wounded, and seven killed by war's end.

Unlike the 7th, the 2nd battalion had emerged from the Somme with no battle honours, and no VC, but had probably deserved both more. War, as in all things, rewards the right narrative, not for the moment including the 2nd Leinsters. However, the battalion possessed one of the finest young officers in the British army. The two main accounts of the regiment, by Whitton and Hitchcock, agree: Alfred Durham Murphy had it all – he was brave, decent, meticulous, humane, intelligent, inspirational, charismatic. Men felt safe in his company and under his leadership. He was to make the 2nd battalion of the Leinster Regiment – already a fine regiment – the basis for one of the most effective infantry regiments in the British army.

Alfred Durham Murphy came of minor Catholic gentry: their home was Ballinamona House, Cashel, County Tipperary, and his father had served in the Leinsters. He had been to a Catholic public school in England, but apparently had not lost his Irish accent. But that he was emphatically and passionately Irish was what particularly appealed to young nationalist soldiers of the Leinsters. For he wasn't just an efficient Irish Catholic: amongst the best, he was also the very best.

It is one of the marks of a great soldier that he is lucky, and Alfred Durham Murphy was certainly that. Men dropped dead beside him while he stood unfaltering. He was hard-working, and his written orders were models of concision and precision. And perhaps most important of all, and not excluding those qualities, his men – usually barely younger than him, and many a good deal older – loved him. He cared for them; in this profession of death, he wanted them to remain alive.

Trench-raids to grab a German for intelligence purposes had become a high-command obsession, and one that Murphy deplored. Nonetheless, when he got an order to grab some prisoners, he complied. His plans covered five closely-typed sheets of paper, and he appointed Paddy Lynch to be the raid's directing officer. Lynch was recently arrived: already a double MC-holder, he was the only son of a successful Catholic businessman from Waterford. Murphy was slightly aloof, studious: Lynch cheerful, gregarious.

Murphy drew up a timetable that covered the movements of the two raiding parties, each of over a dozen men, who were to launch a pincer-movement down a length of German trench. The raid, superintended by Lynch, was successful. A German was taken, with several Leinsters injured, but none killed – in itself a remarkably small bill, for such raids were usually costly in life and unproductive of anything other than casualties and hot air at brigade HQ. The German captive was more than happy to be taken prisoner: a father of ten, he now stood a good chance of surviving the war. Not long afterwards, Hitchcock got an alarm-call from Lynch: a trench mortar had buried three of his men – could he help rescue them? They all dug frenziedly, but incoming shellfire repeatedly interrupted their work, and by the time they got to them, the three men had suffocated: they were Frederick Webb, a Londoner, Michael Duhig from Cork and Joseph Brown from Templemore, Tipperary, whose names have never been published before.

Retaliation for the raid was not long in coming. Paddy Lynch rang Hitchcock soon afterwards to report that a German raid on their trenches was underway, through a vulnerable trench called 'Russian Sap'. The raid was finally repelled, but only after Lieutenant Cecil Mouritz, the son of a Kilbeggan clergyman, had been killed. A frail-looking creature, Mouritz had been able to fire off five shots being himself dying, with his servant O'Neill seriously injured and feigning death at the feet of the intruders. Mouritz had managed to wound a German, who was later found, and put in Paddy Lynch's dug-out alongside O'Neill – who, the moment the stretcher-bearers had gone, unsuccessfully tried to kill him.

Murphy petitioned to have the Russian Sap filled in and abandoned, and General Capper came to adjudicate. He waded through the trench system to find a sentry with head and shoulders well above the parapet, imperturbably watching the enemy lines. Capper sharply told him to keep his head down and asked: 'Have you not got a periscope?'

The sentry eyed the general genially and replied: 'Sure what good would it be, sir? Aren't they just after breaking two on me?'

Christmas day was celebrated with a mass said on an altar of sandbags, officiated amid the snow by the eighteen-stone Father Molony, before the ranks of kneeling Leinsters, with all quiet outside save for a passing whizz-bang. It was the most affecting Christmas that the Protestant officer Hitchcock had ever known.

Two days later an aerial dart killed Captain Paddy Lynch MC & bar, of St John's Hill, Waterford, and fatally wounded thirty-seven-year old Sergeant Michael McCormack, who lived at the corner of Chatham Street and Clarendon Row in Dublin. Lynch in particular was much loved, both for his cheeriness and his military efficiency – a trench-raid without a death was a rare thing indeed – and his death sank the battalion into a deep gloom. Hitchcock removed one of the dead man's collar badges, which he gave to Lieutenant John James Kelly, a journalist from Sunday's Well in Cork, and Lynch's best friend, to send to the bereaved family in Waterford.

The battalion then moved to Vimy Ridge, where Lieutenant Michael Aloysius Higgins, the brother of Kevin O'Higgins, was killed. Some days later the 2nd Leinsters joined the Canadians in their Corps' legendary attack. Again, Lieutenant Colonel Murphy's planning was meticulous and a masterpiece of clarity. It was to be a dawn assault but, as it happened, it took place through a blinding sleet storm that made all objectives invisible.

The battalion Lewis gunners, led by the huge Corporal Cunnningham from Thurles, were unable to see targets, and so, having charged into the German lines, reversed their machine-guns, and holding the barrels, swung their steel butts like knobkerries. Corporal Cunningham charged on, now firing his machine-gun conventionally, and when his Lewis ran out of ammunition, he stood in full view of the enemy, throwing bombs, being hit repeatedly. Finally, and gravely wounded, his arm – among other things – shattered – he made it back to British lines. He was awarded the VC, but did not live to collect it. His widowed mother Johanna had already lost one son to the war. Amongst the dead of the day was Lieutenant John James Kelly, of Sunday's Well.

Of the fifty-three Leinster dead at Vimy, sixteen were transfers from British regiments: four from the traditional West Country, eight from the Royal Field Artillery, and two from the East Surreys. The West Country was drying up a source of replacements; henceforth, non-Irish troops would come infantry-trained gunners as conscript-trained infantry displaced them, and from regiments in the south-east of England. The battalion was now 70 per cent Irish.

The regiment was always on the look-out for soldiers, and the 4th battalion, now stationed in Limerick, kept a watchful eye on ships being paid off, and recruited the now jobless sailors. One of these was a forty-five-year-old American, Henry Hendricks, who proclaimed an interest in serving with an Irish regiment. Few militarily inexperienced men of middle age are remotely suited for soldiering, but it's hard to imagine that a merchant seaman, with maybe some thirty years before the mast, would be able to take to the rigours and discipline of trench warfare. And so in it time it proved.

The year 1917 had begun unpleasantly for the 7th Leinsters. It losses on the Somme had been made good with drafts from Bedfordshire and Sussex regiments. The year's casualties would show that the battalion was now more Bedford than Belfast, yet it was still nearly 60 per cent Irish. The names it employed for its part of the line near Messines – Derry Huts and Clougher Valley – say as much. But it is stretching the imagination to declare that its Irish component was universally nationalist. One of the first officers killed in the year, William Creagh, was the son of a Church of Ireland land agent in Mallow. The next, George Read, was the son of a Church of Ireland maltster. And in the trench mortar attack in which he was killed on 9 March – and though nine of the eleven soldiers killed in the attack were Irish – one of them, George Rennicks from Meath, was of the fundamentalist 'Irish Church', and unlikely therefore to have been a nationalist. However it was composed, the battalion seems to have behaved well during some brisk encounters with the Germans, but perhaps it helped that the previous commanding officer, Lieutenant Colonel Gaye, had been succeeded by a soldier of some renowned vigour – Lieutenant Colonel Stannus, who was the very embodiment of unionist gentry: the son of magistrate, at the age of thirty, he had eight servants to mind his family of four in Baltiboys, a very grand house in west Wicklow.

The two Leinster battalions met for the first time in France that spring while preparing for the forthcoming attack at Messines. The 7th Leinsters, being attached to the 16th Division, had a more prominent role in that attack, in which two of the Farrell brothers were to serve with distinction. After the great mines had exploded, and the German lines were hit by the most savage bombardment the Western Front had yet seen, the battalion charged through the visually impenetrable clouds of smoke that obscured almost everything. Captain Valentine Farrell, noting that a Leinsters' attack was being held up, sent over a party of Lewis gunners to clear the way, which they did successfully. Meanwhile, disaster had struck at battalion HQ: a shell landed in the heart of it, fatally wounding Colonel Stannus, dreadfully wounding the adjutant, Major Acton, and killing the brilliant young trench-mortar officer, a peacetime law-clerk from Maryborough, Major James Roche, whom Colonel Feilding of the Connaughts described as the wittiest men he had ever met. Fortunately, the battalion second in command, though severely shaken, Captain J.A.J. Farrell, brother of Valentine, was able to take Stannus's place. A third brother, Lieutenant G.E. Farrell, was serving as battalion signalling officer.

After Messines, the 16th Irish Division were nominated as 'storm-troops' and allocated to the 5th Army for the forthcoming Third Battle of Ypres. The misuse of the division, so recently named as storm troopers, then used as front-line trench-garrison troops, before being then sent out as attacking troops, is one of the great scandals of the war, both moral as well as tactical. The arrival of a downpour on the first day of the assault does not diminish the responsibility of army commanders for what befell the 16th Division – and the 36th alongside them. Commanders must take circumstances and contingencies into account in the conduct of any battle, and this war does not furnish a more woeful example of a failure to adapt than Third Ypres.

So optimistic was high command that Lieutenant Colonel Buckley sent his mess gear to the forward lines, in the expectation they would soon be in the rear. But the rain that began to fall on 31 July on land where the drainage was destroyed soon created a quagmire. The opening day was spent digging a deep trench under fire, a vile job that cost the battalion one of their finest warrant officers, Company Sergeant Major Patrick Byrne from Dublin. Conditions rapidly worsened, as the battalion advanced to relieve Gordon Highlanders in the frontline trenches. But that unfortunate battalion had simply disappeared in the mud, and had ceased to exist as an entity. So Leinsters then advanced to replace them, hooded in oil-sheets, heavy with packs, rifles, bombs and shovels, platoons at fifty-yard intervals, along a way of horror and butchery.

So 7th Leinsters spent the first week of August 1917 marooned in the swamp that was Frezenberg Ridge. Soon after arriving the troops in the front line were essentially beyond contact with the army behind them. The only communication was by means of 'runners', a term so debased that it would almost be amusing had not the circumstances been so dreadful. The four battalion-companies were under the command of one lieutenant and three second lieutenants.

The official history does not even imply that problems with morals had re-emerged, but the casualty figures suggest otherwise. During one two-day period in the trenches, casualties were one officer killed and two wounded; two other ranks killed, one of them a most promising young NCO, Sergeant Charles Dinsmore, a twenty-three-year old Catholic shop assistant from the Markets area of Belfast. More significantly, fifty-eight other ranks were reported wounded. This is a high wounded-to-death ratio and I suspect this indicates that men were reporting 'injuries' they would not otherwise have taken seriously, and their inexperienced and exhausted company commanders, one of them a second lieutenant, rather than having to deal with recalcitrant semi-malingerers, preferred to send them back as walking wounded. Moreover, these were particularly trying times. The German air force not merely controlled the air, but were free to launch ground-attacks on soldiers clinging onto the edges of their pools of mud. It is hard to sustain the will to fight in such circumstances, and it is certainly impossible now to blame soldiers who failed to do so.

However, the Leinsters' problems were not sufficient to prevent their commanding officer, Lieutenant Colonel Buckley, from roundly congratulating them for their endurance in almost impossible conditions. He told his four company commanders that he had been asked to join in a general protest against the battalion being used in front line duties.

He said that he replied: 'Although I feel it my duty to report that the men of my battalion are really genuinely exhausted, I know that we are living in exceptional days, and we shall make an exceptional effort if called upon to do so.'

The condition of battalions alongside the Leinsters was clearly even worse, for Buckley's words caused the Leinsters' line to be doubled in length. At the end of their ordeal, Buckley wrote to his four company commanders: 'As for me, my heart has bled for you all during these days and nights of trial. I shall thank God when I see you all safely out, and there is no prouder colonel in the whole British Army than I am today.'

These are stirring words but ones that perhaps more reflect his concerns for the morale of his troops than over their fatal casualties. In these three days in the front line, from a battalion now about 900 strong, nine soldiers had been killed – three English and six Irish, and no officers. It is these words, and not the casualties of the time, that have featured so dramatically in almost all Irish military histories of this period. This is not to make light of the astonishingly terrible conditions, but merely to place matters in context. And of course one reason why infantry losses at the time were not as terrible as they might have been is that the German infantry that should have been slaughtering them were also nearly drowning in that very same mud.

On 12 August Captain J.A.J. Farrell took a company of soldiers to the support lines on Frezenberg Ridge. Conditions had eased somewhat, and his company suffered three killed – two British and one Irish, with eleven wounded – an entirely proportionate and believable ratio, no doubt reflecting the moral and mental authority of this officer of the Royal Meaths within the battalion. Contrast this with two killed and *all of fifty-eight wounded* barely a week earlier.

No serious analysis has been written of the amazing Farrell brothers, who when in command, usually succeeded. Throughout their time in the Leinsters, both the 2nd and 7th, most of their soldiers were like themselves Irish and Catholic, giving them a special tribal bond. The Farrells had made their fortune as brewers when that business was dominated by Protestants with better contacts and more influence than these upstart Catholics, but they succeeded because they had drive, purpose and intelligence. Indeed, it is said that Guinness bought the Farrell brewery in Dublin primarily because they wanted the superior Farrell product. The deal with the Farrells was so generous that it enabled them to set up as gentry in County Meath during the 1820s. Nonetheless, across succeeding decades, some of that time spent in Tasmania, the genes of talent remained. Broadbrush strokes for an entire family over generations are usually absurd: yet considering what was to follow, one must wonder about the Farrells.

It was another Catholic officer, Lieutenant Colonel Alfred Murphy, who took the 2nd Leinster, now also attached to the Fifth Army, into action in Third Ypres on 31 July. Their experience and quality marked them out for that most difficult of undertakings, a battalion night attack over broken ground. The men were to advance behind an artillery barrage towards the main line of resistance, called Lower Star Post, but the gunners moved their shell-fall forward too quickly for soldiers to keep up with, as they groped in the dark and fell into freshly made shellholes. Meanwhile, many German defenders in the new 'pillboxes' – the medicinal analogy was just now finding its way into military jargon – on the ridge running alongside Lower Star Post had been unaffected by the British artillery, and were bringing catastrophic enfilading fire on the struggling Leinsters.

Nonetheless, with the artillery-fire now proceeding across the countryside and well out of sight, the surviving Leinsters began to take out the pill-boxes, using double-enveloping tactics in which they had been thoroughly trained. It is one of the many unfortunate myths of the war that soldiers were 'cannon-fodder', whereas in fact they by this time had become highly-trained and thus highly skilled practitioners of tactical fighting. A pill-box that fails to keep the enemy away from its embrasures is a concrete coffin for its inmates, who can expect no mercy from those who have left their dying mates to deal with them.

Dawn had broken to reveal enemy infantry in possession of much of the ridge that was the battalion objective. Fire was opened by the Leinsters at 500-yards range, with rifles, a Vickers, and a Stokes mortar. At that distance, this was suppressing fire, designed to make the enemy profoundly aware of how unhealthy the air around them can be. As with the brothers in the 7th a couple of days later, German air-superiority enabled a spotter plane to bring accurate and devastating artillery fire not merely onto the Leinsters, but also behind them, effectively isolating them from their own lines, and preventing reinforcements. The Leinsters were thus trapped until at least nightfall waiting for a relieving battalion to arrive – which it finally did at dawn the next morning.

The butcher's bill totted up in early August was of eight officers killed or mortally wounded, and twenty-eight other ranks dead; wounded consisted of nine officers and 149 other ranks, and the missing totalled fifty-three. Time would reveal that the OR dead totalled fifty-four, of whom thirty-seven (69 per cent) were Irish. The British component including a diminishing number of West Countrymen, four (7.4 per cent), with the same number of Geordies and RFA each. Making their appearance in the battalion were the first of the British conscripts, three of whom died. The battalion had stood up well in monstrous conditions. All rules being there to be broken, one of the heroes of the mud was 2nd Lieutenant Kyron Dunphy, a twenty-six-year-old Catholic and son of a widowed woman-farmer, Anastatia, who worked a fine-sized property – ninety acres – at Cullohill, King's County. The sons of Catholic strong farmers simply did not join the army: so he, clearly, was an exception. Lieutenant Kyron Dunphy was later to be awarded a Military Cross for his gallantry.

The condign arithmetic of attrition was now telling and irreversible: the thirty-seven Irish dead and unknown numbers of Irish maimed could not be replaced by other Irishmen. The notion of all these many Irish battalions being made good by Britons was becoming absurd. Amalgamations were now inevitable.

If the days of the 7th were numbered, the battalion was steadily improving under the guidance of Lieutenant Colonel G. Buckley. Ordered to launch one of the detested trench-raids, he despatched Lieutenant Weld on a reconnaissance patrol of the target, Tunnel Trench. The raid was a little masterpiece of cunning and deception. Compressed air cylinders were opened, sounding like poison-gas projectors, as meanwhile smoke bombs were released to simulate clouds of gas. The Germans donned their gas masks and took refuge in the tunnel, assuming that no infantry attack could occur until the gas attack had finished. The Leinsters, advancing without gas masks, grabbed two prisoners, both masked, one of whom, baffled at the Leinsters' uncovered faces, asked if the British had invented a gas that would only harm Germans. Captain Dent won a bar to his MC, and Lieutenant Weld won the MC. (In 1998 the latter's grandson, Captain David Foster, formerly an officer in the army of the Republic, and a distinguished and fearless member of the Irish show-jumping team, was killed in a riding accident. I knew him well: and I can honestly say, that in temperament and cheerful humour, he was every inch an officer of the Leinsters.)

This raid was followed by an assault on what was left of Tunnel Trench, led by Captain Valentine Farrell MC, in which many Germans were killed and all of thirty-one taken prisoner. This was part of a general push by the 16th Irish Division as their contribution to the battle of Cambrai, which took 635 prisoners and left 330 Germans dead. Perversely, none of the 16th's battalions were awarded the Cambrai battle honour.

Other matters, however, were now to be in the forefront of the Leinsters' minds. On 6 November Lieutenant Colonel Alfred Durham Murphy DSO MC was with his medical officer and members of battalion HQ attending to the injured in a makeshift hospital when it was hit by a shell. He was killed outright, along with seven other men., including his servant, also from Cashel, Michael Corcoran. In May 1979, when Michael Tierney, a veteran of the battalion, recollected the death of over six decades before, he broke down in tears. For years after the death, men of the Leinsters would gather for a Mass for Colonel Murphy – by common consent the finest and best-loved Irish soldier of the war. He was just twenty-seven. His achievements did not die with him. He laid the basis for a battalion that within the following months was to become one of the finest fighting battalions in the British army.

The dreadful year of 1917 finished with a wholly unnecessary, indeed gratuitous tragedy, caused by ineptitude and indecision. The SS *Aragon*, with replacements for the 1st battalion, was kept waiting in the shipping lanes leading into Alexandria, even though U-boats were known to be active in the area, and after several hours was torpedoed and sunk: among her 610 dead were fifteen men of the Leinsters.

In all, 417 enlisted soldiers died with the four active service battalions of the Leinster regiment in 1917, 158 of them non-Irish. The 2nd battalion lost 236 soldiers dead, 97 of them non-Irish, making that battalion nearly 60 per cent Irish. However, the Irishness of the battalion was only being maintained by transfers from other Irish regiments. The trend towards getting recruits from the east rather than the west of England continued, with forty of the dead coming from the former, and thirty-five the latter. As was evident at Third Ypres, Geordies were also arriving in the death-lists, which for the year included twenty-nine men from Bedfordshire and Sussex, and six conscripts.

In early 1918 Lieutenant Colonel Buckley being unwell – exhausted and perhaps affected by the death in the battalion of his stepson, Lt Jobling – was deemed unfit for further duty, and temporary command of the battalion passed to Valentine Farrell. The strength of the 7th Leinsters now stood at forty-one officers and 504 men – considerably greater than that of the 2nd battalion. Soon afterwards, the two were amalgamated under the aegis of the regular battalion, with 285 men of the 7th switching to the 2nd, and the rest forming into the 19th Entrenching Battalion, whose officers included Captain Valentine Farrell: their general indignation at such a fate can only be imagined. However, as it happens, only one Birr-enlisted soldier was to die with the Labour Corps: Hugh Butler, of Rathcabbin. For the enemy were to have a say in matters, which was, after all, the German way, and the absence from the front line of some many Leinsters soon turned out to be a blessing in disguise.

As part of the process or reorganization of Irish regiments, the 2nd Leinsters under Lieutenant Colonel Weldon had been posted from the 24th to the 16th Division – not a move that was welcome as one might have expected. The 24th were old friends, and the new is always suspect. Everyone knew a German offensive was coming, and with vast armies having been released from the Eastern Front, that it would be massive in scale. What the Germans were planning was actually far greater than anyone on the allied side had anctipated: they had managed to move three great armies of seventy-one divisions of over a million men, with ten thousand guns and mortars, directly opposite the British 5th Army, to effect a breakthrough at the very point in the line held by the 16th Division. All that was bad enough. What the British couldn't have expected, and most particularly the 16th Division, with the 36th alongside, didn't need, was for the god of weathers to turn against them. When the appointed hour arrived, with the 16th covering the line near Ronssoy, the battlefield was shrouded in fog, enabling tens of thousands of enemy storm-troopers to advance unseen. The fog made no difference to the German artillery, which had already pre-registered every British HQ and every British gun-battery.

That was how the battle began, with the most shattering and brilliantly devised bombardment of the war so far. The violence of that first salvo was like a vast earthquake, as the ground erupted, and men's ears almost burst with noise. The effect was as devastating psychologically as it was physically. Few minds could stay sane and composed while tethered in the very heart of the volcano's crater that had been created by the German fire-plan.

No account of the Leinsters' day for the 21st exists, nor will it. The battalion HQ was hit in the first round of artillery-fire, and with its demolition, symbolically anyway, disappeared any possibility of a coherent narrative. Certainly, not many Leinster officers became casualties – two killed and six captured on the first day, with ten men killed. On that same day, sixteen officers in 6th Somerset Light Infantry were captured, and only two were killed, as were sixty-one of their men. For the half dozen battalions of the Manchester Regiment in action on that day, the figures are even more shocking, with fifty-one officers captured, and seventeen killed, along with 386 other ranks. Even more telling was the capture of RFA gunner-officers, well behind the front-line infantry – over a hundred on the first two days of battle. Even the officers of the Garrison Artillery, deep behind allied lines with the heavy guns, lost twenty-one officers over the same period. Little can be read into the ratio of officers to men killed in this offensive: no-one had ever been trained to cope with such an intense artillery bombardment, and it was axiomatic within the British army that if you haven't been trained for something, you can't do it.

Even allowing a wide margin of error in casualty-reporting in such utter chaos, the Leinsters do not seem to have performed badly. After the ten other-rank deaths on 21 March, another ten occurred the next day, and officer deaths increased from two on the first day to seven on the second. In other words, by day two, officers were doing a little too much of the fighting and far too much of the dying, but they were not surrendering. 'There was a retirement,' is all that Whitton would say on the subject: if that is a synonym for a hasty retreat, no-one could disagree with him. But it was not a debacle, which is literally what happens when you break a dammed-up stream: it keeps on going.

Some groups of men unquestionably fought, but the descriptions that Whitton uses – 'Frontal and enfilade fire was poured upon the battalion and heavy casualties were the result' – and 'The cutting was enfiladed by machine-gun fire and the battalion was torn into fragments' – are simply not borne out by the casualties on those first few days. What probably happened is that while officers made heroic – possibly foolish – stands, their men abandoned untenable positions and kept retreating until they found places where they could make a fight of it. No doubt there was panic: but the battalion did not as a whole break, and instead, gradually reformed into small fighting clusters, about which no useful narrative is possible. Six men died on 22 March, all Irish (but one Scots-born), as did an officer, 2nd Lieutenant David Lemon MC, a Presbyterian shipping clerk from Dublin.

No enlisted soldiers died on 24 March, one on the 25th, seven on the 26th, and thirty-nine on the 27th – meaning that the battalion had reformed, and was now taking on the enemy – and that, after what they had been through, is the very definition of bravery. Of these thirty-nine dead, twenty-two were Irish (five of them from Belfast) and British-transfers included seven from the West Country, two Geordies and two from Bedford/Sussex. The coherent whole, however, remained unquestionably Irish. Over the following week, just seven men died, six of them British, but with no particular pre-Leinster regimental background that might suggest unity caused by some other loyalty. That said, the possibility they constituted a die-hard core can't be ruled out, just as it can never be seriously proposed: courageous men, they deserve to be remembered too.

An impromptu formation of the 47th Brigade of the 16th Division was developed around a nucleus of 110 Munsters and 100 Leinsters, withdrawing through Peronne. Attempts to create a defensive line were thwarted by the speed of the German advance: they had crossed the Somme and were between the remnants of the 16th and the main part of the Fifth Army. A detailed account of the molecular activities of the various elements of the Leinsters or the 16th overall would not be fruitful: even the most skilled of military historians are reduced to empty jargon and meaningless hieroglyphs in describing the retreat. When Wellington was asked to provide a description of Waterloo, he replied that one may as well provide one of a ball. To attempt to describe events around the Somme in the last week of March 1918 would be like providing an account of what happened when the Rio Carnival relocated to Mogadishu. Many fine men died, such as forty-year old Captain John William Webster, who was older than most of the men commanding him, and others survived by the skin of their teeth, though gravely wounded, such as the extraordinarily courageous Captain D.P. McCann MC and bar, who was to win a second bar, and survive the war to attend the laying up of the Leinster colours at Windsor in May 1922.

The battalion began to reform around their commanding officer, Lieutenant Colonel Weldon, whose journey had been as exciting, terrifying and exasperating as any. On 8 April the battalion was re-united with their lost brothers – six officers and 113 other ranks – of the 19th Entrenching Battalion: someone in high command was clearly thinking – to be followed by 300 men of the 6th Connaught Rangers. This thus became a second major source of Belfast men into the Leinsters: the first had been through the 7th battalion, which had been 'competing' with the Rangers for men of West Belfast. Now the survivors of the two recruitment-streams were together in a regular battalion of the British army. Another recruit from the Rangers was a man of a slightly higher station: a scion of one of the oldest Irish families, and once Lords of the Isles – John Henry O'Connell de Courcy MacDonnell, of Limerick. And also back with the Leinsters was Captain J.A. J. Farrell.

Meanwhile, the 16th Division was in the process of being broken up; it was a grotesque and unjustified insult, for many battalions of other divisions had performed much worse than any of the Irish battalions, but the slur of Sinn Féin sympathies was too powerful for the division to be allowed to remain in existence.

However, that two battalions were being sent to the 29th (Incomparables), the only all-regular division in the army, reflected well on the perception of their fighting skills. One was the 1st battalion Dublin Fusiliers, which had begun its war with the 29th; the other was the 2nd Leinsters. Thus in defeat and retreat, the battalion had actually been promoted.

The 2nd Leinsters spent the summer being rested and trained for the open-warfare that marked the great departure of the year. Trench warfare is enormously expensive and unproductive, requiring a huge logistical infrastructure to maintain what is, relatively, a thinly spread crust over an enormous distance. And most of the efforts of the soldiers would be spent not on fighting, but maintaining the trench structures and protecting the men's health, both of which would rapidly degenerate without daily efforts. Those days were now over. The men were preparing for open battlefields, with fire-and-manoeuvre advances, in skirmishing order.

Other aspects of life, however, had not improved. On 23 August Private Henry Hendricks, the forty-five-year-old American seaman who had enlisted in Limerick the year before, and had been sent to the 2nd battalion, was court-martialled for repeated acts of desertion. Now aged forty-six, he was found guilty and sentenced to death, and his brigade commander, Brigadier Jackson of the 29th, with a quite gratuitous forceful-ness, attached a damning appendix to the court martial proceedings when they were passed on to high command for deliberation. Brigadier General Freyberg VC opined that Hendricks was one of the worst offenders in the British army. So it was that this merchant seaman, whose services as a soldier were accepted when he was far too old to be converted to an infan-tryman, and who could have been quietly dismissed the service and sent back to the US, was taken out and shot by firing squad, the oldest man to be executed by the British army during the war. There are no doubt words to describe this act; only, I do not know what they are.

On 4 September the 2nd Leinsters showed what they were now capable of when they seized Hill 63, a key and supposedly impregnable German position. At one point during this night attack, most of the Leinsters were pinned down on a road by barrages of machine-guns that were firing blind, with the Germans unaware of how close they were to massacring them. It was Captain Gerald Farrell who found the men cowering there, and managed to extricate them, one by one, in a single file, with him in the lead, and unseen by the German machine gunners. With the battalion re-formed, it was able to launch an attack, led by Valentine Farrell, through and around barbed-wire entanglements that would have stopped less-skilled and less well-led troops.

All three Farrell brothers fought in this engagement, which cost the Leinsters thirty-two men killed and 150 wounded. Of the dead, six were former Connaughts, and eight British transfers. Aside, of course, from the Farrells, one of the officers to distinguish himself (again) in this battle was 2nd Lieutenant Herbert Woods MC MM, a Corkman commissioned from the ranks. Meanwhile, the 1st Royal Dublin Fusiliers nearby had captured the supposedly untakeable Plugstreet Wood, and of the thirty-four dead, all but three were Irish. The mood in Ireland might be swinging in favour of Sinn Féin, but the soldiers at the front were still prepared to fight, and if need be, die in the cause for which they had enlisted. Morale was good, reports Hitchcock – but it was that strange, perverse upbeat-mood of soldiers who are on the warpath, who scent victory, and are prepared to risk life and limb to get it.

Hitchcock is also invaluable for the snapshots of officers that he knew – Catholics such as the Farrells, who at one stage were three of the four battalion company commanders, Denis Hickey MC and Charles 'Manners' Fitzsimons MC (whose name he mis-spells) and from the Church of Ireland 2nd Lieutenant Herbert Woods MM MC. He also supplied details of the plain soldiers who were clearly very dear to him. One of these was Private Coghlan, a dedicated Lewis gunner who regaled the battalion at a camp-concert one night with all ten verses of a song about a bottle of beer, the chorus of which ran: 'Now leave down that, for it doesn't belong to you.'

On 27 September, to the sound of their bagpipers, the 2nd battalion, the Leinster Regiment, took their place in the line for the Fourth Battle of Ypres, the one everyone has forgotten, largely because it was a British victory. Heartened by the ration of rum, the men stood in the inevitable Flanders rain as the artillery crashed overhead, and the night-sky was illuminated the permanent lightning of artillery muzzle-flashes. The pipers marched in fours at Birr Crossroads, playing 'Brian Boru', and shells landed at nearby Leinster Farm: that the Leinsters should be back at these locations nearly four years after they had first named them defies further observation.

The advancing Leinsters passed the graves of Connaught Rangers and Worcesters from November 1914, and in columns of four, they marched on the road to Gheluvelt, passing the living but exhausted forms of Worcesters lying near the last resting places of their colleague from the last time their regiment passed this way. The entire landscape consisted of mud, with here and there the occasional burnt upright shard that was all that was left of a woodland. A distant machine-gunner opened fire. Sergeant Patrick Joyce MM, from Tuam, and formerly of the Connaught Rangers, fell dead. Other men fell wounded, and lay kicking in the long grass, The others continued, the pipers blowing furiously against the din of artillery, the rattle of belt-fed machine-guns putting down suppressing fire into enemy-held territory.

Night fell. Rations and rum came up, they paused, and Private Coghlan drank Hitchcock's health. Then off again, up a slope near the Menin Road, along broken and marshy ground. A burst of German machine-gun fire at the Leinsters. The two-man Lewis team of Private Coghlan and Lance

Corporal Richards steadfastly returned fire, and were themselves then hit.

A night-halt followed, the men improvising cover in the long grass where they lay. They stayed there till dawn, soaking wet and bitterly cold. At first light, some men went looking for the vital Lewis gun and its crew: they found them before the machine-gun nest they had been attacking. The weapon had to be wrenched from the arms of the dead Thomas Coughlan of Dublin, no less possessive in death than he had been in life; beside him lay the body of his faithful comrade-in-arms, Patrick Richards, from the Irish community of Coatbridge in Scotland.

Another bitter night followed, as coal wagons burnt, sending their warmth futilely into the night sky, around them thousands of sodden men shuddered in whatever pools were their beds. Come morning, and the men draped themselves in their groundsheets before heading towards the enemy, in line abreast: Valentine Farrell, Manners FitzSimon and Hitchcock leading their men. The company runner, Private Rice MM, had acquired a German greatcoat, and was nearly shot for his trouble.

Hours passed.

Fitzsimons' platoon got to some craters, but he was shot in the stomach and went down. The men around him stayed firm. Somewhere nearby in the dark and the rain a German breechblock was heard to click, the men lay silent, no doubt heartened by the composure of Sergeant Hackett, and they waited until dawn. In the morning came fresh German shellfire, killing a couple of Farrell's men. The rest waited through the following day, cleaning their guns, and growing colder. The following night was the worst so far – as Hitchcock spent much of it bent double in agony.

Fourth Ypres was winding to a close. The 29th Division, with the Leinsters and the Dubs in their midst, lay encased in mud. It was now 2 October. They had not taken off their boots or anything else since the night of 27 September. And now the Germans were retreating, burning all the Belgian houses as they departed, bequeathing a smouldering waste-land for civilians to inhabit for the coming winter. If you are tempted to wonder about Versailles, follow the conduct of the German army in the autumn of 1918, and the plight of civilians they left behind them: at one stage in their advance, the Leinsters came across half a dozen barefooted women hacking lumps of meat from a long-dead mule, surrounded by nearly naked famished children.

Ten days later, the 2nd Leinsters were to go into action again: to liberate the Belgian town of Ledegem. Louis Daly – who had begun the war with French loaves over the shoulder – was still at home on leave. He should have returned – and would have done, save he had been on the *Leinster*, and though he survived, he was still in Ireland. Frank Hitchcock had been sent on a machine-gun course – much I suspect to his sorrow. And so, the Leinsters would attack without them.

The taking of Ledegem is commemorated every year by its people, and men of the Leinster Regiment now have the posthumous freedom of the town in consequence. Two Victoria Crosses were won. Private Martin Moffatt, a Sligo-man and formerly of the Connaughts, took on a German strongpoint alone, advancing through a hail of bullets, hurling bombs as he went, worked his way round the back of the enemy-held house, killed two there, and forced the surrender of all thirty soldiers within, whom he escorted back to British lines. Sergeant John O'Neill, like Richards, born of the Irish diaspora in Scotland, coming under fire from a field-battery with covering machine-guns, charged it single handed, and captured four field guns and two machine-guns with sixteen prisoners. Four days later, with another man – unnamed: such is the unfairness of life – he routed out about a hundred Germans and sent them fleeing.

There was a price: ninteen enlisted men were either killed or fatally injured during the liberation of Ledegem – privates Myles, Burlace, Duff, Hyett, O'Rourke, McCarthy, Burke, Hood, Earle, Kelly Norman and Crieghton, and corporals McCulla, Connolly and Scott. Twelve of them were Irish, mostly from the small towns at the heart of Ireland, places like Mountmellick, Maryborough and Monasterevin; three were Englishmen from the West Country, two former Dorsets and a Wiltshire, plus a Geordie and a Scot. The dead officers included Lieutenant J. de Courcy MacDonnell of Limerick, and Lieutenant William Henry Coade, a student-accountant of Sydney Parade Dublin. Lieutenant Denis Hickey MC of Fermoy, wounded at Ledgeham, was to die of his wounds on 7 November. But for the sinking of *The Leinster*, Louis Daly might have been in the ranks of the dead.

One Leinster officer, though, who was away from the regiment and died that October, was Lieutenant Colonel Bryan Jones DSO and bar, of Lisnawilly, Dundalk, killed while leading the 15th Royal Irish Rifles of the 36th Division. The end was near. The very last Leinsters actually to die in the war were Private Patrick Kane from Downpatrick and Private Bousfield from Hull, shot dead by their own sentry when his challenge went unanswered on 8 November.

I have intentionally and unapologetically not followed the career of the Leinsters in Salonika and Palestine. Of the 1st battalions sixty-eight deaths there, thirty-five were through illness: and thirty-three deaths in action in three years of war, though good fortune for the living, does not make a good story. Much the same can be said of the 6th Leinsters; twenty-six of the sixty-one dead in the final three years of the war in Salonika and the Middle East were due to illness. The 6th ended the war in France, where the battalion was broken up, the West Countrymen being put into the Gloucesters, and an uncounted number of Irishmen – to their great joy – being transferred to the 2nd battalion.

In the course of the war 1910 men and 158 officers were killed while serving with the Leinster Regiment. They had by no means all chosen to join it; of the 333 Leinsters killed in 1918, 151 were transfers from other regiments. Some 10 per cent of the dead that year were from the English West Country, 7 per cent from eastern counties, 5 per cent were former RFA, 3 per cent were Geordies and under 2 per cent were conscripts. Some 65 per cent were Irish, and 10 per cent of the total were former Connaught Rangers. But the history of this proportion tells its own macabre tale, like a bath with the taps on and the plug missing. Even though ex-Connaughts were killed on the Somme with the Leinsters, of the seventy-two 2nd Leinster killed in the first quarter of 1918, none were former Rangers: there were too few surviving to be evident in the casualty figures.

Following the transfer of 300 Rangers in April, sixteen of the dead in the second quarter of the year were former Rangers, sixteen in the third, and thirteen in the fourth. The bath was inexorably emptying again. The Connaught Rangers therefore supplied 22 per cent of Leinster soldiers for the final five months (1 July – 11 November) of the war. But with the shoe being on the other foot, in the final months of the war, twenty-six out of ninety-five Connaught Rangers – 29 per cent – killed were themselves ex-Leinsters. Indeed, there must have been transfers from one regiment to the other and back again, whose movements have defeated even the the sedulously furious quills of War Office bureaucracy. This was not just an Irish issue: of the 178,000 British soldiers killed in 1918, 117,000 were transferees from their original regiments.

From 21 March 1918 to the end of war, of the 247 Leinster dead, eighty-nine were British born and 158 Irish. The latter were born in ninety-eight places, and only Belfast, Birr, Cork, Drogheda, Dublin, Limerick, provided more than two recruits. This pattern is confirmed by fatalities in the final six weeks, when the Irish dead of the Leinsters came from sixty towns or villages, mostly across the Midlands. Ten from Birr, and in all nineteen from Kings and Queens counties. Amongst these final deaths, there was even one Irish conscript, John Bradley, originally, from Queenstown, but living in Halifax from where he was called to compulsory service and his death.

It's not possible here to say what happened generally to the veterans of the war afterwards. But of some we can speak. So parlous were matters for Protestants in Ireland 1919–23, that Hitchcock gave his clergyman-father a revolver he had recovered from the battlefield, for the old man's own protection. Later, he wrote his masterly *Stand To*, a work of great moral integrity whose intention was to honour private soldier as well as officer, but it appeared too close to the Second World War to enjoy the success it merited. After the war, his brother Rex Ingram became a famous film director, after whom Frank named his son. Frank was a troubled man, and never settled, though he had a son from a brief marriage, also called Rex, whom I met during my researches on this subject and who died in 2014.

Herbert Woods returned to West Cork after the war. After a series of attacks on Protestant houses in the area, he offered to protect the home of his two uncles, the Horneybrook brothers. The IRA did attack the home, and Herbert shot and killed one of the attackers, a man named O'Neill, whose brother was later to shoot Michael Collins. The inmates surrendered after the IRA captured and threatened a maid. The three men were taken away, murdered and buried secretly, their graves never discovered. What happened to them between their capture and their deaths is not known either.

Kyron Dunphy MC resumed his career in the RIC. In May 1920 he escorted a colleague to a doctor's surgery in Limerick. As they emerged they were shot. Kyron Murphy was killed instantly, his colleague fatally wounded. Kyron's older brother never got over the killing, and drank himself to death – but not before losing the ninety-two-acre family farm in Cullohill, County Laois.

Christopher 'Manners' Fitz-Simon recovered from the gunshot wound to the stomach and returned to army life. He transferred to a British regiment in 1922, and as a Lieutenant Colonel with an MC, he retired back to Ireland. His son Christopher Fitz-Simon is the esteemed writer and art historian.

Martin Moffatt VC, whose VC-reception was boycotted, took his own life, a totally forgotten man. Sergeant O'Neill, VC MM, was later commissioned and served in the Home Guard in Britain in the Second World War. He died in in 1942, aged forty-five. Few VCs make old bones.

The four Farrells returned to north Meath to live uneventful, modest lives, their many and extraordinary achievements being forgotten with time, so that today almost no-one is aware of them.

Alfred Durham Murphy's family ended with the war. His brother Eddie was an epileptic, and such was the pagan superstition about this condition that he never married. His life was not, however, without significance; he kept meticulous recordings of the weather in Ballinamona, and they constitute amongst the first statistics of the Irish Met Office.

As I reported, only one former Leinster, recruited in Birr, died with the Labour Corps: Hugh Butler, of Rathcabbin.

Another man from Rathcabbin, Martin O'Meara, serving with the Australians, was awarded the Victoria Cross for going out repeatedly into No Man's Land during the battle of the Somme, and rescuing twenty-five men in conditions of quite incredible violence. He returned to Australia, where he was confined for the rest of his life in a padded cell, often physically restrained by shackles, suffering from a psychotic and homicidal dementia that caused him to be a danger to himself and all round him. He finally died in the asylum at Claremont, Perth, in 1935, aged fifty-one, after seventeen years of forcible confinement.

One might say that Hugh Butler was the lucky Rathcabbin man.

The 2nd battalion finished the war by occupying Cologne. It is not pleasant to read one officer's account of the time. 'The streets through which we passed were simply packed with people: they were standing about eight feet deep on each side. They remained deadly silent as we passed, because "Mr Patrick" was in none too good a humour, and not to be trifled with on any account. Cologne was *his* and not the property of the Germans; he had fought for it, and he had won it, and he was out to let them know that it *was* his, too!'

At 12.59 p.m., 13 December 1918, the 2nd Leinsters began to cross the Rhine: 'The marching of the men was absolutely perfect, couldn't be better, heads erect, chests out, and perfect dressing. Each man knew what was expected of him, and, by Jove, he did it right well! I have never experienced such a peculiar feeling in my life before, and don't suppose ever will again …

'For sheer loutish impertinence, the Hun is the absolute limit. Three attempts were made to break through the ranks of the battalion. The first was made by a tram-driver … Two Leinster men pulled the driver from the platform, and well and truly kicked him. A disbanded soldier attempted to pass between two platoons; an officer of the battalion caught him a direct right in the ear; he fell in the gutter and many a passing kick he got from the men. … Another ex-soldier tried the same game … and he too was left lying in the gutter like a stuck pig. We therefore discovered that there is only one way to treat a Hun. Kick him and beat him and he will show respect.'

Intensely disagreeable as this kind of behaviour reads today, it was done by men within whose regiment lay the lore of 1914, and the dead Abbé Bogeart, and those who had followed the Germany army over the wasteland it had delibertaly created in those conquered territories. Moreover, the Leinster killed no-one.

Just as the opening and most telling words of this account came from the mouth of an ordinary soldier, the final ones properly belong to a couple of his colleagues, as quoted by Whitton but not disrespectfully, for he had the highest regards for the rank and file from the inland counties of Ireland. And rightly so, for had these men, simple men, farmers' labourers and small-town poor, over the previous four years, not shed their blood as freely as the Shannon waters that divide Leinster from Connacht?

As the troops of the battalion reached Mulheim, on the far side of the Rhine, one soldier turned to another.

'Is it far the march is tomorrow?'

'Can't be, the officer says we're in Germany now.'

"'Twas a fine river we crossed today, what's it called?'

'Sure I don't know, better ax the sergeant.'

13. Francis Ledwidge, An Address

'In the beginning was The Word.' So opens the Gospel According to St John. We tell tales, and choose information to fit those tales. As did the authors of the gospel, so do we all.

So, let me begin by stating the obvious: the independent Irish state was born out of the First World War, and as with most births, we have remembered little or nothing of the peri-natal events. All that we know, or think we know, is what the midwives have chosen to tell us: and who in their discreet profession will indulge the personal details of perineal mayhem, bloodshed, torn tissue and obstetric forceps? Which is the reason why a talk like this is even necessary.

The first Irishman to be killed in the Great War, and I choose with a little metropolitan bias here, was Joseph Pierce Murphy of Dublin, one of twenty Irishmen lost when HMS *Amphion* hit a mine off the Hook of Holland and was sunk, taking with her some 120 crewmen. Murphy came from Thorncastle Place, Ringsend, a cul-de-sac of just eleven houses. The first land engagements between the British and German armies occurred a couple of weeks later, outside the Belgian town of Mons. On 23 August about twenty Irish soldiers were killed. One of them was John Corri, aged twenty, of the Royal Irish Regiment, grandson of an Italian choirmaster immigrant who had been first employed to teach the the choirboys of the Pro-Cathedral. And almost unbelievably, John Corri was a neighbour of Joseph Murphy lost on the *Amphion*: the sailor lived at 2 Thorncastle Place, Ringsend, and the soldier lived at 7 Thorncastle Place.

Nearly a million men were to die in empire forces during the war: yet a single small terrace in Dublin provided a victim from the first naval engagement and one from the first one on land. Extraordinarily, such has been the triumph of one narrative, and the amnesia that excluded any alternative, that this amazing truth has been concealed all these years.

And within this process of editing and forgetting, such extraoraordinary stories were lost. For example, one of the officers fatally wounded at Mons was a public-school educated Catholic, Lieutenant John Denys Shine of the Royal Irish, from Dungarvan, County Waterford. He crawled from the battlefield and died in a farmhouse. His two surviving brothers, Hugh and James, already both commissioned officers, were killed within a couple of years, followed thereafter by their mother, Kathleen. Another Royal Irish soldier from Waterford was Private Stephen Collins. He outlived John Shine by a couple of months. He was killed in October, aged sixteen. He has no known grave. His mother Agnes was an illiterate domestic servant. Six of her sons served, of whom another three, Joseph Michael and Patrick, also died.

Now the first local casualty from this particular area of Meath was a Navan-man, Private William Kennedy, of the 2nd battalion, Royal Dublin Fusiliers, who was killed in action on 27 August. That week at least 240 enlisted Irishmen and 20 Irish officers were killed in the fighting in Belgium. And four years on another local man, Private Thomas Farrell, Royal Irish Lancers, from outside Navan, had the melancholy distinction of being the last British soldier to be fatally wounded in the war, again near Mons. He and the last outright British victim of the war, Thomas Ellison of York, were caught in a burst of machine-gun fire as their cavalry unit seized a crossing on the Canal du Nord shortly before the Armistice came into effect at 11 a.m. on 11 November 1918. They were within a couple of hundred yards of where young Corri was killed.

Between the moment when the cold waters of the North Sea closed over young Murphy from Ringsend and Private Farrell's doomed charge for a bridge, there were at least forty-four days in which a hundred Irish servicemen or more were killed or fatally wounded in action. Perhaps the

first such day was on 19 October 1914, when the 2nd battalion, the Royal
Irish Regiment, alone, its orders to withdraw never having been received,
made a final, terrible stand at Lepilly against an entire army corps. Over
150 of its men were killed, and 400 injured: overall, across the Western
Front that day, 50 per cent of all British soldiers killed were Irish. And the
evil work of 19 October lived on long after dusk had descended. Of the
three hundred Royal Irish prisoners taken back to Germany, nearly fifty
were to die in POW camps there.

To pick another terrible day in that usually forgotten year of 1914, 1
November, 26 per cent of all British soldiers killed were Irish, plus one
Cypriot and one Falkland Islander. It really was becoming a world war.

The often-forgotten year of 1915 also had its fell, forgotten days: on
9 May, for example, when 4000 British soldiers were killed, 248 were
Irish dead, some 150 belonging to the 2nd battalion, the Royal Munster
Fusiliers, at Rue do Bois. I say forgotten, but it was not always so: the
painting that the great Belgian artist Matania executed of Father Gleeson
blessing the battalion before it went into action, its ranks now filled with
reservists and the first of the new wartime recruits, was once a commonplace on the walls of homes in Waterford, Cork and Tipperary. The sacrifices of the Munster battalions at Etreux and Le Pilly in 1914, and Rue de
Bois and Gallipoli into 1915, were scorched into the province's communal
memory. A booklet about the destruction of the 2nd battalion, Royal
Munster Fusiliers, with her doomed husband at its head, written by his
widow, Mrs Rickarde, was a bestseller. Yet in time, almost all memory of
the sacrifice of those men was to emulate the fate of the original painting
itself, which was destroyed in the London Blitz, and was forgotten by all
but a few.

An equally comprehensive amnesia was to occlude all memory of the
fate of their fellow Muster Fusiliers in the Ist battalion, who were amongst
the some Irish dead of the battle of Gully Spur in Gallipoli in late June 1915.
Henry O'Desmond O'Hara of the Royal Dublin Fusiliers was to write that
the battered remains of his battalion serving alongside the Munsters were
'in a condition bordering on lunacy when it was all over'.

We can only guess at the family tales that emerged in the coming
years, after the war was over and it was no longer politic to remember the
truth; instead there must have emerged a private and guarded narrative
to be conducted at the hearthside, and nowhere else. What did the future

generations of Cummins hear of their family's war? Professor Cummins of Queen's College Cork had six sons, all of whom served, and two were killed. He had five brothers who also served. Seven Hennessey brothers of Nenagh, lesser-born but of no lesser worth, served, as did the seven Conlon brothers of Hoburn Street, Sligo. I choose these because by happenstance I recently came across them: perhaps half a hundred other families would do as well or as badly, according to how you phrase such matters, each with its own special journey upon its own tragic, particular path.

Consider, for example, the Storeys. Robert Storey, of the 1st battalion Royal Irish Rifles, was home in Dublin on leave in January 1917. He was staying with in-laws, William Brown and his wife, in Myrtle Street, while his own wife Jane boarded a couple of miles away in North Strand with their son. He was due to report to his barracks in Belfast one Sunday evening, prior to returning to the front in France. The couple had tea in the house with the in-laws shortly before Robert's train was to leave. He told her he wanted to speak to her in private, and they went into the hall. Moments later, the Browns heard shrieking and scuffling. Jane Storey staggered into the kitchen, her throat cut. William Brown rushed into the parlour, to find Robert Storey sitting in the armchair in a pool of blood, a razor beside him, having cut his own throat. Both Storeys were dead in seconds. The coroner's inquest the next day concluded that Robert Storey had taken his one life, and that of wife's, while his mind was disturbed. He and his wife were unquestionably victims of the war, yet they are on no known list of casualties; though a soldier, he is not mentioned in the primary record of war-dead, Soldiers Died in the Great War, nor is his grave registered with the Commonwealth War Graves Commission. And of their son, Robbie, we know nothing.

We certainly would know very little of Francis Ledwidge without the pioneering work of Alice Curtayne, whose imprint upon both his life and his poetry lasts to this day. The marginalization and effective concealment of Ledwidge and his poetry, apart from his paean to MacDonagh, within the prescribed texts of independent Ireland constitute a cultural scandal. When in 1987 RTE broadcast a tribute to the poet on the sixtieth anniversary of his death, just about every single detail within the programme was wrong, including the absurd assertion that he never wrote poetry about his war-service. This is of course consonant with the agreed and agreeable fiction that those few Irish in British military service were only there reluctantly; whereas Ledwidge often wrote proudly of his time with the Inniskillings. 'A keen-edged sword, a soldier's heart, / Is greater than a poet's art. And greater than a poet's fame / A little grave that has no name, Whence honour turns away in shame,' refutes the RTE fictions: as does '… we but war when war serves Liberty and Justice, Love and Peace.' In a more peaceful vein, 'The Cobbler of Sari Gueul', written while the author was in the Balkans, and with its echoes of Robert Louis Stevenson and Water de La Mare, is one of the most delightful pieces of verse of the twentieth century, deserving of inclusion in any anthology in English.

Indeed, you could argue that the most important of Ledwidge's poems were written while on active service — though Curtayne's rather tendentious categorizations of his poems conceals this truth, as does her complete exclusion of what she sniffily called 'doggerel': his ballad-room barracks written for his fellow soldiers in Derry. Moreover, the RTE documentary asserted that Ledwidge was an Irish-speaker. This is simply myth-indulgence. He couldn't speak Irish, despite his claims that he could in the 1911 Census. Curtayne furthered this myth by correcting his clumsy attempts at Irish in the poem 'Chanticleer': whereas he had written, 'Mac na Maire Slán', she altered his words in the published poem to 'Mac na H-oige Slán'. It is not the duty of an editor to 'improve' texts, but where necessary to elucidate by means of footnotes.

Curtayne clearly, and I suspect rightly, disapproved of a semi-dramatization of Ledwidge's life, *Bird in the Nest*, written for the Abbey Theatre by Sean Dowling in 1960. Yet deplorable though in its own way it might be, this misrepresentation of Ledwidge conforms neatly with the systemic falsification of Irish history of the twentieth century, in which of course the Abbey Theatre played a central role. It was, after all, the theatre's founder W.B. Yeats who penned one of the greatest and most tendentious, that word again, poetic fictions in Irish literature, 'An Irishman Foresees His Death'. In doing so, he Bowdlerized and sanitized the life of Robert Gregory, artist and warrior. This was the man who liked punching Sinn Féiners, who won a Military Cross for shooting well-defended enemy spotter balloons, pressing home his attacks through intense anti-aircraft fire, and then returning to kill their highly skilled and almost irreplaceable crews as they slowly parachuted to earth. None of Yeats's absurd 'lonely impulse of delight' in either the life or death of Robert Gregory.

So it was entirely consonant with the Abbey's self-prescribed duties as national myth-maker that over time it transmogrified O'Casey's Bessie Burgess into a northern Orangewoman, instead of a Dubliner of the species, the Orange tradition not being suited for the narrative of the new Ireland being created by the post–1916 generations.

In Sean Dowling's theatrical version of Ledwidge's life, the poet becomes a commissioned officer (rather than a private solider, as the poet was) named Tyrrell, and the character of Lord Dunsany, the poet-mentor who had taken the young Ledwidge under his wing, and had watched as his protegee outgrew and outshone him, is represented as D'Arcy, apparently an almost buffoonish caricature. To judge from reviews, most particularly from Seamus Kelly in *The Irish Times,* acerbic northern nationalist who was no friend of the Irish gentry, the play offered a grotesque parody of that caste, which was presented as being all-powerful figures on the Irish political landscape. Whereas, after the passage of Home Rule, the Land Acts, and the reform of the local government, the Irish gentry had become not merely marginalized and politically insignificant, but were heading for economic extinction. The figure of Tyrrell is home on leave at the time of the Easter Rising, and clearly wishes he were part of it, but his overtures to join the insurgents are rejected. Before returning to the front, and inevitable death, he writes an ode to the leaders of 1916, which he leaves with D'Arcy, who in the final scene, in what was no more than a stereotypical cartoon of gentry conduct, ritualistically destroys it.

There you have it in one; the filleting of Irish history of most salient facts, and the reconstitution of the boneless flesh with a fresh skeleton to create the carcase of a fowl that was more suited to contemporary and, be it said, profoundly ungenerous, needs. For, yes, Ledwidge was clearly torn by the Rising and its after-effects: he versified his grief at the death of Thomas MacDonagh, in what became his best-known (indeed, only-known) poem in the Ireland that emerged in the years after his death. In two quite different poems he compared Ireland's constitutional military effort in Gallipoli, and later, the insurgents' own efforts, 'When Sackville Street went down like Troy', to the city of classical legend. On the other hand, he was profoundly proud of his service as a soldier. But of course, only one half of the Janus that was Ledwidge was preserved in the aspic of the national narrative. And the dramaturgically wronged Lord Dunsany, far from destroying any of his poems, remained his posthumous champion.

That said, it would be replacing one myth with another to say that

Ledwidge's motives for enlisting were simple. Like many Irish nationalists, he was appalled by German atrocities in Belgium and France. However, he was also a man with a broken heart. The love of his life, Ellie Vaughey, had fallen for another, Jack O'Neill; according to Curtayne, he was a tall, handsome man who worked at the nearby estate, Townley Hall, where he would appear to have been the chauffeur. Ellie and Jack married in late November 1914. But even in Curtayne's attempt to reveal the truth about Ledwidge, she engaged in fresh mythmaking of her own, asserting that when Ellie gave birth in early June 1915, she did so 'prematurely'. In those days a child could not have survived such a short gestation, whereas Ellie's baby did, but she did not. For what had broken poor Francis Ledwidge's heart was the knowledge that his beloved Ellie had firstly got pregnant out of wedlock, and had then died soon after the birth of her child. In the circular patterns of such stories, her husband Jack then joined the Irish Guards. Did Jack O'Neill ever meet Alice's brother Richard, or any of the Tralee recruits? We shall probably never know. He did survive the war, and Curtayne briefly acknowledges what seems to have been his rather unforthcoming assistance in the preparation of her biography.

As it happens, another cycle of story-telling was to involve the actor who played the young Tyrrell/Ledwidge figure, Vincent Dowling, who seven years later was to father a child with a young UCD student and rising actress, Sinead Cusack. The baby boy was put up for adoption, and many years later, his true mother still unknown, the adult was elected to Dáil Eireann. Up until now, Richard Boyd Barrett TD could not possibly have known of the mythic symmetries and patterns that, if only tenuously, linked his own life with the lives of a cluster of doomed recruits in Tralee in April 1915.

But now he can, as can we all, as the tides of an artificial ignorance withdraw, and leave standing on the foreshore of memory the ghosts of the men and women of a history that simply refuse to be washed away.

14. *Robert Gregory: Airman*

Robert Gregory is perhaps one of the most namelessly famous Irishman in history. Anyone who is poetically literate almost anywhere in the world, and who speaks English, will know the opening lines of 'An Irish Airman Foresees His Death'.

> I know that I shall meet my fate
> Somewhere among the clouds above;
> Those that I fight I do not hate,
> Those that I guard I do not love ...

Robert Gregory's largely anonymous fame – for who outside Ireland knows his name? – has helped obscure the significant role that the Irish played in the Royal Flying Corps from its very inception. Of the hundred aircrew who formed the first deployment to France in August 1914, about 20 per cent were either Irish, or from Irish regiments. The commanding officer of Number 2 Squadron, the first to land in France, Major C.J. Bourke, originally with the Royal Irish Regiment, was from Armagh. His most irresistible subaltern was Lieutenant H.H. Harvey-Kelly, also of the Royal Irish, from County Westmeath. Later emerged Clonmel-born Flight Commander Francis Dominick Casey DSC of the Royal Naval Air Service, killed in 1917, and in the RFC the Cork-born Major 'Mick' Mannock VC DSO and bar, MC and bar, killed 1918, Major George McElroy DFC and two bars, from Dublin, killed 1918, and Major Thomas Hazell DSO MC DFC from Clifden, County Galway, who died in 1946. These final three were in the top five of all RFC/RAF fighter pilots, McElroy and Hazell each are credited with having downed over forty enemy aircraft and Mannock, over seventy – although all of these figures are open to some conjecture. Standing almost alone in the popular memory is the figure of Robert Gregory, whose celebrity is based on a piece of poetic licence that also goes by the name, 'lie'. Such is myth. For it is the deceitful bard not the honest deed that begets enduring fame.

Take the A13 motorway out of Padua towards Vicenza. After several kilometres you'll come to the city cemetery. Enter the main gate, proceed south-east to the middle right, and there in the British plot you'll find a headstone:

In memory of R. Gregory MC, Major, 66 Squadron, Royal Flying Corps, and 4th battalion Connaught Rangers, who died on Wednesday 23 January, 1918.

Even this Commonwealth War Graves headstone has a touch of mythology about it. He wasn't a major, but an acting major and a temporary captain. His substantive rank was lieutenant.

Who is to say that he did not love those he guarded? For he is buried right in the heart of that part of Italy which he visited most frequently as a young and carefree civilian, and loved most, and died guarding. And so, many years later in 1918 in those few weeks before he died, did this artist-soldier manage to visit the Giotto and Titian frescoes in Padua itself, near where his bones now lie?

Did he ever go back to Ravenna, Vicenza and Verona from his airfield at Gosso, where he commanded 66 Squadron? Did he revisit those cathedrals and those galleries that had once visited with his mother and which had inspired him before he became a warrior?

Almost all we know of Robert Gregory comes from Yeats's poems about and to him; and for all the many mentions Robert gets in the first volume of Roy Foster's splendid biography of the poet, he remains an elusive person, tantalizing, remote. It is that very remoteness that enabled Yeats to make the fiction of him, and to write out of the popular narrative the truth about what and who Robert Gregory was. One of Yeats's elegies to Robert – soldier, scholar horseman – he deals in detail with two elements of the reality of Robert, the scholar and the horseman. It merely mentions as an aside that aspect of his life at which he excelled; as a soldier. No public awards came to Robert Gregory, artist or horsemen; but Robert Gregory the warrior won a Military Cross, and was decorated by both the Russian and the French; yet in death an invented Gregory was celebrated by some of Yeats's most beautiful elegies.

In many senses I dislike the most famous of these, 'An Irish Airman Foresees His Death,' for the way it has distorted his memory. To anyone who knows about military motivation, of the duties, the terrors, and the horrors of combat, or better still, who has experienced them (as I have not), it is wretchedly far from the reality of what war is like, especially war in the air.

Yet in one sense we should be grateful for that particular Yeats poem about Robert Gregory, one of four he wrote in his honour. It was, after all, for decades the only public and widely received recognition that Irishmen had actually served in the Great War. However, even this managed to subvert the historical record with its own viral perversion of reality, for it conformed with the already emerging mythology that *real* Irishmen had nothing to do with the war, that in reality it was someone else's war with which the Irish had only an accidental, incidental interest.

Simply because of what was said of him later, most especially within the canon of nationalist mythology, it is time to rescue his life, and his extraordinary courage, from the miasma of poetic myth and of largely pacific legendizing.

Robert Gregory was a real man of his time, a fighting man of extraordinary courage, who as a full and mature adult served in a cause to which he had no legal obligation. His only obvious reason to enlist was his sense of duty. He was approaching middle age when he volunteered for active service as a fighter pilot. So this sense of duty was no ill-formed adolescent thing, no lonely impulse of delight, but the mark of a grown man fully answerable for his deeds.

The earlier Robert Gregory was not least an artist and an athlete. His boxing prowess was such that his mother suggested he teach Lennox Robinson the art of fisticuffs to eject Sinn Féin demonstrators from the Abbey Theatre. He seemed to relish the fight. In a row over Synge's *The Shadow of the Glen* Robert wrote: 'We have won a complete victory over the organized disturbers – Sinn Féin men to a great extent. It was quite necessary that someone should show fight and we are the only people to have done it.'

At Coole Park he played beneath the statue of Maecenas, which had been drawn across Europe by oxen, from Italy. As a young man he and his mother visited Italy every year. They went to Urbino, Ravenna, Ferrara, Venice; and Roy Foster tells us that the architectural influences of those palaces came to be reflected in his set-designs. After New College, Oxford, in 1902, he studied art at the Slade, and he provided the sets for his mother's play *The Twenty-Five*. He didn't confine his artistic output to the stage – he also designed the costumes for Yeats's play *The Hour-Glass* at the Molesworth Hall.

But he was also a young man with other things on his mind; and Foster tells us that he let Yeats down rather badly with the sets of *The Well of the Saints* in 1908. That failure perhaps reflected a certain friction between the two. On reaching his majority in 1902, Robert had inherited the house at Gort. It was now his, not his mother's; and when Yeats came, as he frequently did, he was staying in Robert's house, not Augusta's.

The possession of property can turn anyone's head; and we know from Foster's biography that Robert grew to be increasingly impatient at Yeats's presumptions – to the point that Augusta suggested to Yeats that he supply his own wine in his own decanter for the sake of peace at Coole. A certain awkwardness between the two is understandable. No-one has ever maintained that Yeats was easy.

Aside from these abrasions at Coole, back in Dublin they still worked well together, and Yeats had no hesitation in having his young friend continue to design sets for the Abbey. His enthusiasm for Robert's work was not always shared. 'He thinks or thinks that he thinks so much of them that he speaks as if he was in a Cathedral when he speaks of them,' wrote one non-fan. 'I don't want Robert Gregory's masterpieces,'she added sarcastically.

Robert, his mother and Yeats were emphatically on the one side in their continuing conflict with the more nationalistic school of drama in Dublin. When Maire Garvey was voted off the Abbey Board, Robert was in no doubt what she represented, Lady Gregory said, 'Robert thinks it was worth the whole row to have got rid of Miss G and that she embodies all that is most odious in Irish life,' adding somewhat tellingly, 'These RC's haven't the courage of a mouse, and then wonder how it is we go ahead.'

This dispute was in many senses a forerunner of what lay ahead; that the Gregorys and Yeats were simultaneously creating a theatrical expression of the Irish identity while disliking the actual reality of plain Catholic Irishness when they encountered it, is a commonplace ambiguity. Middle-class nationalists and socialists invariably prefer the image of the plain people they imagine into existence and then romanticize to the grubbier individuals of reality.

The stock the Gregorys came from was a cultured one. Augusta's nephew, Robert's cousin, was Hugh Lane, who was to be claimed in the same cataclysm that was to claim Robert. Though to be sure Roy Foster repeats local folklore that, far from being the son of Sir William Gregory, he might have been sired by the local blacksmith, Seanin Farrell.

William Butler Yeats wasn't alone in admiring Robert. Jack Yeats had been much taken by him at the Gort Show in 1906 in a rather more familiar guise, that of the horse Protestant, and produced one his most famous sketches, of Robert taking a fence on his gelding Sarsfield. This performance entered local mythology, and might very well have enabled William Butler Yeats to draw upon it for his elegy on Gregory's death.

This poem, in addition to being passionate and deeply emotional, was generous: for relations between poet and airman had soured considerably in early 1909 after Robert virtually accused Yeats of nearly causing Augusta's death. But by then the rift over Yeats's endless occupation of Coole Park had been exacerbated by the arrival of Robert's young fiancée, Margaret Parry, who bitterly resented the poet's presence.

All those batty enthusiasms of Yeats's for séances and historical cones and Cathleen the daughter of Houlihan might be entertaining enough in Dublin: but over breakfast in one's own home one might be tempted to tell the poet where he could put his apparitions and his endless mysticism.

Even after Robert came into possession of Coole Park, for years Yeats slept in the master bedroom. His conduct in these matters was not based on ignorance but on his power over Lady Gregory: Margaret Gregory – as she had become – told Lady Dunsany that not merely did she and Robert hate Yeats's presence in their house, but that he knew this, yet had no shame about staying on.

When war came in 1914, men of Robert's gentry caste enlisted in large numbers. Born in May 1881, Robert was thirty-three when war began and it would not have been unreasonable for him to have minded his nearly bankrupt property. However, he had never shown any aptitude for husbandry, and even if he lacked the courage to expel the egomaniacally insensitive Yeats from his house, he was otherwise extremely brave.

While people had no idea of what horrors awaited European civilization, what they did know was that a barbarism such as western Europe had not seen in over a century was being unleashed upon Belgium and northern France. And this was not allied propaganda; the Germans themselves announced with an insensate relish what they had done and were doing in their conquered territories late that summer and early autumn of 1914. Their intention was to intimidate and terrorize Belgium and France into swift surrender. Instead, they aroused an anger that was to sweep the Continent, and much of Ireland too. Robert Gregory, the artist, could not have looked indifferently upon the sack of Louvain, one of Belgium's pearls, and the destruction of its medieval library. Robert Gregory, the son of landowning gentry, could not have been unaware of how his peers were flocking to the colours. Robert Gregory, the Irishman, must have heard the call go out from political leaders of all colours to enlist. Robert Gregory, the father, could not but have read the authentic stories of the murders of children by German invaders, boasted of by the Germans, investigated by the Americans and by Irish nationalists such as Tom Kettle, and proven to be essentially true in subsequent enquiries. If he needed personal reason to detest the Germans, the death of his friend, cousin and fellow artist Hugh Lane on the *Lusitania* might have provided it.

So there is no mystery about why hundreds of thousands of Irishmen enlisted. What I cannot say for sure is which was the most powerful factor behind Robert Gregory decision to join up. Yeats, however, is worse than useless on the subject.

> *Nor law, nor duty bade me fight,*
> *Nor public men, nor cheering crowds ...*

Whereas no law compelled him to fight, a Georgian sense of duty might have done, and for any reason, whether to avenge the violated, to rescue the conquered, or join alongside his peers in what seemed a holy war: and did not the urgings of public men and cheering crowds add impetus to whatever sense of duty he might have felt?

He was commissioned into the Connaught Rangers, and he was not the only representative of the Dublin theatre scene there. That summer, an English comedian was playing in the Gaiety, and he too joined the Connaught Rangers, His name was Stanley Holloway. The Robert Gregory that emerges in the din of war is unlike anything we have seen before. As had many men before him, in battle he found his true metier. Something about his bearing, his individuality, his enterprise, caused him almost from the outset to be recommended as a pilot. 'This officer was earmarked for the Royal Flying Corps early on,' one of the official records states.

It is one of the few written records that have survived. Much of the history of the squadron he served in, 40 Squadron, is missing believed destroyed in the 1940 Blitz. What we have left is fragmentary, and from mixed and often unofficial sources; yet these various parts give us a picture of the real and deadly world that he came to inhabit.

The record shows that his application for appointment to Special Reserve of officers, Royal Flying Corps, was made in mid-June 1915. He put his profession down as artist, and declared that he was both married and of European descent. He reported that he was educated at Harrow and New College Oxford, but made no reference to his time at the Slade, perhaps because art college – notwithstanding the formation of the Artists Rifles – might have seemed, to Flying Corps eyes, as being unmartial.

A RFC report dated 6. 1. 1916 reads: '2 Lt R. Gregory 4 Connaught Rangers, on being commissioned for the Royal Flying Corps and now, if no objection, we should like him to be ordered to the Commdt RFC school of instruction at Reading on the 10th January 1916, for a course of instruction in aviation. He should take Camp Equipment with him.'

Ten days later Gregory joined the RFC at Reading, and was appointed flying officer in June 1916, with orders to join 40 Squadron, stationed at Bruay, near Lens in northern France. There could not be a more dangerous place for a flier, for both the Ypres and the Somme battlefields were within patrolling range. Nor was he a *young* pilot. One of the instructors that summer of 1916 reported his disgust at how old he was getting; he had just turned nineteen. Robert Gregory had turned thirty-seven.

We don't know much about his early days with 40 Squadron, which would turn out to be perhaps the most successful in the Royal Flying Corps. Robert Gregory flew with it for over a year, and being easily the most mature pilot in its ranks, he presumably must have made a contribution to the culture that enabled it to produce some of the best fighter pilots of the Great War.

In February 1917 Robert Gregory was flying an FE 8, a cumbersome beast with its engine behind him, powering a backward-pointing propeller. It had a maximum speed of 80 mph, and was hopelessly outdated at the time, as the Red Baron's triplanes scoured the skies. He was later to report that at 9.15 a.m. he was patrolling between 4000 and 8000 feet when he saw two German aircraft. He did not hesitate.

'FE 8 met two HA (Hun aircraft) two miles north east of Arras. FE 8 dived on the H.A and got within 100 yards and followed down to 4000 ft, firing one large drum at 100 yards range. HA dived steeply and was last seen at about 500 ft, about six miles NE of Arras.'

The odds of two to one against had not daunted him. Greater odds were in store. That March he was on a morning patrol at 10,000 feet near Givenchy in Gohelle when his squadron met a group of seven or eight Halberstadts and Albatross scouts. In the dogfight that resulted he fired a short burst at an enemy aircraft, at thirty yards range, but 'without apparent effect'.

His FE 8 then fired about twenty-rive rounds at under fifteen yards range 'and bullets were seen to enter the fuselage of H.A. H.A. then dived vertically, but FE 8 could not follow him owing to presence of other H.A.'

We should be plain what we're talking about here. The FE 8 had a single forward Lewis gun that had a 47- or a 97-round drum. It fired nearly ten rounds a second, each bullet with a muzzle velocity of 2440 feet per second – or at about half a mile a second – into a man at only fifteen yards range. The term 'lonely impulse of delight' does not begin to encapsulate such an experience.

Sending out obsolete planes such as FE 8s against the rising threat of the German air force was asking for trouble and soon it came. Early in March 1917, nine FE 8 aircraft of 40 Squadron were caught on patrol by Jasta 11, led by Von Richtofen, and all nine were shot down, with four pilots killed. It's not clear if Robert Gregory was one of the nine. He was certainly was on duty at the time, and was one of the most experienced pilots in the squadron. It's unlikely, therefore, that he would have been absent from such a patrol.

There was a motto in the Royal Flying Corps of that time; no empty places at the mess. Fresh pilots, often indecently young and even more indecently under-trained, were rushed in to make good the casualties, so that there was no obvious visible sign of losses. Thus a hastily re-manned

40 Squadron was within days re-equipped with the more modern and effective Nieuport Scouts. The older, more experienced Robert Gregory must have seemed to have been a godlike figure to the beardless lads, barely turned eighteen, now arriving for active service.

Days after getting his first Nieuport Scout, Robert reported his first probable victory in the type. Early one afternoon flying south of Vimy at 15,000 feet he saw two Halberstadts flying among clouds at 12,000 feet. He dived as the enemy flew east, and got on the tail of one of them, firing initially at forty yards, and again closing to some fifteen yards. The enemy plane turned over and was last seen side-slipping into a cloud near Bailleul. Gregory reported that the fight finished at 5000 feet.

In May, flying on an evening patrol at 9000 feet, he encountered a two-seater Albatross with 'a concealed gunner'. He closed with it and fired at its fuselage from below to avoid the attentions of the gunner. The enemy aircraft began to spin out of sight, while Gregory cleared a blockage in his machine-gun. The plane crashed in sight of some Royal Artillery gunners, whose officer confirmed the kill.

Two hours later, flying at 18.000 feet. Gregory attacked three Albatross Scouts at 15,000 feet and another at 17,000. He dived on one and got within twenty yards range and fired half a drum. The plane stalled, nose-dived and span downward through the three enemy aircraft below. Gregory lost sight of it as he attacked another German aircraft.

These reports are bald and in the tradition of military understatement. They do not begin to describe the sensation of imminent death, of circling planes whirling after one another, of the terror of machine-gun bullets ripping into your plane or your body, and the knowledge that if your plane catches fire – and many did, because the fuel tanks were easily punctured, and just as easily ignited – you had two choices. One was to burn alive, thousands of feet up in the sky, and the other to leap to a certain death. (In those days, parachutes were forbidden to fighter pilots, lest they use them frivolously.) There was a third choice, which many pilots are believed to have opted for, which was to shoot themselves with service revolvers rather than to burn to death while the plane spiralled slowly to the ground.

Most of the pilots were about half Gregory's age, with the callow resilience and the sturdy unimaginativeness of youth. Unlike the vast majority of his fellow pilots, beardless teenage virgins, he had a wife and family at home and could have been in no doubt about his likely fate. After all, his squadron had already once been wiped out since his arrival. In just over a month, around April 1917, 1200 British fighter pilots were shot down on the Western Front, all to be replaced by more beardless pilots who in turn would possibly die on their first patrol, either being mercifully riddled with bullets, or being burnt alive as they slowly descended from 10,000 feet, throwing themselves to the charity of two miles of gravity, or ending it all with a Smith and Wesson .45.

Oh truly, no lonely impulse of delight here.

In the summer of 1917 40 Squadron took part in a number of attacks on tethered balloons, which were important targets for either side, because their crews, reporting by radio or by telephone, had an extraordinary insight into what was going on behind enemy lines. They were dangerous targets too, being well guarded by anti-aircraft guns that operated according to carefully-plotted and lethal fire-plans. Unlike fighter-pilots, the highly skilled crews of such balloons were regarded as being so precious that they were equipped with parachutes.

On 9 August 40 Squadron launched a carefully planned attack against hostile balloons in the La Bassee-Arras area. The planes crossed the lines at very low altitude, some pilots flying as low as ten feet to avoid been seen by anti-aircraft observers in the balloons. The aircraft then made a surprise near-vertical attack from below, preventing artillery defences from either spotting then in time, or using their carefully plotted fire-plans to interdict them. It worked brilliantly. Five enemy balloons were destroyed. Similar attacks were launched throughout August by the squadron, which not merely shot down the balloons but their parachuting crews as they floated to safety.

By this time 40 Squadron had in a few months taken on a particular character of its own. Few of its pilots were English. Some were Australian, some Welsh, but most distinctive were the Irish. The man who was to become the most famous RFC pilot of the Great War, Mick Mannock, Cork-born but raised in Britain, arrived at 40 Squadron in April 1917, by which time a large number of Irish pilots were already in its ranks: Robert Gregory himself, of course, and others such as Keen, De Burgh, Mulholland, McElroy. Mannock and McElroy were to be among the highest-scoring fighter aces of the war; and both were killed during its closing days. McElroy won an MC and two bars, the DFC and bar, and Mannock the VC, the DSO and two bars, the MC and bar.

These were to become heroes of the air war, and I suspect that their early flying under Gregory's tutelage was vital to their later successes. For it was during his time with 40 Squadron that Mannock, who went on to become the most skilled tactician of the war, first learnt the art of formation attacking, of covering one another's tail, of pilots supporting one another at almost all times. These were serious fighting men, dedicated to their task of operating in teams.

No lonely impulses of delight here, but a cheerfully ruthless atmosphere in the squadron, as per the diary of Mick Mannock:

May 1917 Ellis did a grand stunt today went over high past Douai and returned comparatively low – meeting two Huns landing at their 'drome ... caused them both to crash by engaging them at once. Met another coming home and brought it down with his automatic pistol ... Morgan got one down in flames today, and Gregory managed to do one in before his gun jammed this evening.

Brown and de Burgh left for England a few days ago. Brown showed signs of nerves – poor chap. I hope they both get soft jobs until the end of the war. McKenzie will be the next to break down I think.

2. 6. 1917 McKenzie came back from leave on the 31st, and was promptly ordered to Home Establishment again. Lucky dog! Capt Keen my flight commander went into hospital today with flu. I hear that Capt Gregory has been awarded the Legion d'Honneur for specially good service. He deserves it!

GOC army visited on May 28 to congratulate squadron on last balloon stunt. He was very pleased indeed, and advised us to shoot at the observers as well as balloons.

Later that year Gregory wrote in Mannock's diary this personal advice: 'Don't let your wires sing, May 27, 1917.' (Singing wires were a sign your wings were about to fold.) Underneath this, Mannock was later to scribble of Gregory: 'Croix de Guerre, Russian Order of St Andrew and St George. Killed in an accident on the Italian front in March (crossed out) Feby 1918.'

Neither date was correct. On 16 October Robert Gregory MC, Legion of Honour, Commander of the Order of St Andrew and St George, took over command of 66 Squadron of the RFC. He was twice the age of most of his pilots. On the 22 October the squadron moved to the Italian front, first to Milan, and then Verona, then to Grossa. And it was after flying out of Grossa on a training mission that his plane fell out of the sky. It is often reported that he was shot down by an ally, an Italian who thought

Gregory's Sopwith Camel was an enemy aircraft. Maybe so: only an ally on this front would have got close to Robert, for he was one of the best pilots in the RFC, and far superior to most of the Austrian enemy. However, family members now suggest that far from being shot down, Gregory had reacted badly to an immunization jab that morning, and lost consciousness while flying.

Whatever its cause, Yeats's response to Robert's death was to write his famous elegy, 'An Irish Airman Foresees His Death'. What is especially striking is the austerity of the language, for in Anglo-Saxon it would have been nearly identical. Place-names aside, only nine words out of 105 have non-Germanic origins. And in that beauty, it is all poetical folderol: for it was to honour the man who had repeatedly hinted into the unhearing and unheeding ears of the greatest poet this country has ever seen, to Go. And the poet didn't leave as requested, but instead grimly stayed on, and to add insult to injury withal, in the master bedroom.

And this obdurately selfish scribe then wrote among the greatest rubbish about aerial combat that has ever been penned, and through it, seized the imaginations not merely of an unknowing public, but also that of almost the entire and thoroughly knowledgeable flying community itself. Which takes us to another great truth about art generally, or in this case, poetry. For art serves a basic human craving to create an aesthetically pleasing form where none naturally exists, to shape a narrative myth out of chaos, and a beauty where in reality there is murder, desolation and despair. It is to create lonely impulses of delight out of emptying a machine-gun into another man's body at fifteen feet, or causing him to burn to death at ten thousand feet. It is the great solace of poets that in their fictions they can find moral truths that console and inspire anyone, even those who know they are reading fictions, but then are able to exult in the beauty of those untruths.

It was not by any means the only tribute Yeats wrote to Gregory. Three years after his death he wrote 'Reprisals'.

> Some nineteen German planes, they say,
> You had brought down before you died.
> We called it a good death. Today
> Can ghost or man be satisfied?
> Although your last exciting year

Outweighed all other years, you said,
Though battle joy may be so dear
A memory even to the dead,
It chases other thoughts away,
Yet rise from your Italian tomb,
Flit to Kiltartan cross and stay
Till certain second thoughts have come
Upon the cause you served, that we
Imagined such a fine affair:
Half drunk or whole-mad soldiery
Are murdering your tenants there.
Men that revere your father yet
Are shot at on the open plain.
Where may new-married women sit
And suckle children now? Armed men
May murder them in passing by
Nor law nor parliament take heed.
Then close your ears with dust and lie
Among the other cheated dead.

Lady Gregory asked for it to be repressed and it was; bafflingly, it remains so to this day, never appearing in the main texts of any of the so-called complete volumes of Yeats poems. Yet Yeats wrote no poem about a pertinent drama engulfing a tennis party at Ballyturin House in Gort on 15 May 1921, attended by British army officers and RIC auxiliaries.

As guests left, a group of some twenty IRA men ambushed them, shooting dead RIC officer District Inspector Blake, a former army officer, and also two army officers with him. The ambushers then ordered the two women in the car to leave. One did so. The other, D.I. Blake's wife, refused, saying she would prefer to stay and die with her husband. The IRA men duly obliged, shooting Mrs Blake five times and killing her.

The sole survivor of the ambush was Margaret Gregory. Was that massacre beyond Yeats' ability to confect and to poetize? Apparently. And what did the Kiltartan poor really think of Lady Gregory and her class? A reflection of what she thought of them? In her own words, we largely know what Lady Gregory thought of the real Irish Catholics she had met, rather than the ones she recruited from mythology and her imagination.

But, even with these clues, we have no idea what stance Robert Gregory might have taken over affairs in Ireland had he survived the war. Would he have been yet another baffled Irish gentry landowner, keeping his head low, knowing that whatever happened, no likely end could leave him happier than before? Would he have sided with his tenants, who the Black and Tans, according to Yeats, were terrorizing randomly and murdering? Or would he have sided with his former colleagues, now serving as soldiers or as RIC men, who were themselves being murdered? Paradoxically, one of those colleagues, now in the RIC Auxiliaries, was that Connaught Rangers officer who in 1914 shared Robert's taste for the theatre, though of a lower-brow variety. He was Stanley Holloway, later world-famous as Eliza Doolittle's father in *My Fair Lady*, which of course was derived from the work of Yeats's good friend, George Bernard Shaw.

I don't know what Robert Gregory would have done had he lived on, but I do know that his deeds have been expropriated by those with a self-justifying, nationalist agenda. He became, through Yeats's versification, and the distorting consensus of nationalist mythology, what he was not: lonely, existential and doomed, fighting for a cause of no meaning. Doomed perhaps, but as one of hundreds of thousands of Irishmen who took the route to war, he was not lonely, nor was his path an existentialist one. As a fighter-pilot he proved to be both a team-player and leader.

He and thousands of Irishmen served the cause for which they had freely enlisted. They do not need poets to explain why they did what they did. They might say that the events in Belgium and France in 1914, the rapes, the butchery, the massacres of thousands. explain almost all. They might also ask why we forgot them, why we forgot the truth of what they were, why we forgot why they did what they did; and they might – with some justifiable anger – ask why we preferred pretty if largely meaningless verse to the awesome, terrible reality of what had befallen them.

The political heirs of those Robert had once expelled from the theatre in time were allowed to banish all memory of him and his kind from the popular imagination, merely for having done their duty to the cause they had sworn to serve. This is the reason I have been relating some facts about the life and deeds of Lieutenant, Temporary Captain and Acting Major Robert Gregory MC, French Legion of Honour, and Commander of the Russian Order of St Andrew and St George, Connaught Rangers, attached Royal Flying Corps

15. *Glasnevin Cemetery*

*To the memory of historian Shane Mac Thomais, who helped
hugely in its preparation and died tragically in March 2014.*

We stand today in the official necropolis of Irish nationalism. It was here
Patrick Pearse intoned his words that have echoed down the decades:
'The fools, the fools, they have left us our Fenian dead, and while Ireland
holds these graves, Ireland unfree shall never be at peace.'

The centrality of these acres to Ireland's republican tradition has not
merely defined that tradition, but defined who of the cemetery's residents
shall be remembered and who shall not. It was thanks to the archival
explorations of the museum curator George McCullough that the secret
dead of Glasnevin were first made known to me. Two decades on, these
hitherto forgotten men are finally being given gravestones.

They are of course Catholic Irishmen who died in the service of the
crown, and whose presence here could never be publicly acknowledged.
We can guess the real reason why with a few figures.

There are 58 Volunteers from the Rising who are buried here; another
48 are Volunteers from the War of Independence: 106 men from the
republican tradition. This is just half the figure for the number of Irish
Catholics and servants of the crown who are buried here, not merely with
no headstones but with no markings to their graves at all. Only the cemetery maps knew the full truth of this extended underground ossuary.

It was an Irish cavalryman, Corporal E. Thomas from Nenagh, of the Royal Irish Dragoon Guards, who fired the first shot of the Great War in August 1914; another cavalryman, Thomas Farrell of Navan, was both last British and Irish soldier to be fatally wounded in that war. His colleague, Corporal Ellison from York was the last British soldier to be killed outright, with moments to go before the ceasefire at 11 a.m. on 11 November 1918.

Farrell's body is buried in Valencienne Cemetery just south of Mons. It offers a useful comparison with Glasnevin, where family discretion – and perhaps even shame – helped keep the secret of this unmarked and unremembered throng. Even in life there was a reluctance to declare the full truth. For example, approximately 0.2 per cent of the residents of Valenciennes served under aliases. Here in Glasnevin the figure is 4 per cent. Just 37 per cent of the soldiers here have family details in the register: the figure for Valenciennes is 80 per cent. And for the seventeen names beginning with 'O', which is most cases in Ireland had only recently been restored as a patronymic, and therefore might stand as a declaration of national identity, only three, or 17 per cent, have family details.

Elisions and deletions are the norm of history making, so we are not unique in deciding not to remember certain things. All societies do the same, consciously or otherwise. A group of men buried here illustrate what I'm talking about. I wonder if their names have ever been recited before. They are Private M. Phibbs. Private Joseph Berry, Private Patrick Duffy, Private M. Johnston, and what these men have in common is that their remains are on the official Commonwealth War Graves list, though of course, for so long without headstones to make their presence here evident, they are not listed in the official catalogue of war-deaths, Soldiers Died in the Great War.

Here we encounter a terrible truth about the truly forgotten soldiers of the Great War: the men of the Labour Corps, which came into existence in January 1917, and into which men were compulsorily drafted from infantry regiments. Because they were not listed as front-line soldiers, they were paid less than gunners, infantry or sappers, and not ceded the rest-time and leave allowed the others. And, as far as I can see, they were worked seven days a week.

Officially, some 5000 British soldiers died in the service of the Labour Corps. For most of these deaths – some 3000 – were not caused by enemy action, or by violence of any kind, but by sickness and exhaustion; that is, they were virtually worked to death, until cardiac exhaustion, rheumatism, pneumonia or tuberculosis made further service impossible. And some 3500 of those listed in SDGW died at home, either from illness contracted at the front, or injury.

That is not the whole story though, for the Commonwealth War Graves Commission accepted many other deaths as appropriate for commemoration after the victims had been discharged from military service for being unfit or wounded beyond recovery. And the Commission lists Labour Corps deaths as 9300 – from which we may deduce that another 4000 men died after discharge, from strained hearts, rheumatic fever and broken bodies. In other words, when of no further use they were discharged so that when they died the War Office was spared the obligation to pay pensions to their families. In all I calculate that some 7000 soldiers were effectively worked to death. These men, in essence military slaves, were subject to martial law and thus the possibility of execution if they resisted or deserted. And if that wasn't bad enough, they were then completely forgotten.

Just fifty-three officers are listed as dying with the Labour Corps – and even here we see the cruel hand of the bureaucratic economies: almost all of them held just temporary commissions; had they lived, they would not have been entitled to the pensions all fully commissioned officers were allowed. Between them they had won just one Military Cross and one Distinguished Conduct Medal. Modest men, unrecognized in life and utterly invisible in death.

In the records of Glasnevin we get to glimpse usually unseen personal tragedies – such as that of Private John Ryan, who in civilian life was a musician. He enlisted as a cavalryman with the South Irish Horse – and of course, as we all now know, there turned out to be little use for cavalry. Instead of joining the 7th battalion of the Royal Irish Regiment, as most of the SIH did, he was transferred to the newly formed Labour Corps in 1917. That year he contracted TB and was sent home – to 41 New Street, Dublin, where he died on 11 November 1917, aged forty-one. He at least is listed in Soldiers Died in the Great War – but what were the cruel vagaries of life that a middle-aged, horse-riding musician should have been turned into a spade-slave, for whom the only escape from military drudgery was death and an unmarked grave in Glasnevin?

However, available evidence suggests that poor Ryan was not typical of the Irish. Contrary to what you might expect, the Irish were not drafted in large numbers into the Labour Corps. For example, twenty-eight

Sheffield-born men died with the Labour Corps, compared to nineteen Dubliners. Admittedly, some Irish infantry battalions were redeployed behind the lines for 'construction work' in the spring and summer of 1918 – duties they detested; even though the 16th Irish Division might have been 'suspect' as Sinn Féin sympathizers, which was why it was disbanded, Irish soldiers generally were still preferred for their fighting qualities

Glasnevin Cemetery, aided by the austere and detailed records that have been kept here, gives us other insights into tragic loss, bureaucratic indifference and national amnesia. Thus we have poor William O'Connor, aged forty-four, of the Royal Dublin Fusiliers, who local officials scrupulously recorded as having died of shellshock in September 1916; he was buried invisibly here but is not even listed as a war-death in SDGW. And we have the quite unspeakable fate of Bernard Moore, from the North Circular Road, Dublin. He joined the Royal Dublin Fusiliers in 1916, but some talent of his was quickly spotted and, aged seventeen, he was transferred to the Machine Gun Corps. On 12 July 1916, at La Boiselle on the Somme, he was hit in the spine by shrapnel and paralyzed from the chest down. He was in due course returned to Ireland to be minded by his brothers and sisters at the family coachworks in 3 North Brunswick Street. He was probably kept there because it was easier to look after him than in the family home with its many steps. Paralyzed and incontinent, he would have stayed for what remained of his life, ended by the merciful intervention of pneumonia in June 1917, aged eighteen. He is not listed in Soldiers Died in the Great War.

Patrick Nolan of the Royal Dublin Fusiliers arrived in France in June 1915. In June 1917 he was sent from the front to Toxteth suffering from 'myalgia' – shorthand for generalized and insufferable agony throughout his body. After a year of probably unsuccessful, certainly unimaginable treatment, he was discharged from the army due to 'infected lungs' in July 1917, with the prognosis that he would need permanent care in a sanatorium. He died at home in May 1918 aged just nineteen. He too is not listed in SDGW.

The only Bartholomew Lynch that I can find in the 1911 Census that would fit the age requirements of what follows was at a boarding school in Mullingar in 1911. His father James was a baker then living in 96 Clanbrassil Street in Dublin, and he was still there when young Bartholomew enlisted in the Royal Dublin Fusiliers under the pseudonym 'J. Hill'. Why, we don't know. But we do know that his boyhood neighbour in 97 Clanbrassil Street, James Melrose, would probably have been aware of the deceit – for he too was a soldier, serving with the Royal Army Medical Corps. He and his wife Annie moved to a tenement in Boyne Street. His health ruined by life in the trenches, young Bartholomew Lynch, serving as J. Hill, was discharged from the army, and on 11 March 1918 died at home, of heart-failure – as so many did. Over a year later his former neighbour James Melrose died of tuberculosis at Our Lady's Hospice, and his remains made the same journey to Glasnevin Cemetery, to be similarly entombed in unsepulchred soil and thereafter forgotten.

Henry Close, an officer in the Dublin Fusiliers, was from a well-to-do Catholic family in Dalkey, his mother a widow who lived off a rental income. His wife Josephine gave birth to a daughter in November 1917, when one third of all birth notices in *The Irish Times* were for children of Irish officers in the British army. Henry Close died of heart disease in 1918, his body consumed by the Glasnevin soil and forgotten. His widow would merely have had a small patch of weeds over which to mourn. When her time came she shared that patch, with its nettles and unheadstoned bones.

One of the Dublin Fusiliers to be buried in Glasnevin encapsulates the fate of the forgotten. Cadet Joseph Simington was the son of works manager of *The Irish Times*, the man responsible for editing the special publication of the newspaper's history of the Rising. Even though *The Irish Times* was then vehemently unionist, its account of the Rising is not merely even-handed but at times strangely sympathetic to the motives of the insurgent leaders. This is particularly evident in the absence in the account of Lieutenant Chalmers about his time as a captive in the GPO, in which he and a couple of Dublin Fusiliers were told to run out of the back, where they were cut down in a volley of gunfire, and apparently killed. This was published in the one of the first editions of the newspaper to appear, but was missing from the *Sinn Féin Rising* handbook. The attack on the Phoenix Park Magazine, and the cold-blooded shooting of young George Playfair, is also absent. Did these deletions indicate a certain editorial sympathy towards the Rising? Certainly, Simington would have been unusual within the newspaper, as a Catholic in a management position.

Whatever the truth, when young Cadet Joseph Simington of the Royal Dublin Fusiliers died in 1918 *The Irish Times* made no mention of his death, and he too went to an unmarked grave. In time the newspaper would embrace and ultimately enforce the amnesia that so systematically and successfully occluded almost all memory of the thousands of Irish dead.

An obscurity conceals the fate of Private J. Kirwan of 183 Parnell Street, who in May 1915 left to catch a train at Amiens Street to rejoin his unit in Belfast. He made it no farther than the North Wall canal basin, where his body was found next day. He clearly preferred to die at his own hand than return to the front. Not even that threat could account for what befell Mark Phibbs of the Leinster Regiment. He cut his throat at home in Russell Square, Drumcondra, in 1919. The only Mark Phibbs in the 1911 Census was a sixteen-year-old grocer's assistant from Corbally, Roscommon, living in Wexford Street, Dublin, listed in neither the Commonwealth War Graves Commission nor Soldiers Died in the Great War.

In the inter-war years, former British soldiers whose families wished to acknowledge their service-history were buried in Grangegorman Cemetery on Blackhorse Avenue. There one will find the graves of Martin Doyle, VC MM, the only holder of Britain's highest military award who was also a member of the IRA. He had won his VC in the battles in September 1918 for a series of actions of almost absurd courage, which involved rescuing wounded soldiers and capturing many of the enemy, plus a troublesome machine-gun and its crew. There are no details of his career in the IRA before he settled down in work with Guinness. He died of poliomyelitis in 1940.

Even more famous was Jack Hunt DSO, DCM, in 1914 a working-class Catholic and former soldier now training the cadets at St Columba's College. Four years later he was an acting Brigadier General who had been recommended for a VC, but who had to settle for a bar to his DSO. It says something about the bizarre, almost dysfunctional priorities that the British army embraced at war's end that Jack Hunt then found himself reduced to the substantive rank of 2nd lieutenant, with a suitably humble pension to match, outranked by men he had commanded in action. Perhaps unexpectedly, one of his best friends in his post-war life was Sir Henry Bellingham, also of the Dublin Fusiliers. His ornate gravestone in Grangegorman offers suitable testimony to the affection and respect with which he was held by his fellow soldiers.

The Second World War saw a return to Glasnevin's habits of subterranean clandestinity – where burials continued, while Grangegorman offered an alternative home. One grave in particular asks a telling question about motivation: air-gunner Sergeant Padraig de Valera McMahon of Munster Street, Phibsborough, died in January 1943, and his apparently disapproving family supplied no details for the cemetery register. Why did this man volunteer to join the most dangerous branch of the British armed services, RAF Bomber Command? The same question arises about Irishmen not buried here such as nineteen-year old Patrick Pearse Murphy from Cork, lost when the HMS *Glorious* battle group was destroyed in June 1940, and RAF navigator Terence de Valera Dignan, killed in action over Germany in January 1943. We can only speculate on the suffering and grief that resulted from such events, as, for example, with the death of Air-Gunner John Whelan, whom we merely know as the foster son of Mrs M. Kenny, aged just nineteen when he was killed on 30 January 1944, one of 192 RAF airmen to die in raids on Berlin that night. Nor should we ever forget the German victims of such raids – hundreds of thousands, burnt alive and blown apart in the murderous raids on what were indisputably civilian targets.

Here too in Glasnevin we see another side to the war: the graves of two Irish Catholic chaplains who died serving the crown. The family of one, Reverend William Gilgunn from County Fermanagh, elected to supply no details of their son in the cemetery register, aged thirty-six when he died. He at least is listed in what is called the Roll of Honour of service deaths during the war, unlike the second chaplain, Thomas Kenny, RAF Volunteer Reserve, who died in September 1945, and is not included in the Roll. Ten per cent of the hundred chaplains who died in this war were Irish – nine from the south and one, Gilgunn – from the north. Kenny's family too declined to supply details of the fate of their son – incidentally, unlike that of his namesake in the RAFVR, and fellow-inhabitant of Glasnevin, Wireless Operator / Air-Gunner Sergeant John Kenny, son of William and Ellen Kenny of Crampton Quay, Dublin, who died of injuries sustained in action and whose body was returned to Dublin for burial.

Auxiliary Territorial Servicewoman Geraldine Mary Fox, who is buried in Glasnevin, gives us a glimpse of the Irish female contribution to Britain's war effort. Some twenty-three Irish women with ATS died, as did thirty Irishwomen of the 188 Queen Alexander Imperial Military Nursing service personnel killed, or 16 per cent, nine of them in a single torpedoing.

So we can see in Glasnevin's lapidary discretion both a metaphor and a memorial to the Irish of the Second World War. The first Irish soldier to be killed liberating the European landmass from the blight of fascist totalitarianism was Major Astley Cooper, of Dundrum, County Tipperary. He is buried along with sixty-two other Irishmen in Catania war cemetery in Sicily. Another fifty Irishmen are buried in Cassino war cemetery, forty-seven in Ranville Cemetery in Normandy, seventy-five in the Reichswald Cemetery, forty-five in Rheinberg, seventeen in Hannover and thirty-three in Berlin – all on active service against the Third Reich.

One of those buried in Reichswald was one of the most outstanding Irish soldiers of the war: Brigadier William 'Jerry' Sheil, DSO and bar, CBE, of Clonee, County Meath. A former gunner, he had gone over as a reserve lieutenant in 1940 when he might easily (and more prudently) have avoided military service. He later served with the 51st Highland Division across North Africa, Italy, Normandy and into Germany. Some years ago one of his soldiers, a Territorial from Glasgow, told me he and his mates – all of them Glasgow Rangers supporters – had never met an Irish Catholic before. The very idea of being commanded by one would once have been simply absurd, but he won them over with his professionalism and passion for the welfare of his men. The darkest hour in the war for them came at its end, when – perhaps typically of him – he gave his driver a break at the wheel of his jeep. As they drove over a hidden mine, Jerry was killed. The driver, sitting in Jerry's usual seat, was uninjured.

As with the First World War, the Labour Corps – renamed with the more exotic title, the Pioneer Corps – continued the ignoble tradition of discharging soldiers after they had nearly been worked to death, and then not including them in the war-lists when the inevitable finally happened. The Army Roll of Honour lists 3484 as having died in the Pioneer Corps, 195 of them Irish. The Commonwealth War Graves Commission acknowledged 4437 Pioneer Corps deaths, an increase of 27 per cent. So, officially 195 Irishmen died with the Corps: but what is the real figure? On the 27 per cent shortfall average, it could well be 248. The following members of the Corps are buried here in Glasnevin, yet are not in the 'Role of Honour': Private Joseph Brazil, husband of Sarah Brazil of Dublin, Private Patrick Fox, forty-two, husband of Brigid Fox of Dublin, Private Patrick Mulvey, husband of Margaret Mulvey of Dublin, and, perhaps most tragic all, Private Michael Hanlon, son of Charles and Teresa, husband of Bridget, who, aged thirty-four, hanged himself at war's end, on 5 October 1945.

For decades these men and women have been forgotten, concealed beneath the unmarbled soil of these acres; now, thanks to the current management of Glasnevin Cemetery, they are finally being remembered and honoured for the cause that – for whatever reason – they served and for which they died.

16. *From* An Irishman's Diary

I. REMEMBRANCE SUNDAY
20 October 1984

There it sits, right in the heart of the national psyche: implacable, unregenerate, unforgiving, forgetting no past injustice; ever-sensitive of betrayal, it suspects treachery in every attempt to modify the received canon of nationalism and perceives only vile hearsay in every attempt to embrace broader notions of Irishness than those exemplified by the men in 1916. One flag, one people, one form of nationalism, one single, unwavering loyalty, one noble band of heroes, and in effect, one permissible religion. The Truth.

It is one seamless garment, admitting no adulteration by other cloths. And those born on the same island who do not choose that particular weave automatically become part of some alien fabric, forever isolated. There can be no accommodation with those who belong to that alien fabric, no reconciliation, nor even peace. For they do not acknowledge the single Truth.

World wars come and go. Whole populations are herded to camps set in distant forests, where they are vaporized into the skies over central Europe; cities are levelled and their populations burnt alive; armies in strange uniforms strut in other people's capitals, and country after country is enslaved, their treasures looted, their peoples subjugated, their patriots murdered.

But in Ireland there remains one Truth, unique and inviolable, one band of heroes, solely one cause to serve: and those who wear any uniform not associated with that Truth cease somehow to be Irish; their valour neglected; their deaths ignored. For such matters are unrelated to the Truth; and memorials to such men are a violation of the Truth, which allows of service to solely one flag, one loyalty, one form of nationalism – one tribe.

And the very essence of this Truth is hatred – hatred for England, to be sure, and Englishness, but more than that: the real hatred is for those who do not share that hatred. Traitors. Lackeys. Worse than the Brits.

We have been seeing a great deal of the Truth of late, all to do with the army's participation in last year's Remembrance Service in St Patrick's Cathedral. That event has been the subject of such misunderstanding, and, much worse, such deliberate misrepresentation, that I despair. For the whole business arose out of a desire for reconciliation, no more; and in how many countries in the world would a desire for reconciliation lead to so much acrimony?

And the acrimony is there because the Truth is at work. Though by no means are all those opposed to army involvement in Remembrance Sunday motivated by hatred. They are disturbed at what they feel is a submission of national honour to a foreign flag and a foreign organization.

If that were true in spirit or deed, I would agree with their objections; but it is not true. There was only one national flag in evidence in the St Patrick's service, last year, and that is our own; and it was not, as one writer recently suggested, in an obscure part of the cathedral. It was next to the pulpit.

But I recognize an honest doubt is at work for many people on this matter, and uneasiness that the army and the flag are not being put to proper purpose. I assure them; if they were present at St Patrick's they would almost certainly recognize there was no ground for such qualms.

But for the adherents of the Truth, there can be no such reassurance. Their hatred burns unquenchably. No quarter to be given, no ground yielded. Simple desires for reconciliation are incomprehensible to the devotee of the Truth.

For them, there is the grim litany of history, the Nicene Creed of the Truth – the Penal Laws, the Fencibles and their pitch-caps of 1798, the evictions and the Famine. Coercion, the Curragh Mutiny, the 1916 executions, the Black and Tans, Partition, and the North; all unfinished business on the agenda, and business which can never be finished while the Truth holds the memory fast.

And it seems that the simple desire of Brian Clark, the British Legion organizer, and the Taoiseach to sponsor a bit of reconciliation has failed thanks in large degree to the Truth. Where an attempt to reconcile causes controversy, reconciliation is defeated. The Truth still has a veto.

At the time of writing this I do not know whether the army will be actively participating in the Remembrance Sunday commemorations. But I shall certainly be present in St Patrick's that day, for mine is a typical family. One close relative served in the post office garrison in 1916; his father was in the British army unit besieging the GPO. Another relative, whose father had been an RIC man, was an active IRA man in 1919-1921 and a close companion of Charlie Dalton, brother of Emmet. Another relative joined the British army during the Second World War. He is buried in North Africa – his brother subsequently was to become Fianna Fail attorney general. Another relative served with the Irish Guards right through the drive through France, Belgium, Holland and northern Germany, and rather surprisingly, survived. The fortieth anniversaries of the deaths of his colleagues and friends have been rather frequent of late.

It is not dishonour for the army to honour any such men before the national flag.

II. ST COLUMBA'S COLLEGE AND THE GREAT WAR
27 April 1993

Perhaps few institutions reveal more about a society than its schools, and perhaps no school reflects the changes in Irish society over the past century more than St Columba's College, which this year celebrates its 150th birthday.

Take up a copy of the splendid *A Portrait of St Columba's College* by Patrick Wyse Jackson and Ninian Falkiner, and look at the sections covering the start of the century. The school is 100 per cent male and 100 per cent Church of Ireland. Not even a Methodist or Presbyterian darkened the door, for those were days of deep class and religious sensibility. And just look at the photograph of the cadet corps in 1914, all those well-scrubbed Protestant boys from nice families throughout Ireland, often sons of the rectory, Cecils and Percivals and Archibalds, under the stern command of H. Apil sitting there in the middle of the picture.

But there is a germ of things to come, situated just on the outskirts of the picture, on the very flank of the rows of boys, not sitting down with the other adults, but standing, almost an afterthought. That person is Jack Hunt, the drill sergeant. Oh, how the boys must have mocked him behind his back, this working-class Catholic, the son of an unskilled labourer. How they must have scorned his manners and his 'abominable' Liberties accent. What fun they must have had in the dorm attempting to mimic his parade-ground voice and having to stuff pillows into their mouths to suppress their mirth.

Weeks after that photograph was taken the world was a different place and the school was about to embark upon a journey of travail and sorrow equalled by probably no other school in the land. Nearly 400 pupils enlisted for service in Europe's civil war, for such a small school an extra-ordinary number. Somebody else enlisted too, Jack Hunt, their old drill-master, back in the colours with his old regiment, the Dublin Fusiliers.

There now. Look at that picture on page forty-nine; how many of them are doomed? Of course the first Columbans to die are not in the picture. They would have been professional soldiers. Probably the first was Charles Rodney Spedding, who fought with the Irish Rifles and died on 19 September. The next day another Columban, Robert Burton Benison, was killed with the Connaught Rangers. By now the joy that had greeted the outbreak of war was diluted as the names of the dead were read out at school assembly.

Some ex-Columbans marched off to Landsdowne Road to join the footballers' D Company of the Dublin Fusiliers. One of them was Arthur Crookshank from Dundrum, killed on the evil ridge of Kiritich Tepe Sirt in Gallipoli. Other Columbans were to be among the first victims of gas in warfare; James Neville Herbert Murphy, gassed to death with the Dublin Fusiliers at Ypres on 10 May 1915; a week later followed by Ralph William Gore Hinds with the Inniskillings.

A year later gas killed Eric Edge Beatty and by this time the harvest of Columbans had grown enormously. And 1 July 1916 lay ahead, the first day of the Somme, which was to claim Alfred Middleton Blackwood

Rose-Cleland with the Dublins and, through its three months of Calvary to the last day, when Hugh Gordon Stamper of Newtownmountkennedy, also with the Dublins, was killed.

And what of Jack Hunt, the working-class lad with the Liberties accent? He is now a commissioned officer, adjutant, no less, of the Eighth Dublin Fusiliers; beneath him are all sorts of Columbans, who are doubtless baffled at this turn of events. By the end of the conflict sixty-seven Columbans were dead, a calamitous loss for an already demographically declining community. Some of them are in the photograph: Nathaniel Hone of the Irish Rifles, aged eighteen, killed on the first day of the Somme, certainly is. So too is Herbert Coles Kennedy, son of Reverend H.B. Kennedy of Corrig Castle, Kingstown, who died of wounds at war's end, aged nineteen.

But no Columban equals their drill master in achievement. Jack Hunt, the labourer's son, is now an acting Brigadier General, much decorated by Britain and by France.

Four years later, and another war briefly visits St Columba's – irregulars en route for sanctuary as the Civil War breaks out. Relations are clearly cordial. They pose for photographs, and the boys gather around for the jape. What a lark. And, while the photographs of anti-Treaty IRA men are being taken (miraculously they and a receipt for bicycles from Liam Ui Cleirigh survived to make it to the published history), Jack Hunt is on his way to the Curragh to take charge of training the new Free State Army, the foes of the anti-Treaty lads in the Columba's photographs.

What better man – private, sergeant, adjutant, major, battalion commander, brigade general – to train a new army, and, amazingly and sadly, completely forgotten today. But the bedrock of that army, its culture of discipline and courage that have been testified to all over the world, was in part laid by Jack Hunt.

Move on from the photograph of the cadets to the sixth form of 1991. There is a Pedlow there, as there almost certainly was in the 1914 picture (that Pedlow, a Dublin Fusilier, died a month before the war's end). And just out of the picture in the 1991 shot, doubtless, is Ninian Falkiner; his kinsman George Falkiner was most probably in the original picture, for which there are no names, and was killed under Jack Hunt's command in the mud and slime before Vampire Farm, near Ypres, in August 1917.

III. SHOT AT DAWN
12 September 1989

The names have never appeared before. They are not on the official lists for the war dead. They are not on Ireland's Memorial Records for the Great War. In death they have achieved a noneness that any totalitarian state would envy. From that noneness, that undeserved, inhuman oblivion into which they have been cast, the time has now come to rescue them.

These are the men who died before the firing squads in the Great War. Of the 312 soldiers the British army disposed of by that method, mostly for the offences of desertion of cowardice, the following were Irishmen or were serving in Irish regiments: T. Cummins, A. Smythe, B. O'Connell, Irish Guards; J. Brennan and B. McGeehan, King's Liverpool Regiment; J. Cassidy, R. Hope, T. Hogan, J. Seymour and J. Wishart, Inniskilling Fusiliers; P. Sands, S. McBride, J. Crozier, J.E. McCracken and J. Templeton, Irish Rifles; G. Hannan and J. Carey, Irish Fusiliers; T. Hope, H. Hendricks and P.J. Downey, the Leinsters; T. Davis and J. Graham, the Munster Fusiliers; A. Rickman and S. Byrne, Dublin Fusiliers; J. Wilson, Canadian Expeditionary Force.

The injustice that befell these men was twofold. The first was their actual fate of being brought before the wavering rifles of their comrades at dawn. The second has been the unchanging attitudes of the British authorities then and ever since. They have become non-persons. The files of their courts-martial remain closed. Their names are omitted from all lists of the war dead. It was then and has remained a quite monstrous scandal.

It is a scandal that has been falteringly peered at through the years as successive authors have tried to establish details of the horror stories associated with those men's deaths. But since the files were closed, there appeared to be no way the full story could be told.

The judge, Anthony Babbington, some years ago was given permission to read certain files provided he did not name the victims; but he had access to only a limited number of files, and research into the victims' genuine family circumstances could only be possible with knowledge of the men's names.

Nonetheless, the account that Judge Babbington wrote was powerful enough to compel one to read it through tears of rage. Yet the identity of those men remained a secret.

No more. Two researchers, Julian Putkowski and Julian Sykes, have cracked open the secrecy surrounding those executions, simply by exploiting the blind cumbrousness of bureaucracy. For although there was no list of the executed, the authorities did produce a complete medal list of all those who served in the Great War. Every soldier who served – and there were millions – was given at least a general service medal, even posthumously; except, that is, those men who were executed. And against their names is the remark: executed.

From that bureaucratic indiscretion began the two Julians' enormous research project, which has taken them over twenty man-years in labour, and which is shortly to be published under the title *Shot at Dawn* by Wharncliffe Publishing of Barnsley in Yorkshire. It is a devastatingly meticulous examination of the workings of a military machine, quite noticeably more brutal than its equivalent in the French or German armies.

'It was a long job simply because nobody gives anything away on the subject,' said Julian Sykes. 'Even the indexes to the files are not available. People want to keep the whole matter under wraps, and nobody in authority will say otherwise. I put it down to ignorance, arrogance and old-fashioned ideas.'

As the two Julians progressed with their research they kept on thinking that they had come to the very worst possible case; only to be proven wrong the next day. Of accounts of shell-shocked soldiers, who very possibly had heard of the deaths of their brothers in action, breaking under the strain and deserting, if only very briefly; of how, overwhelmed by the circumstances of their court-martial, they would decline to give evidence on their own behalf, and of how incompletely and indifferently they might be defended by an officer with no knowledge of either military of civilian law.

And then sentenced to death. That sentence was reviewed all the way up to the commander in chief, for the greater part of the war. Douglas Haig. And in 312 cases the outcome would be execution.

Take for example Private Hope, of the Leinsters, from Longford, who deserted in 1915. He told the court he had done so on hearing his two brothers had been killed in action. He was not defended. He was shot in February 1915. An even more astounding, not to say wicked, decision touched upon the fate of twenty-year-old Private Patrick J. Downey, from Limerick, who was serving with the Leinster Regiment in Salonika. He refused to stand-in for parade, and then refused to put on his cap; and he too court-martialled, and the presiding officer, his own CO, decided that this wartime volunteer-soldier should be shot, because 'morale in the unit was poor'. The officer in question was Captain Robert Otway Mansergh, of Rock Lodge, Ballyhooley, County Cork, kinsman of Senator Martin Mansergh.

Downey was a survivor of the Gallipoli campaign. So too was Albert Rickman. A non-Irish soldier with the Royal Dublin Fusiliers, he had taken part in the famous V–Beach landings, and then fought in the far more ghastly campaign that followed. Futile is a word freely used about the Great War but it wholly applies to Gallipoli. One thousand enlisted soldiers of the 1st batallion, Royal Dublin Fusiliers, had landed in April: by the time of withdrawl, some 572 were dead. The remains of the batallion were transferred to France, and on the first day of the battle of the Somme it again suffered several hundred casualties.

The next day, with the battalion was recovering its dead and wounded, Rickman deserted. And he too in due course was caught, tried and shot; and it is almost certain that his family in Hampshire was never informed of the monstrous injustice done to their son.

The cover up concerning the killings of those men even extended to their death certificates, which in the cause of death column might just record the illuminating item: dead. The two Julians had to perform huge amounts of work to uncover the mountain of detail in *Shot at Dawn*, sifting through thousands of birth and death certificates at Somerset House.

It is a devastating indictment of military injustice.

And thus we may add to the list of the Irish dead of the Great War another two dozen or so names; perhaps those who are responsible for Islandbridge Memorial Park could place an addendum to the existing records, and so end the condition of noneness of the men who were shot at dawn.

IV. WILLIE REDMOND
7 November 1998

'What I want to ask, in all simplicity, is this – whether, in face of the tremendous conflict which is now raging, whether, in view of the fact that apart from every other consideration, the Irish people, North as well as South, are upon the side of the Allies and against the German pretension today, is it not possible from this war to make a new start; whether it is not possible on your side, and on ours as well, to let the dead past bury its dead, and to commence a brighter and a newer and a friendlier era between the countries?'

Thus spoke William Redmond MP in March 1917 during his last speech to the House of Commons before departing for the Western Front. His heartfelt words moved the Commons deeply.

None of the members listening to him on that last parliamentary day of his life could possibly have imagined that the war that had consumed so many lives, and was to consume so many more, including that of the impassioned speaker before them, far from constituting a new start from reconciliation in Ireland was to provide merely fresh, and often vigorously exploited, opportunities for misunderstanding, hatred and murder.

Willie Redmond's unit, the Royal Irish Regiment, was serving near Ypres with the 16th Irish Division. That division was largely drawn from the pre-war Irish National Volunteers; and the division alongside it was the 36th Ulster Division, drawn from the pre-war Ulster Volunteer Force. To the surprise of outsiders, the two divisions got on exceedingly well, though it was of course no surprise to their members.

Aside from the Irishness they held in common – and unionist identity in 1917 as still an emphatically Irish quality – their morale was high. Both divisions had fought in fierce battles in 1916, with 16th Division casualties (nearly 2700 dead) actually higher than those of the 36th (nearly 2000).

They were distinctly different from the other British army division. An English officer with the Connaught Rangers, Rowland Feilding, said of his men that they would do nothing if ordered; if asked, they would do anything. 'I can never express in writing what I feel about [them],' he said in a letter home. 'Freezing or snowing, or drenching rain; always smothered with mud; you may ask any one of them, any moment of night or day, 'Are you cold?' or 'Are you wet?' and you will always get but one answer. The Irishman will reply – always with a smile – "Not too cold, sir," or "Not too wet, sir."'

He was as much impressed by his Irish officers, cheery, friendly, open towards outsiders, and his trench mortar officer, a former barrister on the Midland Circuit, James Patrick Roche, born in Kerry, but then resident in Monasterevin, who he regarded as the wittiest raconteur he had ever met, as well as being a superb soldier: 'As bridge mortar officer, a genius.'

Whenever Roche was about to utter one of his quips, a small grin would settle on his face, lingering afterward when the jest was complete.

Perhaps the finest soldier in the 36th Ulster Division alongside the 16th was Henry Gallaugher who, during the fighting on the Somme the previous summer, had personally killed six snipers, later collecting twenty-eight injured men from No Man's Land.

His letters home to Manorcunninghman were farmer's letters and spoke not so much of war but of the fields of Donegal and the prospects for the coming flax harvest.

That spring of 1917 the two Irish divisions were put through intensive training for the coming assault on the German-held Flanders villages of Messines and Wijshaete, beneath which sappers had burrowed miles of tunnels to plant a score of huge mines beneath enemy trenches.

They played football together, and officers visited one another's messes, sometimes discussing their political differences, and by all accounts ending their conversations in the best of humour. They were confident young men, rightly proud of their military prowess and their identity.

On the morning of 7 June 1917 the men of the two divisions prepared to go over the top. Some of the Dublin Fusiliers said a decade of the Rosary for the Germans they were sure were going to die in the coming minutes. At 3.10 a.m., while the nightingales were still singing in Rossignol Wood, nearly a millions pounds of high explosive detonated beneath the enemy positions, obliterating numerous strong points, and causing one of the largest man-made explosions so far in history.

Simultaneously, British artillery opened fire on German positions, and the two Irish divisions rose from the trenches and advanced over the ground still quaking from the detonations, through the falling debris, which killed many of them.

Surviving German artillery and the redoubtable German machine -gunners opened up on the advancing soldiers, and in their separate engagements Redmond and Gallaugher were hit, the latter's arm being shattered. Both insisted on continuing. 'This'll do me rightly,' declared Gallaugher as he threw away his useless rifle and continued his advance. Both were hit again. Redmond was brought back to his lines by stretcher-bearers from the 36th Ulster Division, under the command of a Lieutenant Paul, from Howth. Both Gallaugher and Redmond died of their wounds. Paul himself was to die shortly afterwards.

Casualties were, by the deplorable standards of that time, remarkably light, but a single shell had fallen into a group of Irish officers. Lieutenant Col. Feilding came across their corpses and lifted the sandbag covering a face. 'It was discoloured by the explosion of the shell that had killed him, but otherwise was quite untouched, and it wore the same slight smile that in life used to precede and follow his wonderful sallies.'

Captain James Patrick Roche MC, aged twenty-nine, son of Stephen and Elsie Roche, of Monasterevin, brilliant wit and a gallant soldier, was dead.

Both divisions suffered cruel losses, but their spirits were high. They had participated in a stunning victory; they could not know that ahead of them, side by side yet again, lay the pure Calvary of Third Ypres, where they were – in common with so many British divisions – to be squandered in one of the most appalling campaigns of history.

But in a way even more grievous was to be their place in mythology; the Ulsters were already on their way to immorality within the unionist population of Ireland, but the 16th Irish Division, composed overwhelmingly of Irish nationalists and whose casualties had exceeded those of the Ulsters by the time it was disbanded in 1918, was destined for four score years of neglect and amnesia. Indeed, many of its members were to be murdered at home simply because they had served in the British army.

Flanders was where together the two divisions were victorious; Flanders, two months later, was where, in the smothering and bitter swamplands of Frezenberg Ridge, they were united in defeat; Flanders is where, next Wednesday, some eighty years after the end of the war which consumed so many Irish volunteers of all political colours, their common sacrifice will be commemorated jointly by the heads of state of Britain and Ireland; and Flanders is where Willie Redmond's farewell words to the Commons seem finally to be coming true.

V. WILLIAM ORPEN
11 April 1996

What happened to William Orpen? How did he come to be so neglected, though he is clearly the greatest Irish artist of the twentieth century?

Others of his generation, such as McGonigal and Keating and Yeats, remained cherished and in the forefront of popular consciousness.

But Orpen vanished, until that is, Bruce Arnold's magnificent, reputation-rescuing biography of 1981, with the accompanying retrospective exhibition at the National Gallery.

What happened to Orpen was, of course, a fate that he shared with much else from the period in which he worked. It was the time when a new state was being created, and those who had identified with the historical processes that led to the formation of that state came to be incorporated in popular mythology and common memory.

And those who did not, unionists like Orpen, constitutional nationalists and those policemen, civil servants, soldiers, who had served the former regime, vanished from the *dramatis personae* of Irish collective recall.

All societies do this, picking and choosing their heroes by conscious and unconscious processes, abandoning certain individuals to obscurity, for no clear reason other than that they did not fit the required templates of historical suitability.

And so Ireland forgot the one true artist of unquestionable genius whose works will be collected and cherished by non-Irish people in one hundred years' time.

Nobody seeing the latest Orpen publication, the reprint of *An Onlooker in France* (1921, 1996), could be in any doubt about his greatness as an artist. His genius shines through every brushstroke, every touch of pencil on a line drawing, every light he places in the eye of a sitter.

He had lightness of touch and seriousness of purpose simultaneously; he was witty and sombre, had a sublime sense of composition, and technically was gloriously skilled.

But of course these skills, though heaven sent, could achieve nothing unless refined and improved on so that each line represented an expression of artistic intention, executed according to intellectual principles that the artist himself understood.

This is one of the reasons Orpen is a joy to behold. The mind intends, the eye envisages, the hand performs and, in performing, creates something new that feeds the mind, hand and eye that created it. That is what one feels whenever one contemplates an Orpen work – the sheer dynamisms of the artistic process.

That is the reason even those potentially dull portraits of the seated, posing generals contain so much to enchant: creative genius at work. And according to *An Onlooker in France*, more than mere creative genius.

When Orpen was painting General Plumer, a buffoonish-looking figure who was also the most brilliant general of his time, Plumer's cockney batman insisted on making his own contribution to the portrait.

Just as Orpen declared the general was perfect as he was, the batman spoke up. 'No he ain't, not by a long chalk,' and proceeded to pull out the creases in Plumer's tunic, saying, '"Ere, you just sit up proper – not all 'unched up the way you are. What would Her Ladyship say if I let you be pained that way?"'

Later the batman returned and laid a hand on Orpen's shoulder, saying, 'Look up at me.' Orpen obliged while the batman scrutinized the work.

'Won't do,' he sniffed. 'You wants keeping up to the mark,' promptly vanishing and then returning with a huge glass of port.

Thus was the portrait of Herbert Plumer begun, and pretty much thus was it completed. It is outwardly a straightforward enough composition. But there is a great and gentle humour in the eyes. It is a true reflection on his character: there was not a man more concerned about the welfare of the men he led than Plumer.

Orpen's greatness shines in the quick sketch of the soldier in the dentist's chair or the more carefully-composed works called 'Scenes from the Trenches' – the shell-shocked Highlander, the naked, insane figure of a man who has been blown up, or the Dubliner in the South Irish Horse, resting on his way to Arras.

Some of his war work was meticulously precise – a drawing of a heavy gun and its tractor-tow is almost photographic in its detail; yet some of his watercolours are impressionistic in their vigour and use of light.

And some of his work in this volume must constitute some of the great and most devastatingly accurate portrayal of war – 'The Madwoman of Doual,' with the eponymous figure sitting amid the ruins of her town, a surviving crucifix on a fragment of wall behind her and around her the assorted figures of baffled townsfolk and a brace of indifferent, exhausted soldiers – provides a truly haunting, unforgettable vision of the lunacy Orpen was witnessing as an official war artist.

Orpen was much more than that, of course, both before and after the hostilities; but the humanitarianism that informed his art was never more evident than during this era. He came to worship the ordinary soldiers he was painting.

He could write, too.

Of the Somme in summer he said, 'The dreary, dismal mud was baked white and pure – dazzling white. White daisies, red poppies and a blue flower, great masses of them, stretched for miles and miles. The sky was a dark blue and the whole air, up to a height of forty feet, thick with butterflies …

'Through the masses of white butterflies, blue dragonflies darted around; high up the larks sang; higher still the aeroplanes droned. Everything shimmered in the heat. Clothes, guns, all that had been left in confusion when the war passed on, had now been baked by the sun into one wonderful combination of colour – white, pale grey and pale gold …'.

VI. MENIN GATE AND MARY MCALEESE
18 November 1998

The moment that spoke most powerfully to the future came after the opening of the Round Tower at the Peace Park at Messen, when the two bands marched together to the nearby town hall. There they were, the No. 1 Band of the Army of the Irish Republic, the kilted pipers of both traditions almost indistinguishably cocky in their saffron swagger as they played 'Killaloe'. Wonderful.

But there were still hard blows for ecumenists. For example, no SDLP anywhere; army buglers were not permitted to play the 'Last Post' at the Menin Gate; and Foreign Affairs had declined the invitation to the President to lay a wreath during the Menin memorial service. Moreover, there were wreaths galore at the next Peace Park from unionist-controlled councils in the North; even a personally laid wreath from David Trimble for the nationalist 16th Division sixty miles away on the Somme – but no wreaths at all from the SDLP nor from any councils in the Republic.

So is this what reconciliation is all about? That outsiders are expected to participate in the authorized ceremonies of Ireland, but that our President, or our army, is not expected to join those outsiders in their places and services of memorial? That the SDLP remains absent from both? In all of our reconciliations with those we have been opposed to, must we not merely travel to those places unexamined and uncommemorated within our own political cultures, even as we make comparable journeys to other people's sensitivities?

We are told that President McAleese was not allowed to lay a wreath at Menin Gate because there was to be an imperial ceremony there. 'Imperial'? Not so imperial that the Indians, the Sri Lankans, the Bangladeshis felt they could not lay wreaths; not so imperial that the ANC government of South Africa felt unable to lay wreaths to South Africa's own graveless thousands, black and white; not so imperial that clusters of turbaned Sikhs could not mumuringly gather and touch the names of the sepoys and havildars lost on the Flanders swamplands and now carved imperishably on the stones of the memorial.

Our President seems to have had none of the difficulty of the mandarins of Foreign Affairs in making the journeys her office and her own humanity demands of her; and the very great pity of it all is that there is no radio or television record of her greatest moment, which came not during the ceremonial opening of the tower, with King Albert and Queen Elizabeth (which was comprehensively televised) but later, at Messen town hall, after the military march back from the Peace Park.

The cold words written on a page cannot convey the moral and emotional power of the President's speech. She was truly majestic. She did not lecture, hector or moralize, but her words were at once but gentle and firm, kind but strong, as she spoke of the men who, as she herself said, were doubly tragic: they fell fighting oppression in Europe, and their memory fell victim to a war for independence at home in Ireland. She is a north Belfast Catholic and nationalist, and the Royal Irish Regiment present for her opening of the Peace Tower contains in its entirety the Ulster Defence Regiment so distrusted by people of her background. What greater evidence could there be of her own full and unequivocal enthusiasm for our long overdue rapprochement of history than this?

She is not alone. Many Irish soldiers had come at their own expense to be present, in uniform, both for the memorial service at the Menin Gate that morning and for the opening of the Memorial Park that afternoon, not in criticism of the splendid traditions of their own army, but merely to acknowledge the courage and sacrifice of an earlier generation of Irish soldiers; and their commander in chief did them proud. Is it wrong to hope that representatives of our army will in the future march with the armies of all the other nations of Europe to commemorate the dead – our dead and theirs – of the Great War?

Regardless of that, one deeply painful truth must be considered: the uniform of the army brass section frankly resembles that of a colliery band from Merthyr Tydfil on a wet day during a miners' strike in 1948. It certainly compared horribly with the dashing uniforms and headdress of the Royal Irish. Is there some unwritten code that detects military virtue in sartorial mediocrity? If so, it was violated splendidly and comprehensively by the differently uniformed army pipers who in style and military bearing were the match and more of their opposite numbers in the Royal Irish. To be sure, getting it right for the brass will not come cheaply; but nor, I'm sure, does getting it wrong.

One spectator at this affair has for many years written of the disgraceful neglect of the Irish of the Great War, though naturally never seeking public acknowledgment for his. He certainly did not expect any mention from the President, about whom he had been less than courteous, but he did rather wistfully hope some passing reference to his role over twenty years might have been made by some other voice during the ceremonies. Not a sausage. The glory lay elsewhere, and he became as invisible as once had been those he had written about.

VII. EUROPE'S CIVIL WAR
11 November 1993

It is only because we view the First World War through the uniquely horrible lens of the Second World War that we do not see the Great War for what it was: politically the most destructive war in the history of civilization. Four empires – Romanov, Hohenzollern, Habsburg and

Ottoman – came crashing down at its conclusion and the unresolved issue of European domination in due course helped bring down two more, the French and the British.

Europe in 1914 entered a period of flux that has not yet passed. The First World War was the first step in the creation of the American empire.

Seventy-five years on, since the war ended, that empire is now beginning to wane, and the centre of gravity of imperial ambition is shifting east, to Japan and, more impressively, to China.

The political states of democratic Germany, Finland, Poland, Ireland, Czechoslovakia, Austria, Hungary, Yugoslavia and the Soviet Union came into existence in the aftermath of the war. Another, Israel, was conceived though not yet born. Others, Syria, Lebanon, Iraq, took shape under new masters. European statesmen then thought permanence had been achieved.

The reverse has been the case. Germany, Poland, Austria and Hungary have since changed beyond recognition. Irish boundaries are still bloodily disputed. Czechoslovakia and Yugoslavia are no more, the Jewish populations of central Europe have been exterminated and the millions of ethnic Germans of Mitteleuropa, the cultural architects of the region, have been murdered or been herded back to Germany.

And the sad and sorry territories of the Soviet Union in the aftermath of the war were only beginning a journey of almost insupportable suffering and death that even yet gives no sign of ending.

The Europe of the Empires that began the war was one in which only France was not ruled by a monarchy; European states were largely multi-ethnic, and, by subsequent standards, extraordinarily peaceful, had virtually no secret police or intelligence agencies, pensions, private insurance, private telephones, vacuum cleaners, domestic electricity or racism, other than anti-Semitism; and outside Russia, even that was almost entirely nonviolent. There were seven postal deliveries a day. Even clerks had servants. The franchise – where it was meaningful, that is in France, the United Kingdom, Italy and Scandinavia – excluded women, as did most paid employment, especially skilled. The poor were grindingly, wickedly poor; the rich were comparably contrastingly rich.

It was an international Europe in which passports were virtually unknown and unnecessary. French was the language of international politics and diplomacy. Throughout European societies ran incredibly delicate fissures of class distinction. The ocean-going steamship characterized

Europe perfectly: stokers toiled like coolies in the abomination of the holds, but a stoker, first class, lorded it over a stoker, second class, a mere worm in comparison. And so the class distinction proceeded upwards by minute but awful degree until it reached the luxuriant splendours of the ornamental castle of drones.

It is not surprising that such societies engendered murderous class hatreds. Throughout the multi-ethnic empires of Ottoman, Hohenzollern, Habsburg and Romanov, in which nationality meant nothing and loyalty everything, another and more potent force than class was stirring in its nest, and has stayed with us to this day, flailing and vicious: the aspiration that political boundaries should be synonymous with those of the tribe, particularly and ungenerously defined.

Socialism, feminism, nationalism were all gnawing in the vitals of these ethnically tolerant but politically reactionary empires as they collided in 1914. Few in authority thought it would be a long war. They were wrong.

It was Part One of the Great European Civil War of 1914-1945. When it erupted, mankind's killing machines had the range of an artillery or naval shell – twenty miles or so. Aircraft were kites powered by motorcycle engines, at best able to lift two men a couple of thousand feet for a few miles. The British had about fifty of them. Battlefield communications were by flags. Foot soldiers advanced to take position, their path cleared by cavalry. Battleships ruled the seas.

Just four years later all was changed. Appalling, unthinkable technologies had transformed war and mankind forever. Killing range had changed from the score of miles of an artillery shell to four-engined, seven-man Handley Page bombers capable of dropping over a ton of bombs on Berlin a thousand miles away from East Anglia. The British alone possessed 22,000 combat aeroplanes. Communications had been revolutionized. Radio-telephones had appeared; so, too, had complicated devices that could tap distant telephones. Cavalry was militarily extinct. Enemy positions were taken by steel, by artillery, by 'tanks', a concept and a word unknown in 1914, and by the even more revolutionary and unheralded ground-attack aircraft directed by said radio-telephone.

By 1918 submarines and aircraft carriers, another entirely new term and concept since 1914, had usurped the strategic authority of the seas, though the battleship did not know it yet. The greatest revolution in the history of war had just taken place. The invention of the strategic rocket by the Germans and the release of the abominable secrets of the atom by the allies in the Second World War merely added a layer, and a virtually unusable arsenal, to the means of warfare created in the four years after 1914. Every conventional war since 1918 has employed the principles established then.

New consensuses were forged in that war, not least in the English-speaking world, that it was the final war. Other and more realistic consensuses emerged; for instance, that the rat-infested hovels of major European cities were unacceptable homes for returning soldiers. A political ruling class that had been subalterns in the trenches transformed the nature of politics. Allied with a reformist, rather than revolutionary, trade union movement, it created welfare states throughout Europe.

Women were freed from domestic service to work in factories once men had been press-ganged into the armies of Europe.

Different countries remembered the war differently. The British created a myth of a lost generation and a war to end all wars: the French, with twice as many dead, remembered and repined. Neither country could fight another war unaided.

The Germans, incredibly, proved to have the stomach for more war, largely by forgetting that the German Grand Army had been defeated in – though not driven from – the field by the British in particular. The Germans blamed their defeat, instead, on the Jews, who were, in fact, among their greatest patriots. A Jewish officer gave Hitler his Iron Cross.

The Americans, whose battlefield contribution had been relatively negligible (and thus casualties light) forgot that too, and were convinced they won the war. Accordingly, none of the self-doubt and terror of casualties, which assailed the British and French when the European civil war re-erupted in 1939, worried the USA high command when it was induced to join the fighting in 1941.

And such simple human considerations certainly never troubled the high command of the Soviet Union, which had been liberated from tiresome and effete bourgeois scruples by the Marxist-Leninist putsch of October 1917, subsequently falsified as a revolution. The techniques of authoritarianism, of social discipline, of industrialized murder, perfected by the Marxists in the post-Romanov regime, were infinitely worse than anything the much-reviled czars had done. They were copied in detail by the Nazis and remain a helpful blueprint for tyranny anywhere.

Yet, seventy-five years on, some lessons seem to have been learned: but as foreigners again burn alive in Germany, who can say which ones? French and German leaders hold hands at Verdun, and a Franco-German-Belgian army brigade stands by to repel, well, somebody.

Certain words still echo with sickening resonances: the Somme is no longer a river, a poppy is no longer just a flower, and gas will never again be a friendly means of lighting and cooking.

We cannot, in our tenure on this planet, unlearn the techniques of murder we mastered in less than half a decade . It is not just in Bosnia that the reverberations of the Great War rock the ground beneath the feet of humanity. The war to end all wars lives with us yet.

APPENDIX

FATALITIES AMONGST NCOS & ENLISTED MEN
IN IRISH INFANTRY REGIMENTS, 1914–1918

THESE FIGURES DO NOT INCLUDE COMMISSIONED OFFICERS,
OR IRISHMEN IN OTHER INFANTRY BATTALIONS, OR IN RAMC,
ENGINEERS, GUNNERS, ET CETERA

IG = Irish Guards	RIrRg = Royal Irish Regiment
RDF = Royal Dublin Fusiliers	LR = Leinster Regiment
RIrF = Royal Irish Fusiliers	CR = Connaught Rangers
RInnF = Royal Inniskilling Fusiliers	RIrRi = Royal Irish Rifles
RMF = Royal Munster Fusiliers	

1914									
	IG	RDF	RIrF	RInnF	RMF	RIrRg	LR	CR	RIrRi
AUG	–	47	25	39	91*	50	–	20	7
AUGUST 6TH. HMS *AMPHION* SUNK. SOME TWENTY IRISH SEAMEN ARE KILLED									
AUGUST 20TH. PRIVATE JAMES RYAN KILLED BY A TRAIN ON SENTRY DUTY AT FOTA. FIRST IRISH SOLDIER KILLED ON DUTY									
24TH MAY, RETREAT FROM MONS. LT MAURICE DEASE OF WESTMEATH WINS FIRST VC									
*27TH, 2ND MUNSTERS IN LAST STAND AT ETREUX									
SEPT	63 *	13	14	28	07	37	04	61*	37
*IRISH GUARDS AND CONNAUGHT RANGERS LOSE HEAVILY DURING THE BATTLE OF THE AISNE									
OCT	33	18	43	76	03	183*	140#	56	204
*2ND ROYAL IRISH REGIMENT MAKE LAST STAND AT LE PILLY AND IS ALMOST COMPLETELY WIPED OUT									
#2ND LEINSTERS LOSE HEAVILY AT PREMESQUE									
19/20 OCTOBER; 50% OF ALL BRITISH ARMY DEATHS ARE OF IRISHMEN									
NOV	228*	25	28	62	44	03	18	189*	53
*IRISH GUARDS AND CONNAUGHT RANGERS SUFFER GRIEVOUS LOSSES DURING THE FIRST BATTLE OF YPRES									
DEC	10	25	08	04	68	07	07	15	39
1915									
	IG	RDF	RIrF	RInnF	RMF	RIrRg	LR	CR	RIrRi
JAN	12	15	11	06	26	16	21	04	35
FEB	38	19	36	04	14	39	61	16	24
MARC	15	15	59	20	18	64	74	20	168*
*ROYAL IRISH RIFLES IN BATTLE FOR NEUVE CHAPPLLE									
APRIL	14	319*#	120	38*	88*	58#	60	86	30
*1ST DUBLINS. MUNSTERS AND INNISKILLINGS LAND AT GALLIPOLI, 24 APRIL									
#GAS ATTACKS ON 2ND DUBLIN FUSILIERS AND ROYAL IRISH AT YPRES									

MAY	103	320*#	88	377*	252*+	195#	129	09	264*

*BLOODY BATTLES DECIMATE IRISH BATTALIONS IN GALLIPOLI

#GAS ATTACKS IN YPRES ON 2ND DUBLINS AND 2ND ROYAL IRISH

+2ND MUNSTERS DESTROYED AT RUE DE BOIS, AUBERS RIDGE

JUNE	05	176	35	56	38	21	25	14	84
JUL	06	70	30	53	29	10	24	12	34
AUG	18	288*	236*	306*	368*	61*	134*	190*	110*

10TH IRISH DIVISION LAND AT SUVLA BAY. ALL THE IRISH BATTALIONS ARE ENGAGED IN RUINOUS WARFARE. THE REMAINS OF THE IST MUNSTERS, DUBLINS AND INNISKILLINGS ARE DESTROYED IN THE ATTACK ON 'SCIMITAR HILL'

SEP	84	54	29	30	42	21	31	31	107
OCT	78	30	12	09	34	24	12	17	22
NOV	13	30	07	21	24	06	14	12	31
DEC	09	62*	30	42	28	09	09	122*	36

*6/7 DECEMBER 10TH IRISH DIVISION IN BATTLE OF KOSTURINO IN MADECONIA

1916

	IG	RDF	RIrF	RInnF	RMF	RIrRg	LR	CR	RIrRi
JAN	10	23	11	16	15	13	14	70	48
FEB	08	16	16	13	19	12	19	16	34
MAR	08	23	27	49	30	07	37	44	47
APRIL	21	279*	106*	134*	46	32	45	*88	83

*GAS ATTACK ON 16TH IRISH DIVISION AT HULLUCH, FRANCE, APRIL 26–30

EASTER RISING

MAY	10	28	64	72	43	27	23	48	91

31 MAY. BATTLE OF JUTLAND. 5000 BRITISH DEAD, 200 IRISH

JUNE	19	44	46	50	73	42	34	24	118
JUL	26	204	308	958	80	157	28	38	1.273

THE SOMME BEGINS; FATAL CASUALTIES FOR I JULY ONLY ARE

	134	227	802		906				
AUG	03	32	42	113	70	31	62	16	78
SEPT	303#	268*	176*	177*	248*	207*	106*	103*	152*

* 3–9 SEPT, 16TH IRISH DIVISION BATTALIONS ATTACK AT GUILLEMONT AND GINCHY ON THE SOMME

#BOTH IRISH BATTALIONS GUARDS ATTACK AT GINCHY IN MID-SEPTEMBER AND SUFFER HEAVILY

OCT	12	215	112	38	40	14	18	10	98
NOV	12	115	20	75	21	15	08	09	45
DEC	16	17	17	23	21	18	09	04	29

1917									
	IG	RDF	RIrF	RInnF	RMF	RIrRg	LR	CR	RIrRi
JAN	07	16	21	81	10	13	17	23	26
FEB	08	78	27	40	12	09	15	22	44
MAR	34	61	10	17	20	07	27	16	84
APRIL	02	104	108	98	14	32	73	15	47
MAY	14	65	89	85	05	12	11	06	44
JUNE	17	52	48	97	13	53	69	29	289
16TH AND 36TH DIVISIONS IN ATTACK ON MESSINES RIDGE, 6 JUNE									
JUL	101	28	24	45	21	11	68	26	81
THIRD YPRES STARTS 31 JULY/ I AUGUST									
AUG	40	275*	236^	557*	34*	103*	57*	40*	755*
16TH AND 36TH DIVISIONS IN THIRD YPRES, I AUGUST TO 17 AUGUST, LOSING 1100 MEN DEAD ON 16 AUGUST ALONE									
SEPT	69	22	23	45	4	18	12	03	29
OCT	118*	65	13	18	12	09	08	03	31
*IRISH GUARDS IN THIRD YPRES									
NOV	92#	63*	128*	117*	128*	38*	30*	39*	204*
*16TH AND 36TH DIVISIONS IN BATTLE OF CAMBRAI									
#IRISH GUARDS IN BATTLE OF BOURLON WOOD									
DEC	40	28	17	101	28	64	30	13	101
1918									
	IG	RDF	RIrF	RInnF	RMF	RIrRg	LR	CR	RIrRi
JAN	07	10	11	17	03	13	04	04	27
FEB	03	08	11	12	10	06	10	06	11
MAR	81	287	123	387	176	220	79	96	498
KAISERSHCLACHT GERMAN OFFENSIVE, STARTING 21 MARCH, HITTING ALL IRISH UNITS									
APRIL	95	48	124	42	12	20	28	03	184
16TH IRISH DIVISION BROKEN UP									
MOST IRISH BATTALIONS WITHDRAWN FROM FRONT-LINES FOR REBUILDING									
MAY	32	60	18	46	10	15	20	05	6
JUNE	09	25	28	18	09	11	27	06	82
JUL	06	16	30	52	14	37	09	07	67
AUG	30	31	45	80	09	108	27	05	74
8 AUGUST; BATTLE OF AMIENS, AND ALLIED 100 DAYS OFFENSIVE BEGINS									
SEPT	41	74	96	109	56	133	71	12	156
OCT	35	253	160	373	91	98	51*	110	292
*2ND LEINSTERS WIN TWO VICTORIA CROSSES LIBERATING LEDEGEM									
ALL IRISH BATTALIONS IN AGAIN ACTION FOR THE FIRST TIME SINCE MARCH									
NOV	07	43	23	100	44	45	06	22	28
2ND MUNSTERS TAKE FOREST OF MORMAL 4 NOVEMBER									
II NOVEMBER, 10.59, PRIVATE THOMAS FARRELL, OF NAVAN, LAST IRISH OR BRITISH SOLDIER TO BE FATALLY WOUNDED, IS SHOT NEAR MONS. HE DIES THE NEXT DAY									

Index